Prayer in John's Farewell Discourse

Prayer in John's Farewell Discourse

An Exegetical Investigation

SCOTT ADAMS

☙PICKWICK *Publications* • Eugene, Oregon

PRAYER IN JOHN'S FAREWELL DISCOURSE
An Exegetical Investigation

Copyright © 2020 Scott Adams. All rights reserved. Except for brief quotations in critical publications or reviews, no part of this book may be reproduced in any manner without prior written permission from the publisher. Write: Permissions, Wipf and Stock Publishers, 199 W. 8th Ave., Suite 3, Eugene, OR 97401.

Pickwick Publications
An Imprint of Wipf and Stock Publishers
199 W. 8th Ave., Suite 3
Eugene, OR 97401

www.wipfandstock.com

PAPERBACK ISBN: 978-1-5326-8683-2
HARDCOVER ISBN: 978-1-5326-8684-9
EBOOK ISBN: 978-1-5326-8685-6

Cataloguing-in-Publication data:

Names: Adams, Scott, author.

Title: Prayer in John's farewell discourse : an exegetical investigation / Scott Adams.

Description: Eugene, OR: Pickwick Publications, 2020 | Includes bibliographical references.

Identifiers: ISBN 978-1-5326-8683-2 (paperback) | ISBN 978-1-5326-8684-9 (hardcover) | ISBN 978-1-5326-8685-6 (ebook)

Subjects: LCSH: Bible—John—Criticism, interpretation, etc. | Bible. John, XIII, 31-XVII, 26 | Prayer—Biblical teaching

Classification: BS2615.2 A33 2020 (print) | BS2615.2 (ebook)

Manufactured in the U.S.A. NOVEMBER 29, 2022

Contents

Permissions | vii

Acknowledgements | ix

Abbreviations | x

CHAPTER 1   Introduction | 1
CHAPTER 2   Jewish Prayer | 12
CHAPTER 3   Greco-Roman Prayer | 42
CHAPTER 4   Prayer in the Synoptics and Acts | 52
CHAPTER 5   A House of Prayer: Analysis of John 14 | 69
CHAPTER 6   Prayer that Produces: Analysis of John 15 | 104
CHAPTER 7   Plain and Persistent Prayer: Analysis of John 16 | 135
CHAPTER 8   The Prayers of Jesus: Analysis of John 6:11; 11:41b–42; 12:27–28; 17; 19:28, 30 | 161
CHAPTER 9   Conclusion | 198

Bibliography | 219

Permissions

Scripture quotations marked ASV are taken from the American Standard Version of the Bible.

Scripture quotations marked ESV are taken from the ESV® Bible (The Holy Bible, English Standard Version®), © 2001 by Crossway, a publishing ministry of Good News Publishers. All rights reserved. Used by permission.

Scripture quotations marked KJV are taken from the King James Version of the Bible.

Scripture quotations marked NASB are taken from the New American Standard Bible® (NASB), © 1960, 1962, 1963, 1968, 1971, 1972, 1973, 1975, 1977, 1995 by The Lockman Foundation. www.Lockman.org. Used by permission.

Scripture quotations marked NIV are taken from the Holy Bible, New International Version®, NIV®. © 1973, 1978, 1984, 2011 by Biblica, Inc.™ All rights reserved worldwide. The "NIV" and "New International Version" are trademarks registered in the United States Patent and Trademark Office by Biblica, Inc.™ Used by permission of Zondervan.

Scripture quotations marked NKJV are taken from the New King James Version. © 1982 by Thomas Nelson. All rights reserved. Used by permission.

Scripture quotations marked RSV are taken from the Revised Standard Version of the Bible, © 1946, 1952, 1971 by National Council of the Churches of Christ in the United States of America. All rights reserved worldwide. Used by permission.

All Old Testament Hebrew Scripture quotations are taken from BHS Deutsche Bibelgesellschaft Stuttgart Morphological Data, © 2004 Westminster Theological Seminary. All rights reserved. Used by Permission.

All Old Testament Greek Scripture quotations are taken from LXX Deutsche Bibelgesellschaft © 1935, 1979. All rights reserved. Used by Permission.

All New Testament Greek Scripture quotations are taken from NA27 Deutsche Bibelgesellschaft, D-Stuttgart, © 1993, 1994, 1998, Morphological Database, © 2006 Logos Research Systems, Inc. All rights reserved. Used by Permission.

Acknowledgements

THIS BOOK IS THE abbreviated form of my Ph.D. dissertation which was written under the guidance of Dr. Jan van der Watt (Radboud University, Netherlands). When searching for topics to research, Dr. Jan and I agreed that the topic of prayer in John's Farewell Discourse was one that had not been adequately examined by scholars. Therefore, in 2013 I began the task of researching the topic, reviewing the literature, and seeking to set forth what I envisaged was the function of prayer in the Farewell Discourse. I am deeply indebted to Dr. Jan for the excellent oversight and guidance he provided in my Ph.D. program. He has labored in the Johannine vineyard for decades, and I am thankful for the opportunity to have gleaned from his expertise and scholarly wisdom. Additionally, I want to acknowledge and express my gratitude to Ryan Lytton (M.A.) for his helpful review of this book. His suggestions, once implemented, improved the clarity and quality of my work in several respects. Finally, I would like to thank my wife, Kelly, for her encouragement over the years as I wrote my dissertation and prepared this book for publication. I could not have completed these works without her support.

Scott Adams

Abbreviations

General and Bibliographic

ASV	American Standard Version
bis	twice
ch.	chapter
ESV	English Standard Version (primary)
KJV	King James Version
LXX	Septuagint
NASB	New American Standard Bible
NIV	New International Version (2011)
NKJV	New King James Version
NT	New Testament
OT	Old Testament
RSV	Revised Standard Version
TDNT	*Theological Dictionary of the New Testament*. Edited by Gerhard Kittel and Gerhard Friedrich. Translated by Geoffrey W. Bromiley. 10 vols. Grand Rapids: Eerdmans, 1964–76.

Hebrew Bible / Old Testament (including Septuagint)

Gen	Genesis

Exod	Exodus
Lev	Leviticus
Num	Numbers
Deut	Deuteronomy
Josh	Joshua
1–2 Sam	1–2 Samuel
1–2 Kgs	1–2 Kings
1–2 Chr	1–2 Chronicles
Ezra	Ezra
Neh	Nehemiah
Ps	Psalm
Prov	Proverbs
Song	Song of Songs
Isa	Isaiah
Jer	Jeremiah
Lam	Lamentations
Ezek	Ezekiel
Dan	Daniel
Hos	Hosea
Joel	Joel
Mic	Micah
Zech	Zechariah
Mal	Malachi

New Testament

Matt	Matthew
Mark	Mark
Luke	Luke
John	John
Acts	Acts

Rom	Romans
1 Cor	1 Corinthians
Eph	Ephesians
Phil	Philippians
1–2 Thess	1–2 Thessalonians
1–2 Tim	1–2 Timothy
Heb	Hebrews
Jas	James
1 John	1 John
Rev	Revelation

Deuterocanonical Works and Septuagint

Sir	Sirach/Ecclesiasticus
2 Macc	2 Maccabees
4 Macc	4 Maccabees

Dead Sea Scrolls and Related Texts

Number	Abbreviation	Name (and Alternative Names)
1QapGen ar	Genesis Apocryphon	
1QH^a	Hodayot^a *or* Thanksgiving Hymns^a	
1QM	Milḥamah *or* War Scroll	
1QS	Serek Hayaḥad *or* Rule of the Community	
1QSb		
1QS34–34bis		
4Q285	Sefer Hamilḥamah (*olim* Serekh Hamilḥamah) *or* War Rule	
4Q286–290	Ber^{a-e}	Berakot *or* Blessings

ABBREVIATIONS

4Q325	Cal. Doc. Mishmarot D (*olim* Mishmarot D)	
4Q327	cancelled (see 4Q394 frags. 1–2; Cal. Doc. D [*olim* 4Q327; Mishmarot E^b])	
4Q372	4QapocrJoseph^b	
4Q400–407	4QShirShabb^{a-h}	Songs of the Sabbath Sacrifice^{a-h}
4Q408	4QapocrMoses^c?	
4Q414	4QRitPur A	Ritual Purity A, formerly Baptismal Liturgy
4Q444	Incantation	
4Q503	4QpapPrQuot	Prières quotidiennes *or* Daily Prayers
4Q504–506	4QDibHam^{a-c}	Dibre Hame'orot^{a-c} *or* Words of the Luminaries^{a-c}
4Q507–508	4QPrFêtes^{a-b}	Prières pour les fêtes^{a-b} *or* Festival Prayers^{a-b}
4Q509	4QpapPrFêtes^c	
4Q510–511	4QShir^{a-b}	Shirot^{a-b} *or* Songs of the Sage^{a-b}
4Q512	4QpapRitPur B	Ritual Purity B
4Q560	4QExorcism ar	
4QH$^{a, b}$		
4QH^{a-f}		
4QM$^{a, b, e}$		
4QPs^f	"Apocryphal" Psalms	
4QS503	Daily Prayers	
4QTLevi ar^b		
8Q5	Hymn	
11QBerakhot		
11QPs^a	"Apocryphal" Psalms	
11Q17	ShirShabb (unopened scroll)	

11Q19	11QT^a	Temple Scroll^a
11Q20	11QT^b	
11Q21	11QT^c?	
11Q22	paleoUnidentified Text	
11Q23	CryptA Unidentified Text	
11Q24	Unidentified Text ar	
11Q25	Unidentified Text A	
CD	Cairo Genizah copy of the Damascus Document	

Other Ancient Sources

Athenaeus

Deipn.   *Deipnosophistae*

Cicero (Marcus Tullius)

Inv.   *De inventione* (*On Invention*)

Josephus

A.J.   *Antiquitates judaicae* (*Jewish Antiquities*)

Plato

Symp.   *Symposium*

Philo Judaeus

Spec. 4   *De specialibus legibus* IV (*On the Special Laws* 4)

Quintilian

Inst.   *Institutio oratoria* (*Institutes of Oratory*)

CHAPTER 1

Introduction

IT WAS REPORTED THAT a doctoral student at Princeton once asked Albert Einstein, "What is there left in the world for original dissertation research?" He replied by saying, "Find out about prayer. Somebody must find out about prayer."[1] In this book I have taken up the task of "finding out" about the topic of prayer in John's Farewell Discourse in particular for three reasons: First, while much has been written on prayer, generally, relatively little has been written that critically sensitizes Johannine prayer against the backdrop of the Jewish, Greco-Roman, and Christian religious traditions that the Fourth Gospel is situated in and surrounded by. Second, scholarly commentaries[2] that examine the Johannine text may be exegetically engag-

---

1. Einstein quoted in Yancey, *Prayer* 3.

2. Concerning the enormous quantity of works produced on the Fourth Gospel, Diehl is right to say, "To jump into the water of Johannine research is like putting a row-boat into the Atlantic. That said, the questions concerning the Fourth Gospel, like ocean waves, just keep coming, begging for more research" ("Puzzle of the Prayer," 20). Notwithstanding, it is necessary to offer a brief summary of the more important Johannine commentaries. Dodd devotes brief attention to Jesus' prayer in chapter 17 and seeks to relate it to the preceding discourses (*Interpretation of the Fourth Gospel*, 417–22). Brown interacts with key prayer passages in the Farewell Discourse (John 14:12–14; 15:7–8, 16; 16:23–24, 26) and briefly examines the nature of asking in Jesus' name and the topic of "greater works" (*Gospel According to John [XIII–XXI]*, 633–735). Naturally, Brown provides an extensive analysis of chapter 17. Yet outside of his work on this chapter, prayer is not treated in any significant detail. The same holds true for commentaries/works produced by Hendriksen, *Exposition of the Gospel According to John* (1953); Barrett, *Gospel According to St. John* (1962); Bultmann, *Das Evangelium des Johannes* (1964); Schnackenburg, *Gospel According to St. John* (1982); Haenchen, *Commentary* (1984); Carson, *Gospel According to John* (1991); Becker, *Das Evangelium nach Johannes* (1991); Brodie, *Gospel According to John* (1993); Witherington, *John's Wisdom* (1995); Culpepper, *Gospel and Letters of John* (1998); Malina and Rohrbaugh, *Social-Science Commentary* (1998); Moloney, *Glory Not Dishonor* (1998); Schenke,

ing in certain respects, but they typically fail to examine the function of prayer in the Farewell Discourse amidst the matrix of circumstances and themes that make it relevant for the "implied" and "intended readers."[3] Finally, to my knowledge there are no substantial, scholarly works that juxtapose the prayers of Jesus in John chapters 6, 11, 12, 17, and 19 with the topic of prayer located in chapters 14, 15, and 16. Therefore the analysis that follows seeks to fill in some of the research gaps that remain in order to more fully discern and appreciate the function of prayer in the Farewell Discourse.

History of Research

Of course, a comprehensive overview concerning the research of prayer is beyond the scope of this book since discussions about prayer are as ancient as the practice itself.[4] Therefore the following summary centers on the more important works that were published in the mid- to latter part of the twentieth century. In 1967, Joachim Jeremias published a work entitled *The Prayers of Jesus*. This analysis contains three essays that center their attention on God the Father as *Abba*, the daily prayer life of Jesus, prayer in the primitive church, and the Lord's Prayer in light of recent scholarship. While Jeremias's work does include a discussion of God as Father in both

---

Johannes Commentar (1998); Beasley-Murray, *John* (1999); Wilckens, *Das Evangelium nach Johannes* (2000); Wengst, *Das Johannesevangelium* (2001); Keener, *Gospel of John* (2003); Köstenberger, *Encountering John* (2002); Köstenberger, *John* (2004); Beutler, *Das Johannesevangelium* (2013); Thyen, *Das Johannesevangelium* (2015); Schnelle, *Das Evangelium nach Johannes 4* (2016).

3. The "implied reader" is not a person but rather a character that emerges from the Fourth Gospel as the documents unfolds. The "intended reader" is the Johannine community. The implied author addresses the so-called implied reader in the plural in 19:35 and 20:31 (ἵνα καὶ ὑμεῖς πιστεύ[σ]ητε, ἵνα πιστεύ[σ]ητε, and ζωὴν ἔχητε ἐν τῷ ὀνόματι αὐτοῦ, respectively).

4. Some of the more notable books that address prayer in general include those written by Heiler, *Prayer*; Hammerling, *History of Prayer*; Zaleski and Zaleski, *Prayer*. Books that examine Greek religion/prayer include Pulleyn, *Prayer in Greek Religion*; Burkert, *Greek Religion*; Charlesworth et al., *Lord's Prayer*. Some of the more noteworthy treatments of OT and Jewish prayer are Jacobs, *Jewish Prayer*; Martin, *Prayer in Judaism*; DiSante, *Jewish Prayer*; Reif, *Judaism and Hebrew Prayer*; Thompson, *I Have Heard Your Prayer*; Werline, *Penitential Prayer*; Balentine, *Prayer in the Hebrew Bible*; Elbogen, *Jewish Liturgy*; Miller, *They Cried to the Lord*; Hammer, *Entering Jewish Prayer*; Steinsaltz, *Guide to Jewish Prayer*; Hoffman, *My People's Prayer Book*; Brueggemann, *Great Prayers of the Old Testament*; Horst and Newman, *Early Jewish Prayers in Greek*; Penner, *Patterns of Daily Prayer*; Matlock, *Discovering the Traditions*; Camp and Longman, *Praying with Ancient Israel*.

the Old and New Testaments, it is void of any notable analysis concerning the unique Johannine distinction of prayer to the Father in Jesus' name.

In 1979, Bingham Hunter published a dissertation entitled "The Prayers of Jesus in the Gospel of John." Most notably, by analyzing passages that highlight Jesus' prayers to the Father, he filled in some gaps that Jeremias and others had left unaddressed. In particular, Hunter analyzes the prayer report of John 6:11, 23, along with the prayer passages located in 11:41b-42, 12:27-28, and chapter 17. Most helpful is his analysis of the Johannine prayer vocabulary and his rather lengthy treatment of the prayer materials in John 17. However, Hunter's work lacks any substantial analysis of the prayer passages in John 14-16.

Several decades later, in 1994, a collection of essays titled *The Lord's Prayer and Other Prayer Texts from the Greco-Roman Era* was published. Edited by James H. Charlesworth with Mark Harding and Mark Kiley, this work discusses the meaning of *Abba*, the Lord's Prayer, and Matthean theology as well as other notable Jewish and Christian prayer texts. Most notable is the book's inclusion of a collection of works "written from the historical-critical point of view that treat the subject of prayer, especially in the Judeo-Christian and Greco-Roman traditions, as a religious phenomenon."[5] Finally, this work includes a generous bibliography of treatments on the Hebrew Bible and Jewish, New Testament, early Christian, Greco-Roman, magical, Gnostic, Hermetic, Manichaean, and Mandaean texts.

About the same time, Oscar Cullmann published a work entitled *Das Gebet im Neuen Testament* ([1994] 1997) that gave fuller attention to the topic of prayer in the NT. In this work, Cullmann examines prayer in the Synoptic accounts, the Pauline corpus, the Fourth Gospel, the Johannine letters, as well as prayer in Acts, 1 Peter, James, Hebrews, and Revelation. His work also addresses more practical topics that relate to the difficulty of praying and objections to praying, as well as discussions on prayer as it relates to God's foreknowledge, immutability, and omnipotence. Furthermore, Cullmann devotes considerable attention to the Johannine concepts of prayer in spirit and truth and prayer in Jesus' name. Like other authors, Cullmann states what prayer is but offers no penetrating analysis concerning how it functions in light of Jesus' departure. While much space is devoted to prayer in Jesus' name, the link between prayer and bearing fruit / performing greater works is passed over rather briefly.

In 2000, Robert Karris published an introduction to the latest scholarship on NT prayer entitled *Prayer and the New Testament: Jesus and His Communities at Worship*. He interacts with prayer passages from a wide lens,

---

5. Charlesworth et al., *Lord's Prayer and Other Prayer Texts*, 105.

including selections from Luke-Acts, the Fourth Gospel and 1 John, the Pauline Corpus, the hymns of Revelation, and the Letter of James. His work includes significant interaction with a variety of scholars working in the field of NT. While he only devotes three pages to discussing prayer in the Farewell Discourse, Karris offers a helpful treatment of prayer in John 17 and 19:28, 30. While Karris's discussion concerning the link between prayer passages in John 14–16 and Jewish tradition that celebrates individuals who have intercessory power is insightful, his rather brief, three-page analysis leaves many gaps open for further discussion.

A fresh analysis of prayer appeared on the scene in 2001. This work edited by Richard Longenecker is entitled *Into God's Presence: Prayer in the New Testament*. It includes contributions from notable scholars including, but not limited to, David Aune, Richard Bauckham, I. Howard Marshall, and N. T. Wright. Like the aforementioned treatments of prayer, this work also covers a wide spectrum of NT texts. Of special note, Andrew Lincoln provides a uniquely enriching chapter that analyzes prayer in the Fourth Gospel. In particular, he highlights the Evangelist's portrayal of Jesus' relationship with the Father and discusses how prayer functions within that relational context. He further interacts with how prayer functions in the Farewell Discourse and links prayer to several of the dominant themes in John chapters 14–16. Yet in the final analysis, Lincoln fails to sensitize the text in light of Jewish, Greco-Roman, and Christian prayer traditions. Further, his treatment lacks any significant discussion concerning prayer and friendship with God and overlooks the link between the Paraclete, prayer, and Jesus' mission through the disciples.

This was followed in 2006 by Karl-Heinrich Ostmeyer's work *Kommunikation mit Gott und Christus: Sprache und Theologie des Gebetes im Neuen Testament*, which offers an analysis of how each of the NT authors used the terminology of prayer to elucidate the nature of communication that takes place with God and Christ. The uniqueness of this work centers on its analysis of the variegated profile of NT prayer that is constructed by a wide spectrum of terms and concepts. As such, his work shows the unique theologies and Christologies that are reflected in prayers throughout the NT. Ostmeyer offers an analysis from the following NT literature: die unumstrittenen Paulusbriefe, die deuteropaulinischen Briefe und der Hebräerbrief, Katholische Briefe (ohne Johannesbriefe), Synoptiker und Apostelgeschichte, das Johannesevangelium und die Johannesbriefe, and die Offenbarung des Johannes. Insofar as the Fourth Gospel is concerned, Ostmeyer examines terms that relate to prayer/communication, but he does not offer a thorough examination of how these terms relate to the more dominant themes that spiral through the Farewell Discourse.

A book by Jerome Neyrey entitled *Give God the Glory: Ancient Prayer and Worship in Cultural Perspective* (2007) examines prayer by bringing cultural materials into the discussion in order to see things "the way the early Christian community did."[6] In this work, Neyrey, following the influence of Bruce Malina in *The New Testament World: Insights from Cultural Anthropology* (2001), examines various prayer materials in light of social science communication theory.[7] He provides general characteristics of prayer and then provides the basic but necessary questions of communication, namely: Who says what to whom, when, how, and why? In addition to examining various prayer texts in the NT in general, Neyrey's most notable contribution centers on his cultural treatment of the prayer materials in John 14–17. In particular, he examines these chapters in two directions of worship: (1) speaking to God (i.e., through prayer) and (2) listening to God (i.e., prophecy, homily, and oracles of salvation/judgment). Accordingly, with particular attention given to John 4 and 14–17, Neyrey sees fluid relationships established through Christ as the "place" where worshipful communication occurs. He further highlights the "dwelling" motif (15:4, 5b, 7) in terms of loyalty/faithfulness and envisions it in light of several relational models such as kinship (father, son, household) and patron-broker-client relationships. In light of my research, Neyrey's discussion of worship/prayer has proved most insightful, and his conclusions will be utilized and interacted with throughout the present work.

In 2009 a book entitled *Das Gebet im Neuen Testament* was published that contains a collection of papers given at the Fourth European Orthodox-Western Symposium of Biblical Scholars in Sâmbăta de Sus, Romania. This work includes entries that discuss various aspects of prayer in the NT. In particular, two essays relate (in varying degrees) to prayer in the Fourth Gospel. First, in his work entitled "Prayer to Jesus in the New Testament," Vasile Mihoc pays special attention to how Jesus was worshipped as being truly God. He makes his case by drawing from Pauline, Johannine, and other NT materials. Mihoc concludes his position by stating, "The New Testament Christ is at the same time the one who prays, as true man, and the one who hears the prayers, as true God."[8] In the final analysis, there is little in Mihoc's work that contributes to one's understanding of the nature of prayer in the Farewell Discourse. To be sure, he firmly establishes the nature of the one addressed in prayer, but he leaves unaddressed the question of how prayer

---

6. Neyrey, *Give God the Glory*, 4.
7. Neyrey, *Give God the Glory*, 10.
8. Mihoc, "Prayer to Jesus in the New Testament," 183.

to Jesus is relevant in light of his absence and subsequent mission through the disciples.

A second important work that appears in *Das Gebet im Neuen Testament* is by Karl-Heinrich Ostmeyer entitled "Prayer as Demarcation: The Function of Prayer in the Gospel of John." Ostmeyer presents a step forward in discerning the function of prayer in the Johannine materials. In addition to examining prayer in relation to the place of worship in the Fourth Gospel, Ostmeyer also examines the usage of ἐρωτάω and αἰτέω in relation to prayers offered by Jesus and the disciples. As such, he points out that Jesus never uses αἰτέω in his prayers to the Father but instead employs the term ἐρωτάω. Conversely, the serviceable term for the disciples' prayer to the Father is αἰτέω, not ἐρωτάω. He sees the careful selection of terms as indicative of demarcation in the Fourth Gospel, that is, the Johannine limitations of how one may approach God in prayer. Jesus prays directly to God, but the disciples pray to God by asking (αἰτέω) in the name of Jesus. He states moreover, "Jesus and his disciples pray in different ways. The disciples do not pray like their fellow-Jews. Anyone who belongs to Jesus can be identified as such by the way in which he prays."[9]

While Ostmeyer establishes his case concerning the so-called "new" way of praying via one's relationship with Jesus, there is more work to be conducted concerning how this genre of prayer functions within the demarcated boundaries of Johannine worship. Why does one pray within this relationship? What are the implications of such prayer? What precisely can one expect when offering prayer in Jesus' name? How do the topics of indwelling, persecution, friendship, and the Paraclete further enhance one's understanding of demarcation? This is but a small sample of the questions that remain in regard to the function of prayer in the Fourth Gospel.

In 2014, Reidar Hvalvik and Karl Olav Sandnes edited a work entitled *Early Christian Prayer and Identity Formation*. This book analyzes the wide spectrum of NT prayer passages/terms and seeks to discover how they contributed to the religious identity of those who were exposed to them. Notable questions that set the agenda for this work include but are not limited to the following: "In which ways was identity in nascent Christianity shaped by prayer?"; "How did the believers pray?"; "In what ways does prayer, and practices associated with prayer, provide insight into an ongoing process of identity formation?"; and "Did prayer among the Christ-believers make any difference with regard to gender and status?"[10]

---

9. Ostmeyer, "Prayer as Demarcation," 247.
10. Hvalvik and Sandnes, *Early Christian Prayer*, 7.

INTRODUCTION

Among all of the contributions to this work, Larry Hurtado's entry, "The Place of Jesus in Earliest Christian Prayer and Its Import for Early Christian Identity," is the most relevant to this study due to its interaction with select Johannine prayer texts/terms. In addition to discussing Jesus' role as intercessor, advocate, prayer teacher, role model, and the recipient of prayers, Hurtado also devotes attention to Johannine prayer terms (ἐρωτάω and αἰτέω) and the centrality of Jesus' name in religious identity and expression. However, lacking from his analysis is a meaningful discussion concerning how the centrality of prayer in Jesus' name fleshes out in religious identity (outside of the act of praying itself). In particular, his work overlooks the practical corollaries that relate to discipleship, worship, and the advancement of God's mission through prayer in the name of Jesus. As such, Hurtado's work, while an important contribution to the topic of Christian prayer, leaves room for further analysis of prayer in the Fourth Gospel.

Interpretative Approach

In chapters 2–4 of this book, I will provide a survey of the Jewish, Greco-Roman, and Christian prayer traditions. However, I will not provide an in-depth exegetical analysis of the prayer texts from these traditions. Instead, I will rely on secondary sources to form conclusions and utilize primary sources as illustrations. The interpretive approach I will take grows out of the historical approach, which examines the religious text and makes conclusions based on the text.[11] Meeks explains, "Since we do not meet ordinary early Christians as individuals, we must seek to recognize them through the collectivities to which they belonged and to glimpse their lives through the typical occasions mirrored in the texts."[12] In this approach, the aim is to read and analyze Christian, Jewish, and Greco-Roman texts on their own terms as they stand. When juxtaposed carefully, these religious texts aid the reader in discovering possibilities concerning how the Johannine community may have viewed prayer in general.[13] While such texts may not offer a direct link to prayer in the Fourth Gospel, they may serve to strengthen and

---

11. See Malherbe, *Social Aspects of Early Christianity*.

12. Meeks, *First Urban Christians*, 2.

13. Meeks says, "To write social history, it is necessary to pay more attention than has been customary to the ordinary patterns of life in the immediate environment within which the Christian movement was born." He continues, "The task of a social historian of early Christianity is to describe the life of the ordinary Christian within that environment—not just the ideas or the self-understanding of the leaders and writers" (*First Urban Christians*, 2).

enhance the overall portfolio of prayer as presented by the Evangelist at the conceptual level.

My position is that the Fourth Gospel was finalized in the last decade of the first century, most likely in Ephesus.[14] I will keep this assumption in mind as I analyze the text and discuss the relevant social materials. My exegetical approach to the Johannine text (in chapters 5–8 of this book) involves a synchronic, intratextual method that seeks to ascertain the fullest meaning and implication of the text as it is read closely in its present form. Terms will be examined in the immediate context of the passage (i.e., syntagmatic context) in which they appear in order to better understand the sentences, paragraphs, and pericopes they form. I will also consider the paradigmatic meaning of terms and concepts as they are seen throughout the Fourth Gospel.

Furthermore, I will pay close attention to the literary context in which various prayer passages appear (e.g., the narrative reports, the Farewell Discourse, etc.) and will also explore the immediate and surrounding social and historical contexts. Bruce Malina's work entitled *The New Testament World: Insights from Cultural Anthropology* (2001) is consulted, cited, and integrated in the chapters that follow. Of course, Malina's approach is not without criticism. Burge says, "One problem with studying the New Testament communities in this manner is that little direct evidence tells us about the character of early Christian life."[15] With this in mind, the categories and paradigms that Malina provides are tentatively integrated. Thus, care will be exercised when discussing and comparing various social and religious phenomena that are not explicitly enunciated in the text. In particular, given the religious and social expression of the first century CE, the analysis that follows will provide interpretative possibilities concerning the topic of prayer in the Fourth Gospel.

Finally, a diachronic analysis would be in order to fully appreciate the prehistory of the Farewell Discourse. But the following analysis is best described in the words of Moloney as one that concentrates on the world "in the text" and attempts to show "how the story has been designed and told in order to influence the world in front of the text."[16] A careful study of the Farewell Discourse provides us with clues to the church's interior struggles,

---

14. For helpful discussions, see Beutler, *Das Johannesevangelium*, 13–16, 67–68; Van der Watt, *Introduction to the Johannine Gospels and Letters*, 110–19; Brown, *Gospel According to John (I–XII)*, xxiv–ciii; Keener, *Gospel of John*, 81–148; Carson, *Gospel According to John*, 68–86; Culpepper, *Gospel and Letters of John*, 29–41; Haenchen, *Commentary on the Gospel of John Chapters 1–6*, 67–90.

15. Burge, *Interpreting the Gospel of John*, 30.

16. Moloney, *Glory Not Dishonor*, 13.

challenges, and needs that the implied author sought to address. In the face of hostile circumstances, the implied author reminded his readers that, although Jesus would not be physically present, God's mission would succeed through them since Jesus remained with them in Spirit and was, therefore, just a prayer away.

Overview of the Present Work

In what follows, chapters 2–4 provide an overview of Christian, Jewish, and Greco-Roman paradigms of prayer against which the materials of the Fourth Gospel will be read and analyzed: (1) How did the Jews pray? (2) What was the nature of Christian prayer? (3) What was the content and form of Greco-Roman prayer? These are the broader questions that will draw forth insights into the nature of prayer within these traditions. Moreover, chapters 2–4 provide specific questions that seek to sensitize the reader to the exegetical discussions that follow. By elucidating the nature of prayer within the aforementioned traditions, one will be more aptly suited to compare and contrast prayer within the Fourth Gospel.

Chapter 5 examines how John 14 contributes to the Johannine profile of prayer. Hence, this chapter initiates the exegetical discussion concerning how the disciples will function and communicate with God in light of Jesus' physical absence. Key questions addressed in this chapter include the following: (1) What are the prerequisites to answered prayer? (2) By what means may the disciples perform "greater works"? (3) What is the significance of prayer in Jesus' name? (4) How does the Father/Son family dynamic contribute to Johannine prayer? (5) What are the roles of the Paraclete, and how do these roles relate to prayer? In short, this chapter initiates the work of detecting the interrelationship between prayer and other major themes that gradually develop in the Farewell Discourse. In particular, I will analyze the topics of faith in Jesus, the disciples as the new dwelling place of God, Jesus' departure and return via the Paraclete, and how these realities equip the disciples to offer prayer in Jesus' name. Further, this chapter explores how prayer serves as the means by which greater works are accomplished through the disciples who have faith in Jesus.

Chapter 6 will analyze how John 15 contributes to one's understanding of the theme of prayer in light of the metaphorical imagery of the gardener, vine, and branches. Attention will be given to examining the consequences of the disciples' union with Jesus in general and how remaining in this relationship provides the grounds for answered prayer. Key questions that are answered in this chapter include the following: (1) How does the viticultural imagery of John 15 contribute to the topic of prayer? (2) Why is remaining in the vine the prerequisite to answered prayer? (3) What is the nature of friendship with Jesus, and how does it relate to prayer? (4) How does the concept of παρρησία relate to Johannine prayer? (5) How does the Paraclete contribute to prayer in the face of persecution? As will be seen, the topic of faith in Jesus is explicitly addressed in John 14 in the context of Jesus' departure and the disciples' performance of greater works. In John 15 the topic of faith is assumed in the context of remaining in Jesus and bearing fruit for God and friendship with God. Hence, as chapter 15 unfolds, one will see clearer evidence concerning the function of prayer as it appears within the context of union with Jesus and other supplementary themes. In particular, attention will be given on the one hand to the consequences of remaining in Jesus, and on the other hand to the consequences of failing to remain, and then to how each consequence relates to prayer, bearing fruit for God, and bringing glory to God.

Chapter 7 seeks to examine how prayer is understood in light of dominant themes that spiral through John 16. In particular, this chapter examines how the Paraclete and prayer function together in God's salvific mission in the world. Key questions answered in this chapter include the following: (1) How does the spiraling of topics through the Farewell Discourse serve to elucidate the Evangelist's view of prayer? (2) What is the relationship between prayer and the work of the Paraclete? (3) What is the nature of the temporal duration that may exist between the disciples' asking in prayer and their receiving from God? Further, this chapter examines the nuances of the unique time period between Jesus' death and reappearance through resurrection, the privilege of approaching the Father directly in prayer, and how the fullness of joy relates to answered prayer. As will be shown, this chapter builds on John 14–15 in its discussion of how prayer in Jesus' name provides the disciples with the confidence necessary for approaching the Father. Although Jesus will be physically absent, his mission will continue through his disciples who prove to be fruitful in the world as they proceed into hostile circumstances.

Chapter 8 covers the various prayers of Jesus that are scattered through the Fourth Gospel. As such, this chapter analyzes Jesus' thanksgiving prayer at the episode of the feeding of the five thousand in 6:11 (a prayer report in the narrative), his prayer of thanksgiving that precedes the raising of Lazarus in 11:41b–42, his prayer of boldness toward his death in 12:27–28 (a prayer attributed to Jesus), his so-called prayer-report in John 17, and his prayer from the cross just prior to his death in 19:28, 30. The total analysis of these passages aims at highlighting Jesus' intimate relationship with the Father and answering the following questions: (1) When did Jesus pray?

(2) What was his posture in prayer? (3) How did Jesus honor the Father in his prayers? (4) What is the nature and purpose of Jesus' prayer in chapter 17? (5) How are we to understand Jesus' final words from the cross?

Chapter 9 provides a brief summary of the exegetical conclusions from all of the previous chapters and offers a systematic description of prayer in the Fourth Gospel, generally, and in the Farewell Discourse, particularly. The aim is to synthesize the materials in a manner that elucidates the uniqueness of Johannine prayer and how it functions within and contributes to Jesus' mission in the believing community. In short, this final chapter brings together the collective research of this book in order summarize the nature and purpose of Johannine prayer.

CHAPTER 2

Jewish Prayer

A CURSORY OVERVIEW OF Jewish prayer reveals that it was offered both in public and in private (Dan 6:10; Neh 9:5–37) and was offered in a variety of postures and positions (Josh 7:6; 1 Chr 17:16). Prayer occurred when divinity and humanity collided in intimate dialogue. In the space of prayer, confession was made, requests were presented, requests were granted, and praise/thanksgiving was offered. This space was, in its very essence, the place of frank and earnest dialogue with God. But one must ask how such communication could occur between such disparate parties? The bipolarity between heaven and earth is of special relevance for the study of Jewish prayer. The Scriptures posit a God who rules the heavenly realm and a world that has fallen out of his rule. Nonetheless, in his work entitled "The Suffering of God," Terence Fretheim says that "God does move freely back and forth across the realms of the world, while heaven is 'unreachable from the earth.' Yet, unreachability ought not to be interpreted in terms of unaffectability."[1] As such, the God who is in heaven graciously accommodates those on the earth who have rebelled against his rule. Most striking is God's inclination to enter into the space of relationship with the subjects of his rule and his unswerving allegiance to open his ears to the cries of his people. For example, the psalmist writes:

הַטֵּה אֵלַי ׀ אָזְנְךָ מְהֵרָה הַצִּילֵנִי (Ps 31:3[2])

וַאֲנִי ׀ אָמַרְתִּי בְחָפְזִי נִגְרַזְתִּי מִנֶּגֶד עֵינֶיךָ אָכֵן שָׁמַעְתָּ קוֹל תַּחֲנוּנַי בְּשַׁוְּעִי אֵלֶיךָ: (Ps 31:23[22])

עֵינֵי יְהוָה אֶל־צַדִּיקִים וְאָזְנָיו אֶל־שַׁוְעָתָם: (Ps 34:16[15])

---

1. Fretheim, THE SUFFERING OF GOD, 39.

With these examples in mind, the topic of metaphorical speech comes into focus. A metaphor is necessitated when the literal meaning of a word in the sentence is incongruent with reality, absurd, contradictory or irrelevant. The incongruence that exists between the temporal and the transcendental, between the physical and the metaphysical, creates a gap. But that gap may be closed through the implementation of metaphorical language in which God is drawn into the reality of human dialogue. God speaks, but not as humans speak. He listens, but not with human ears. He acts, but not with human hands. The very nature of anthropomorphic speech is designed to lessen the communicative disparity that exists between God, whom Jerome Neyrey calls the "superior receiver" and humankind, who he calls the "subordinate sender."² Notwithstanding, the Scriptures labor to demonstrate that the God of heaven is interested in, inclined toward, and interactive with his people on the earth.

Accordingly, Balentine remarks that "metaphors promote the understanding of divine-human relatedness. It is significant that they also function as foundational arguments in the effort to describe who this God is in contrast to other gods."³ The psalmist says,

¹⁵ עֲצַבֵּי הַגּוֹיִם כֶּסֶף וְזָהָב מַעֲשֵׂה יְדֵי אָדָם׃

¹⁶ פֶּה־לָהֶם וְלֹא יְדַבֵּרוּ עֵינַיִם לָהֶם וְלֹא יִרְאוּ׃

¹⁷ אָזְנַיִם לָהֶם וְלֹא יַאֲזִינוּ אַף אֵין־יֶשׁ־רוּחַ בְּפִיהֶם׃ (Ps 135:15–17)

The God of Israel is aware of and involved with his creation. The false gods, by virtue of not possessing life, are by necessity unaware of, uninvolved with, and unable to respond to human discourse. The contrast between Yahweh and the pagan gods is best illustrated in the episode of Elijah and the prophets of Baal (1 Kgs 18). Yahweh hears and responds (vv. 37–39); the false gods are deaf and do not respond (vv. 26–29).

Furthermore, in the divine dialouge the transcendent God ("You") condescends into the relational space of prayer in a manner that is both relatable and understandable. The nature of such dialogue is circumscribed for us most clearly in the Psalms. Brueggemann cites Psalm 86, where the strong independent pronoun "You" (אַתָּה) is employed for special emphasis:

אַתָּה אֱלֹהָי (v. 2)

כִּי־אַתָּה אֲדֹנָי טוֹב וְסַלָּח וְרַב־חֶסֶד לְכָל־קֹרְאֶיךָ׃ (v. 5)

כִּי־גָדוֹל אַתָּה וְעֹשֵׂה נִפְלָאוֹת אַתָּה אֱלֹהִים לְבַדֶּךָ׃ (v. 10)

---

2. Neyrey, *Give God the Glory*, 9.
3. Balentine, *Prayer in the Hebrew Bible*, 35.

וְאַתָּה אֲדֹנָי אֵל־רַחוּם וְחַנּוּן אֶרֶךְ אַפַּיִם וְרַב־חֶסֶד וֶאֱמֶת: (v. 15)

עֲשֵׂה־עִמִּי אוֹת לְטוֹבָה וְיִרְאוּ שֹׂנְאַי וְיֵבֹשׁוּ כִּי־אַתָּה יְהוָה עֲזַרְתַּנִי וְנִחַמְתָּנִי: (v. 17)[4]

The "You" of the Psalms is also the "You" of the rest of the biblical narrative. Although this pronoun אַתָּה is not always used, it is implied in the context of prayer. The one praying is the "subordinate" sender ("I"); Yahweh is the "superior" receiver ("You"). When the pray-er enters into the space of prayer with God, a message is communicated. Following Neyrey's description of prayer, the message might be in the form of "petition, adoration, contrition, or thanksgiving."[5] The medium of the message might be "verbal or substantive or both." As will be demonstrated below, the space of prayer was not occupied out of religious duty but out of a desire to express oneself emotionally, spiritually, and physically. Such expressions were not always calculated but rather were spontaneous and reactive to one's situation in life. The discussion that follows explores how subordinate senders postured themselves before God as they sought to communicate their message.

The Postures of Prayer

Within the space of prayer, the OT reveals that individuals communicated to God in a variety of verbal/oral forms. In such cases, one's body language and posture reveal the nature of one's disposition and attitude before God.[6] In some of the examples below, the act of praying is not explicitly stated but rather assumed. At the very least, the following examples demonstrate the general postures that were assumed before God in response to certain crises, other significant events, and/or worship:

וַיִּקְרַע יְהוֹשֻׁעַ שִׂמְלֹתָיו וַיִּפֹּל עַל־פָּנָיו אַרְצָה לִפְנֵי אֲרוֹן יְהוָה עַד־הָעֶרֶב הוּא וְזִקְנֵי יִשְׂרָאֵל וַיַּעֲלוּ עָפָר עַל־רֹאשָׁם: (Josh 7:6)

וַיָּבֹא הַמֶּלֶךְ דָּוִיד וַיֵּשֶׁב לִפְנֵי יְהוָה וַיֹּאמֶר מִי־אֲנִי יְהוָה אֱלֹהִים וּמִי בֵיתִי כִּי הֲבִיאֹתַנִי עַד־הֲלֹם: (1 Chr 17:16)

וַיֹּאמְרוּ הַלְוִיִּם יֵשׁוּעַ וְקַדְמִיאֵל בָּנִי חֲשַׁבְנְיָה שֵׁרֵבְיָה הוֹדִיָּה שְׁבַנְיָה פְתַחְיָה קוּמוּ בָּרְכוּ אֶת־יְהוָה אֱלֹהֵיכֶם מִן־הָעוֹלָם עַד־הָעוֹלָם וִיבָרְכוּ שֵׁם כְּבוֹדֶךָ וּמְרוֹמַם עַל־כָּל־בְּרָכָה וּתְהִלָּה: (Neh 9:5)

וַיְמַהֵר מֹשֶׁה וַיִּקֹּד אַרְצָה וַיִּשְׁתָּחוּ: (Exod 34:8)

---

4. Brueggemann, *Psalms and the Life of Faith*, 36.

5. Neyrey, *Give God the Glory*, 9.

6. See Hvalvik, "Praying with Outstretched Hands," 78, 82.

Whether one kneels or stands, a common posture of OT prayer involves the lifting of one's hands toward heaven. For example:

וַיַּעֲמֹד לִפְנֵי מִזְבַּח יְהוָה נֶגֶד כָּל־קְהַל יִשְׂרָאֵל וַיִּפְרֹשׂ כַּפָּיו: (2 Chr 6:12)

וּבְפָרִשְׂכֶם כַּפֵּיכֶם אַעְלִים עֵינַי מִכֶּם גַּם כִּי־תַרְבּוּ תְפִלָּה אֵינֶנִּי שֹׁמֵעַ יְדֵיכֶם דָּמִים מָלֵאוּ: (Isa 1:15)

קוּמִי ׀ רֹנִּי בַלַּיְלָה לְרֹאשׁ אַשְׁמֻרוֹת שִׁפְכִי כַמַּיִם לִבֵּךְ נֹכַח פְּנֵי אֲדֹנָי שְׂאִי אֵלָיו כַּפַּיִךְ עַל־נֶפֶשׁ עוֹלָלַיִךְ הָעֲטוּפִים בְּרָעָב בְּרֹאשׁ כָּל־חוּצוֹת: (Lam 2:19)

The examples above are not exhaustive, but they sufficiently illustrate the range of postures assumed by individuals in the OT. As such, one's posture of prayer is often related to his situation in life. Lying prostrate or falling on one's face demonstrates a sense of grief, bitterness, and/or anguish. Sitting conveys an attitude of contemplation or bewilderment before God. Standing may convey a sense of confidence and eagerness to address God in worship and/or prayer. Bowing one's head demonstrates a sense of humility and wonder. And finally, the lifting/spreading of one's hands conveys a sense of desperation before God in prayer.

Prayer, Sacrifice, and the Temple

A survey of the history of Jewish prayer reveals that from the earliest eras of Jewish history to the First Temple Era there did not exist a universally rigid prayer formula in content or in practice. Steinsaltz notes, "The majority of people prayed whenever the need arose, whether in response to their inner emotions, or in times of distress, or when they had some special petition to make to God."[7] Thus, prayers throughout the biblical record may be characterized as the pouring out of one's soul to God rather than the recitation of words from a prayer book. Most obvious to the reviewer of the biblical account, it seems, is the personal nature of prayer in the Hebrew Scriptures, which, by necessity, focused on relationship rather than religious rigidity. The worshipper was free to approach God without an intermediary in honesty and freedom. Thus, the concept of *paressia*, or boldness of speech, was part and parcel of this sort of prayerful dialogue. The worshipper could approach God directly and honestly without resorting to formalities and/or flattery.

However, did prayer continue to be practiced in the aforementioned manner, or did it morph into a more structured, regimented form in later

---

7. Steinsaltz, *Guide to Jewish Prayer*, 47.

eras of OT history? The evidence suggests that during the First Temple Era, prayer continued to be offered freely without liturgical rigidity. Certain scholars have noted that there was no regular prayer service during the First Temple Era.[8] Further, there is no direct, scriptural imperative that prescribed and/or mandated prayers in the cultic regime itself. However, while this was true of prayer in general, *the offering of sacrifice and the establishment of the temple* did have a *gradual* but *informal* influence on the practice of Jewish prayer. But it cannot be overstressed that these elements did not immediately create a demand for a regimented approach to prayer. Rather, they served to form a theological perception in the minds of certain Jews that pre-existing forms of spontaneous prayer could be further enhanced. Penner's research shows that spontaneous praying did not preclude offering prayer at certain times of the day, particularly in conjunction with sacrifice. He remarks that "from a variety of both geographically and chronologically diverse texts . . . spontaneous prayer was often recited in conjunction with, or timed according to, the sacrifices of the daily cultic services." He explains:

> Within the daily service, the *minḥah* sacrifice in particular was often described as efficacious. In 1 Kgs 18:37, for example, Elijah cries to the Lord "Answer me!" at the time of the evening sacrifice (1 Kgs 18:36: עלות המנחה), and God responded with the necessary fire to consume his sacrifice (1 Kgs 18:38). This contrasts with the opposing prophets who were unable to gain the attention of Baal through their prayers and sacrifices (also עלות המנחה): "But there was not a sound; no one answered, and no one was listening" (1 Kgs 18:29).[9]

He continues:

> Even when it is not offered, sacrifice continued to provide a framework for how to pray. A text exemplary of this relationship is Ps 141:2, where, although still clearly subordinate to sacrifice, prayer is said at the time of the evening *minḥah* offering:

> Let my prayer be counted as incense (תפלתי קטרת) before you, and the lifting up of my hands as an evening sacrifice (מנחת ערב).[10]

Following Penner's research, passages that link sacrifice and the offering of incense abound in the OT.[11] But he also points to examples in Luke-

---

8. Wylen, *Jews in the Time of Jesus*, 85.
9. Penner, *Patterns of Daily Prayer*, 38.
10. Penner, *Patterns of Daily Prayer*, 38.
11. Penner, *Patterns of Daily Prayer*, 40–41.

Acts where prayer is linked to activities within the temple. For example, Luke 1:8–10 states:

> 8 Ἐγένετο δὲ ἐν τῷ ἱερατεύειν αὐτὸν ἐν τῇ τάξει τῆς ἐφημερίας αὐτοῦ ἔναντι τοῦ θεοῦ, 9 κατὰ τὸ ἔθος τῆς ἱερατείας ἔλαχε τοῦ θυμιᾶσαι εἰσελθὼν εἰς τὸν ναὸν τοῦ κυρίου, 10 καὶ πᾶν τὸ πλῆθος ἦν τοῦ λαοῦ προσευχόμενον ἔξω τῇ ὥρᾳ τοῦ θυμιάματος.

Further, Acts 3:1 states:

> Πέτρος δὲ καὶ Ἰωάννης ἀνέβαινον εἰς τὸ ἱερὸν ἐπὶ τὴν ὥραν τῆς προσευχῆς τὴν ἐνάτην.

Finally, the following quotation from Penner is lengthy, but is necessary to cite in order to read his argument in precise terms. He writes:

> That the author of Luke-Acts had in mind a correlation between prayer and the evening *minḥah* sacrifice is made explicit in the Cornelius episode in Acts 10:1–4. Here we read that at the ninth hour Cornelius received a vision in which an angel tells him that his prayers (and almsgiving) have gone up "as a memorial offering before God" (cf. also Acts 10:30). Luke's reference of a "memorial offering" to describe Cornelius's prayers recalls the same term used to describe the *minḥah* offering as a "memorial portion" (אזכרה; cf. Lev 2:2, 9, 16; 6:8 [15]). The term "memorial portion" is used also in conjunction with the incense offering that is part of the ritual of the temple bread in Lev 24:5–9 (v. 7: לאזכרה). Because incense is the common ingredient in both the *minḥah* and temple bread sacrifice, it stands to reason that it is the presence of incense in these sacrifices that allows them to be considered a "memorial portion," the pleasing odour of which ascends and causes God to "remember" the one sacrificing/praying (cf. also Sir 38:11; 45:16).[12]

What, then, is the significance of praying at the time of the daily sacrifices (*minḥah* sacrifice in particular)? Penner says, "Generally, it seems that the preeminence and potency of sacrifice gave added weight to the performance of prayer."[13] But more specifically, he says: "(1) the *minḥah* sacrifice contained incense, the burning of which was a high-point in the daily service, and (2) the *minḥah* sacrifice had widespread popularity." To summarize Penner's reasons further, he says that the *minḥah* offering and the burnt offering were offered together, but the *minḥah* offering maintained a different status (as seen repeatedly in Leviticus) as being "a most holy part

---

12. Penner, *Patterns of Daily Prayer*, 41.
13. Penner, *Patterns of Daily Prayer*, 41, 43.

of the offerings made to the Lord by fire."[14] In addition to be regarded as the "memorial portion" of the offering that was pleasing to God (אזכרה; Lev 2:2, 9, 16; 5:12; 6:8 [15]; Isa 66:3 [מזכיר לבונה]), Penner says that the *minḥah* "contained a mixture of incense that was especially pleasing and thus had the effect of generating divine goodwill towards the worshipper. Thus, we see that when incense is present, the offering has an anamnestic quality that garnered divine attention (cf. Lev 2:2, 9, 16; 6:8 [15], 24:7)."[15] He concludes by saying, "In addition to the goodwill associated with incense, the *minḥah* and incense sacrifices could be offered by anyone for any number of reasons, and were not subjected to the restrictions associated with the centralization of the cult in Jerusalem, at least not to the same degree."[16] In the final analysis, this summary elucidates a link that exists between sacrifice, the offering of incense, and prayer. Although the OT Scriptures do not strictly prescribe that prayers be offered in conjunction with sacrifice, they do describe situations in which this took place (Dan 9:21), which indicates that the worshippers saw the sacrificial enterprise as enhancing their prayers. Therefore, it is not surprising to see throughout the biblical narratives individuals offering prayer at the time of daily sacrifices.

Moreover, a link between *prayer and sacrifice* is also seen during the Second Temple Era in the institution of the *ma'amadoth*. Berkovits observes that this institution consisted of the daily gathering of "selected groups of men who met in prayer during the offering of the sacrifices in the Temple."[17] This enterprise was established to ensure the people's participation in the sacrificial event. Elbogen explains, "In order to mark the sacrifice as a communal undertaking, it had to be offered in the presence and with the participation of the community. And since it was impossible for the entire people to be in attendance in Jerusalem for the sacrifice, the 'prophets in Jerusalem' divided them . . . into twenty-four courses [or 'standing posts']."[18] Thus, men were appointed for one week every half year to "stand over" the sacrifice at the temple. Thus, representatives held four services (morning, additional, afternoon, and Closing of the Gates) in which prayer and Torah readings took place. Accordingly Jeremias writes, "Part of it accompanied the priests and levites to Jerusalem and was present during the sacrifice as representatives of the people. . . . The other part remained at home, and during its priestly course's week of service assembled in the synagogue to

---

14. Penner, *Patterns of Daily Prayer*, 41–42.
15. Penner, *Patterns of Daily Prayer*, 42.
16. Penner, *Patterns of Daily Prayer*, 43.
17. Berkovits, "From Temple to Synagogue and Back," 139.
18. Elbogen, *Jewish Liturgy*, 190.

read the scriptures and pray, thus participating in the Temple service from a distance."[19] Thus, in time the sacrificial enterprise of the temple became informally linked with prayer. As the place/space where sacrifices were offered and the presence of God dwelt, the temple stood as a reminder that God was accessible and his ear was inclined to his people, even for those who were not in close proximity to the temple sacrifice. Although not physically present to the place where God's name dwelt, certain individuals, by virtue of prayer, could participate in the sacrificial offering.

Finally, a link between *prayer* and the *temple* is seen in Solomon's prayer of dedication. As seen in 1 Kings 8:1–11, Solomon assembled the people of Jerusalem to formally dedicate the temple. The ark was carried into the temple, sacrifices were presented, and the glory of the LORD filled the temple. Thus, this opening address and its consequences seem to suggest that the main emphasis of the temple rested on it being a dwelling-place/space for God. As such, the temple not only provided the "turf" where sacrifice was offered but the temple also served as the "conduit" through which prayers were "channeled heavenward."[20] Moreover, the majority of references to prayer in 1 Kings 8 involve God "hearing" and "forgiving" the people's sin when they prayed toward the temple. For example:

אֵת אֲשֶׁר יֶחֱטָא אִישׁ לְרֵעֵהוּ וְנָשָׁא־בוֹ אָלָה לְהַאֲלֹתוֹ וּבָא אָלָה לִפְנֵי מִזְבַּחֲךָ בַּבַּיִת הַזֶּה: [31]

וְאַתָּה ׀ תִּשְׁמַע הַשָּׁמַיִם וְעָשִׂיתָ וְשָׁפַטְתָּ אֶת־עֲבָדֶיךָ לְהַרְשִׁיעַ רָשָׁע לָתֵת דַּרְכּוֹ בְּרֹאשׁוֹ וּלְהַצְדִּיק צַדִּיק לָתֶת לוֹ כְּצִדְקָתוֹ: ס [32]

בְּהִנָּגֵף עַמְּךָ יִשְׂרָאֵל לִפְנֵי אוֹיֵב אֲשֶׁר יֶחֶטְאוּ־לָךְ וְשָׁבוּ אֵלֶיךָ וְהוֹדוּ אֶת־שְׁמֶךָ וְהִתְפַּלְלוּ וְהִתְחַנְּנוּ אֵלֶיךָ בַּבַּיִת הַזֶּה: [33]

וְאַתָּה תִּשְׁמַע הַשָּׁמַיִם וְסָלַחְתָּ לְחַטַּאת עַמְּךָ יִשְׂרָאֵל וַהֲשֵׁבֹתָם אֶל־הָאֲדָמָה אֲשֶׁר נָתַתָּ לַאֲבוֹתָם: ס [34]

בְּהֵעָצֵר שָׁמַיִם וְלֹא־יִהְיֶה מָטָר כִּי יֶחֶטְאוּ־לָךְ וְהִתְפַּלְלוּ אֶל־הַמָּקוֹם הַזֶּה וְהוֹדוּ אֶת־שְׁמֶךָ וּמֵחַטָּאתָם יְשׁוּבוּן כִּי תַעֲנֵם: [35]

וְאַתָּה ׀ תִּשְׁמַע הַשָּׁמַיִם וְסָלַחְתָּ לְחַטַּאת עֲבָדֶיךָ וְעַמְּךָ יִשְׂרָאֵל כִּי תוֹרֵם אֶת־הַדֶּרֶךְ הַטּוֹבָה אֲשֶׁר יֵלְכוּ־בָהּ וְנָתַתָּה מָטָר עַל־אַרְצְךָ אֲשֶׁר־נָתַתָּה לְעַמְּךָ לְנַחֲלָה: ס (1 Kgs 8:31–36) [36]

As it stood, the temple was the place where God's name dwelt (1 Kgs 8:17–19, 20, 29). In this understanding, the covenant name of God was

---

19. Jeremias, *Prayers of Jesus*, 71.
20. Balentine, *Prayer in the Hebrew Bible*, 82.

linked to the very place where God was said to dwell among his people.[21] Further, as 1 Kings 8 is read in light of the exile and destruction of the temple, one would naturally be reminded of its relationship to God's willingness to hear their prayer. Balentine observes, "With the destruction of the temple in 586 BCE, this advocation of a 'Name Theology,' as von Rad calls it, serves as one means of securing access to God even when the temple can no longer function as the place of worship."[22] Deuteronomy 12:5 and 12:13–14 require bringing sacrifices to the place or space where God has chosen for his name to dwell. Yet the emphasis of 1 Kings 8 rests on the temple being a place of prayer. Werline points out that the author of 1 Kings pens an ideology of prayer in chapter 8 that is "especially suited for his nation's situation."[23] He says:

> He does this by creating a scene that depicts the Temple as originally dedicated as a place of prayer, especially penitential prayer in response to punishment for sin. . . . The author maintains that even without the Temple the people can continue to practice the activity for which Solomon dedicated it—prayer. Thus, Israel gains a way to expiate sin without Temple sacrifice: repentance and penitential prayer toward the Temple.

With this emphasis in mind, the name of God might serve as a reminder concerning both the character and covenantal promises of God. Prayer in light of the place (or turf) that bore God's name would enable his people to achieve certain "results" in the form of God's pardon, promises, and provision, their situational crisis notwithstanding.

Questions

1. Spontaneous and free outpouring of the heart is seen in various OT prayers. Is this the case in the Fourth Gospel? Is there any evidence of fixed prayers in the Johannine tradition?

---

21. De Vries says that in Deuteronomistic ideology, "the Name" refers to "a hypostasis or extension of Yahweh's true being, but not the Deity in the fullness of his being (vv. 28–29). Accordingly, the temple served as a listening-post or sounding board, continually receptive to any prayer that may be directed toward it (v. 29b; cf. vv. 30, 33, 35, 42, 44, 48)" (1 Kings, 125).

22. Balentine, Prayer in the Hebrew Bible, 82.

23. Werline, Penitential Prayer in Second Temple Judaism, 28. This assumes an exilic date for the final form of 1 Kings 8, especially in light of the statements concerning the people of God being "in the land of their enemy" (vv. 46, 48).

2. Penner demonstrates that Jewish prayers were spontaneous, but oftentimes offered in conjunction with the timing of the sacrificial enterprise. Does the Fourth Gospel make this connection? How does prayer and sacrifice relate in the Fourth Gospel?

3. In light of 1 Kings 8, Jewish prayer could be offered toward the temple that bore God's name. How does God's name relate to prayer in the Fourth Gospel?

4. The emphasis in 1 Kings centers on the temple being a place of prayer. What emphasis does the Fourth Gospel place on the temple? Does it connect prayer to the temple? How does prayer in the temple change in light of Jesus?

5. The theme of confession of sin is present in 1 Kings 8. Does the Fourth Gospel link confession of sin and prayer?

6. What is the Johannine sentiment toward worship in light of particular geographical locales?

Prayer in the Synagogue

Thus far we have examined the space of prayer, which consists primarily of the human/divine relationship, one's physical location notwithstanding. However, as noted above, the temple became identified as the physical locale where God's name dwelt and the place toward which the people would pray. But the temple was not the only place where sacred dialogue occurred. Although it is impossible to be certain, an informal connection between prayer and the synagogue probably developed[24] some time during or after the exile. As is widely known, a shift took place concerning Jewish worship during the Babylonian exile when the destruction of Jerusalem precluded sacrificial and cultic atonement in the temple. Thus, the event of the exile gave rise to the concept of the synagogue and to religious practice within. Martin says that it was at the time of the exile that Jews, "now separated from the Temple, the one legitimate center for the offering of sacrifices, would gather informally on Sabbaths and festivals under the leadership of prophets such as Ezekiel, as well as other teachers, for prayer and the reading

---

24. Hammer follows the commonly held view that the synagogue developed during the Babylonian exile when worship was forced to take a different form and expression (*Entering Jewish Prayer*, 66). Yet the question of how one is to worship in a foreign land was answered by the development of the synagogue. In fact, Hammer contends, "Had it been possible to offer sacrifices in Babylon, the synagogue might never have emerged" (*Entering Jewish Prayer*, 67).

and exposition of Scripture."[25] Berkovits observes further, "Of necessity, in Babylon prayer replaced the sacrifice. In its manifold consequences this development amounted to a major religious revolution. The sacrifice could only be offered by the priest; prayer was expected of everyone.... Every Jew now became actively associated with the religious service."[26]

In Jesus' day, the synagogue functioned as a place of reading, teaching, and preaching. The Torah scroll provided the content from which the synagogue audience was instructed. Finkel says that Torah readings occurred on the Sabbath, at festivals, and every Monday and Thursday. He remarks, "The people's trust in and commitment to the Lord God was displayed in their hearing of the words of Torah. But their trust and commitment was also fortified by public preaching."[27] In the NT it is said that Jesus spent time preaching, teaching, and healing in the synagogues (Matt 4:23; 6:2, 5; 9:35; 12:9; 13:54; Mark 1:39; 3:1; 6:2; Luke 4:15; 6:6; John 18:20). The book of Acts presents Paul frequenting the synagogue to preach and teach (9:20; 13:14–41; 14:1; 17:1–3, 10–17; 18:4; 19:8). As might be expected, the synagogue functioned as a place of prayer. Concerning the NT evidence, Jesus warns of praying like the hypocrites (Matt 6:5) and does so in the context of praying in the synagogue. A "place of prayer" existed near Philippi (Acts 16:13, 16), which functioned as a gathering place (or possible synagogue) for Jews and Gentile worshippers. However, out of approximately fifty-seven references to the synagogue in the NT, only a few passages mention prayer in connection with it. Therefore, one must look beyond the NT in order to understand how prayer related to and functioned within the synagogue.

Moreover, the evidence suggests that Jews prayed several times a day and did so in various venues within the period of the second temple. Greeven remarks, "Regular prayer, two or three times a day, is attested fairly early. It is presupposed in Acts 3:1; 10:9, and indirectly in Matt 6:5. Josephus (b. 37/38 CE) refers to the thanksgiving (*A.J.* 4.212) which goes up to God twice a day and he appeals to Moses, so that the habit must have been common in the first Christian century."[28] The actual number of times that prayers were offered notwithstanding, the main point is that Jews prayed in various places at various times. One could pray virtually anywhere he chose, whether at home or in the synagogue. Therefore, the most one can say is that an informal link existed between the synagogue and prayer. While the synagogue functioned as a house of prayer in some locales, it was not the

---

25. Martin, *Prayer in Judaism*, 5.
26. Berkovits, "From Temple to Synagogue and Back," 139.
27. Finkel, "Prayer in the Jewish Life," 58.
28. Herrmann and Greeven, "εὔχομαι, εὐχή, προσεύχομαι, προσευχή," *TDNT* 2:801.

definitive place of prayer for all Jews in the Second Temple Era. The lack of explicit NT data concerning prayer in the synagogue may be puzzling to some. One might imagine that the plethora of reference to the synagogue in general would yield numerous examples of prayer (that is, if it were a regular practice within the synagogue). Yet this is not the case. Accordingly, as one looks beyond the NT documents for evidence that prayer in the synagogue was a binding practice for Jews during the first century, he will discover that such evidence is lacking.

Questions

1. A central component of the synagogue was the Torah. Does the Fourth Gospel emphasize the commandments of God? If so, how does the Evangelist link them with prayer?
2. As noted above, in light of the destruction of the first temple and the abolition of cultic sacrifice, the synagogue participants were transformed into a praying community. What is the scope of prayer in the Fourth Gospel? Is prayer presented as a private or communal activity?
3. In conjunction with various locales, the synagogue served as a place/house for prayer. Does the Fourth Gospel associate prayer with any particular place? In light of Jesus' instruction in the Farewell Discourse, how is the concept of the believer as a home/house related to prayer?
4. The synagogue served as a place of education and learning. In what manner does instruction take place in light of Jesus' departure to the Father? In what ways is education linked to prayer?
5. How would expulsion from the synagogue affect prayer in the Johannine community?

The Shema and the Tefillah

The Shema and Tefillah maintain a prominent place in the history of Jewish prayer. What is the nature of these addresses to God? When were they offered and in what contexts were they offered? These are the questions that will be addressed below. By analyzing these prayers, one is able to obtain a better understanding of the profile of Jewish prayer.

The Shema consisted of three passages from the Hebrew Scriptures (Deut 6:4-9; 11:13-21; Num 15:37-41). The first passage is the most important and foundational for all that follows in the text and in subsequent religious practice. In fact, Jeremias says that Deuteronomy 6 contains "a phrase which was regarded as the basic creed throughout the Jewish world of the time of Jesus."[29] While the Shema is more precisely identified as a creed than a prayer, it nonetheless played a vital role in Jewish religious life and provided an ancient foundation for Jewish prayer in particular. Hammer observes that the Shema was "compiled at some point during the Second Temple period in order to provide an opportunity to listen daily to God's word through chosen paragraphs from the Torah which both represented the whole and presented three basic dogmas about Judaism's belief in God."[30]

The Shema was recited every day for devotional purposes by priests who served in the temple. According to Hammer, "Its Torah sections were recited twice daily by pious individuals during the Second Temple period, at least as a private devotion."[31] It was recited in the morning at *Shaharit* and in the evening at *Arvit*. Jeremias says, "The custom of reciting the creed in the morning between dawn and sunrise and in the evening after sunset is first attested in the second century BCE by the Letter of Aristeas (145–100 BCE). It was observed in Palestine as well as in the Diaspora. The Essenes and the Therapeutae, too, had prayers at sunrise and in the evening."[32] The Shema was also referenced by Philo (*Spec.* 4.141), Josephus (*A.J.* 4.212), and Qumran (1QS 10.10).

The foundation of the Shema, as might be expected, is grounded in 6:4a, which states, ":שְׁמַע יִשְׂרָאֵל יְהוָה אֱלֹהֵינוּ יְהוָה | אֶחָד" The term *Shema* itself means, "hear" or "listen." DiSante says, "The command is so important, and summarizes all the others to such an extent, that Israel and, later, Judaism would turn into its privileged act of faith. But what is it that is to be heard? What is the object of this radically important 'listening'? 'The Lord our God is the only Lord.'"[33] These words are followed by the commandment:

⁵ וְאָהַבְתָּ אֵת יְהוָה אֱלֹהֶיךָ בְּכָל־לְבָבְךָ וּבְכָל־נַפְשְׁךָ וּבְכָל־מְאֹדֶךָ:

⁶ וְהָיוּ הַדְּבָרִים הָאֵלֶּה אֲשֶׁר אָנֹכִי מְצַוְּךָ הַיּוֹם עַל־לְבָבֶךָ:

⁷ וְשִׁנַּנְתָּם לְבָנֶיךָ וְדִבַּרְתָּ בָּם בְּשִׁבְתְּךָ בְּבֵיתֶךָ וּבְלֶכְתְּךָ בַדֶּרֶךְ וּבְשָׁכְבְּךָ וּבְקוּמֶךָ: (vv. 5–7)

---

29. Jeremias, *Prayers of Jesus*, 67.
30. Hammer, *Entering Jewish Prayer*, 128.
31. Hammer, *Entering Jewish Prayer*, 122.
32. Jeremias, *Prayers of Jesus*, 68.
33. DiSante, *Jewish Prayer*, 53.

But how does such love manifest? What did this mean practically? Petuchowski says, "For you may search the Bible from the beginning to the end . . . and you will not find a single command which says: 'Thou shalt pray!' What you will find, however, is a verse, Deuteronomy 11:13, which tells Israel 'to love the Lord your God, and to serve Him with all your heart and with all your soul.'"[34] Therefore the author's audience may not have viewed the commandment to love the Lord as an explicit reference to prayer, but in time this seems to have been one of the reasonable expressions of such love and service to the Lord. As will be shown below, love for God and obedience to God are the qualifications for effectual prayer. Deuteronomy 11:13–21 says,

13 וְהָיָ֗ה אִם־שָׁמֹ֤עַ תִּשְׁמְעוּ֙ אֶל־מִצְוֺתַ֔י אֲשֶׁ֧ר אָנֹכִ֛י מְצַוֶּ֥ה אֶתְכֶ֖ם הַיּ֑וֹם לְאַהֲבָ֞ה אֶת־יְהוָ֤ה אֱלֹֽהֵיכֶם֙ וּלְעָבְד֔וֹ בְּכָל־לְבַבְכֶ֖ם וּבְכָל־נַפְשְׁכֶֽם׃

14 וְנָתַתִּ֧י מְטַֽר־אַרְצְכֶ֛ם בְּעִתּ֖וֹ יוֹרֶ֣ה וּמַלְק֑וֹשׁ וְאָסַפְתָּ֣ דְגָנֶ֔ךָ וְתִֽירֹשְׁךָ֖ וְיִצְהָרֶֽךָ׃

15 וְנָתַתִּ֛י עֵ֥שֶׂב בְּשָׂדְךָ֖ לִבְהֶמְתֶּ֑ךָ וְאָכַלְתָּ֖ וְשָׂבָֽעְתָּ׃

16 הִשָּֽׁמְר֣וּ לָכֶ֔ם פֶּ֥ן יִפְתֶּ֖ה לְבַבְכֶ֑ם וְסַרְתֶּ֗ם וַעֲבַדְתֶּם֙ אֱלֹהִ֣ים אֲחֵרִ֔ים וְהִשְׁתַּחֲוִיתֶ֖ם לָהֶֽם׃

17 וְחָרָ֨ה אַף־יְהוָ֜ה בָּכֶ֗ם וְעָצַ֤ר אֶת־הַשָּׁמַ֙יִם֙ וְלֹֽא־יִהְיֶ֣ה מָטָ֔ר וְהָ֣אֲדָמָ֔ה לֹ֥א תִתֵּ֖ן אֶת־יְבוּלָ֑הּ וַאֲבַדְתֶּ֣ם מְהֵרָ֗ה מֵעַל֙ הָאָ֣רֶץ הַטֹּבָ֔ה אֲשֶׁ֥ר יְהוָ֖ה נֹתֵ֥ן לָכֶֽם׃

18 וְשַׂמְתֶּם֙ אֶת־דְּבָרַ֣י אֵ֔לֶּה עַל־לְבַבְכֶ֖ם וְעַֽל־נַפְשְׁכֶ֑ם וּקְשַׁרְתֶּ֨ם אֹתָ֤ם לְאוֹת֙ עַל־יֶדְכֶ֔ם וְהָי֥וּ לְטוֹטָפֹ֖ת בֵּ֥ין עֵינֵיכֶֽם׃

19 וְלִמַּדְתֶּ֥ם אֹתָ֛ם אֶת־בְּנֵיכֶ֖ם לְדַבֵּ֣ר בָּ֑ם בְּשִׁבְתְּךָ֤ בְּבֵיתֶ֙ךָ֙ וּבְלֶכְתְּךָ֣ בַדֶּ֔רֶךְ וּֽבְשָׁכְבְּךָ֖ וּבְקוּמֶֽךָ׃

20 וּכְתַבְתָּ֛ם עַל־מְזוּז֥וֹת בֵּיתֶ֖ךָ וּבִשְׁעָרֶֽיךָ׃

21 לְמַ֨עַן יִרְבּ֤וּ יְמֵיכֶם֙ וִימֵ֣י בְנֵיכֶ֔ם עַ֚ל הָֽאֲדָמָ֔ה אֲשֶׁ֨ר נִשְׁבַּ֧ע יְהוָ֛ה לַאֲבֹתֵיכֶ֖ם לָתֵ֣ת לָהֶ֑ם כִּימֵ֥י הַשָּׁמַ֖יִם עַל־הָאָֽרֶץ׃ ס

This passage likewise contains the imperative and qualification to love God as well as the command to study, teach, and bind the author's words on one's hand and forehead. But the main thrust of this passages centers on the theme of reward and punishment. DiSante says that this passage is built on three main propositions:

> The first proposition makes a conditional statement about the real world: "if you obey . . . he will give" (vv. 13–15). . . . The

---

34. Petuchowski, *Understanding Jewish Prayer*, 18.

second proposition consists of a lengthy command/exhortation (vv. 16–17) which puts negatively the ideas which the preceding proposition expressed in positive terms.... The Third proposition consists of a series of commands (vv. 18–21) which in substance repeat Deut 6:6–9: the duty of having the divine commandments always in mind (v. 18), even in a corporeal way by means of the *tefillin*; the duty of teaching and transmitting them day after day to one's children (v. 19); the duty of observing them in one's home (vv. 20–21), using the *mezuzah* as an aid.[35]

Hammer remarks that the opinions of the rabbis involved viewing this passage as implying that God "made the Land of Israel heavily dependent on the rains in order to assure that people would be conscious daily of their need for God and grateful for His gifts."[36] In his view, the rains or lack thereof, represented reward and punishment. If the people obeyed the commands passed to them, they would certainly reap a tangible benefit. On the other hand, if they disobeyed, they would certainly fail to reap a tangible benefit. Thus, the author reminded his audience to not forget the words that were spoken. To do so would have devastating consequences. It is likely that one of the primary ways by which a Jew remembered the commandments was by reciting them in prayer. In this manner, prayer led to obedience and obedience led to blessing (or the granting of certain favorable "results"[37]).

The commandment to wear *Tefillin* is mentioned in several passages in the Hebrew Scriptures (Deut 6:4–9; 11:13–21; Exod 13:11–16). Tradition says that only men may wear the *Tefillin* and only during daylight hours (barring Shabbat and holy days). According to Steinsaltz, many of the regulations concerning the form and structure of the *Tefillin* were passed from tradition rather than directly from the Torah. Notwithstanding, the passages above were written down on parchment slips and inserted in *Tefillin* boxes made of hard leather that were worn on the arm and head.[38] He says:

> The name *Tefillin*—form the word *Tefillah*, prayer—apparently derived from this custom of wearing them during prayer services. In the Torah, they are known by the unique term *Totafot*, as well as by the more general words for "sign" and "reminder." Some *Rishonim* and *Aharonim* have offered different explanations for the term *Tefillin*: i.e., as being derived from the root

---

35. DiSante, *Jewish Prayer*, 60.
36. Hammer, *Entering Jewish Prayer*, 126.
37. Neyrey, *Give God the Glory*, 9.
38. For a discussion of the dimensions of the Tefillin boxes, see Steinsaltz, *Guide to Jewish Prayer*, 353.

TFL, meaning "combination" and "connection," or from the root PLL, which means "sign" or "testimony."[39]

Accordingly, Steinsaltz says, "The biblical passages embody several of the basic essentials of the Jewish faith: the belief in God, love of God to the point of self-sacrifice, reward and punishment, the exodus from Egypt, the election of the people of Israel, and their inheritance of the Land of Israel. ... The *Tefillin* thus contains the essential principles of God's law, together with the injunction to continue studying it, and to preserve and observe it. Hence the commandment is a 'remembrance' and a 'reminder.'"[40] Therefore it is not difficult to detect how such an external sign would serve to remind the people of God about the necessity of walking in obedience and not forgetting the God who redeemed them. To live as a Jew involved being both knowledgeable and mindful of these realities and praying accordingly.

The final passage is Numbers 15:37–41, which states:

³⁷ וַיֹּאמֶר יְהוָה אֶל־מֹשֶׁה לֵּאמֹר׃

³⁸ דַּבֵּר אֶל־בְּנֵי יִשְׂרָאֵל וְאָמַרְתָּ אֲלֵהֶם וְעָשׂוּ לָהֶם צִיצִת עַל־כַּנְפֵי בִגְדֵיהֶם לְדֹרֹתָם וְנָתְנוּ עַל־צִיצִת הַכָּנָף פְּתִיל תְּכֵלֶת׃

³⁹ וְהָיָה לָכֶם לְצִיצִת וּרְאִיתֶם אֹתוֹ וּזְכַרְתֶּם אֶת־כָּל־מִצְוֹת יְהוָה וַעֲשִׂיתֶם אֹתָם וְלֹא־תָתוּרוּ אַחֲרֵי לְבַבְכֶם וְאַחֲרֵי עֵינֵיכֶם אֲשֶׁר־אַתֶּם זֹנִים אַחֲרֵיהֶם׃

⁴⁰ לְמַעַן תִּזְכְּרוּ וַעֲשִׂיתֶם אֶת־כָּל־מִצְוֹתָי וִהְיִיתֶם קְדֹשִׁים לֵאלֹהֵיכֶם׃

⁴¹ אֲנִי יְהוָה אֱלֹהֵיכֶם אֲשֶׁר הוֹצֵאתִי אֶתְכֶם מֵאֶרֶץ מִצְרַיִם לִהְיוֹת לָכֶם לֵאלֹהִים אֲנִי יְהוָה אֱלֹהֵיכֶם׃ פ

The concept and practice of making of tassels/fringes[41] on the corner of one's garments may be foreign to the modern ear. What does this practice signify and/or symbolize? Hammer explains, "The fringes contained a thread of deep blue . . . a symbol of divine royalty, comparable to the purpose of Roman nobility. Seeing them reminds us of how we are supposed to live in the sight of God. The fringes are a commandment whose only importance and meaning is to remind us of all the commandments."[42] DiSante draws attention to the *tallit* (a cape in the form of a scapular), which serves as a reminder (like the *Tefillin*—tassels or fringes) and "obeys a

---

39. Steinsaltz, *Guide to Jewish Prayer*, 349–50.

40. Steinsaltz, *Guide to Jewish Prayer*, 354.

41. Hammer says, "In biblical times these fringes, or tzitzit, were not worn on some special garment, as they are today, but were attached to the corners of everyday garb where they could easily be seen" (*Entering Jewish Prayer*, 127). For a discussion on the essential regulations for making tzitzits, see Steinsaltz, *Guide to Jewish Prayer*, 344–45.

42. Hammer, *Entering Jewish Prayer*, 129.

theological-pedagogical logic, being a sign and instrument of holiness. It is not simply an aid to remembrance of what the Lord wills, but makes the wearer live in the holiness to which the Lord calls."[43] Therefore, the apparel reminds the people of God of what they have heard and how they are to respond in lifestyle and practice.

The Tefillah

The Tefillah[44] ("the prayer") originally consisted of eighteen short benedictions (or prayers) recited three times a day, morning, afternoon, and evening. Dating to several centuries before the destruction of the Second Temple in 70 CE, the Tefillah was the primary prayer for the Pharisees of second-temple Judaism. It was also known as the Amidah ("Standing [Prayer]") or the Shemoneh Esreh ("Eighteen [Benedictions]") and was customarily recited after the recitation of the Shema without a break. Following closely with the themes of the Exodus, the Tefillah contains benedictions (or blessings) that follow a threefold pattern: (1) praise (first three); (2) petition (twelve or thirteen); and (3) thanksgiving (final three).[45]

The following outlines the structure of the Tefillah:[46]

---

43. As noted by DiSante, *Jewish Prayer*, 62.

44. Ariel says that the term *tefillah* "is derived from the Hebrew root *pll*, which means 'to judge,' 'to intercede on behalf of someone,' or 'to hope.' Tefillah therefore implies an act of self-judgment or intercession on one's own behalf before God, or the expression of hopeful sentiments" (*What Do the Jews Believe?*, 188).

45. Crump, *Knocking on Heaven's Door*, 110.

46. DiSante, *Jewish Prayer*, 87.

A.	Three Opening Benedictions (1–3)		
		1. Thou art God	Praise of God
		2. Thou art mighty	
		3. Thou art holy	
		Therefore we ask:	
		4. Understanding	Spiritual Blessings
		5. Repentance	
		6. Forgiveness	
		7. Personal freedom	Material Blessings
		8. Health	
		9. Well-being	
		10. Reunification of the scattered	
B.	Thirteen Intermediate Petitions (4–16)		
		11. Integral justice	Social blessings
		12. Punishment of enemies	
		13. Reward of the just	
		14. The new Jerusalem	
		15. The messiah	
		16. Hearing of prayers	
C.	Three Final Benedictions (17–19)	Therefore:	
		17. Restore worship in Jerusalem	Thanksgiving to God
		18. Accept our gratitude	
		19. Grant us peace	

The pattern above begins with praise, continues with requests (spiritual, material, and social) and then concludes with thanksgiving. In particular, the opening prayer (*Avot*, "The Fathers") says:

> Blessed are You,
> Lord our God and God of our fathers,
> *God* of Abraham,
> *God* of Isaac,
> And *God* of Jacob,
> Great, mighty and revered God,
> God high above all,
> You who bestow loving kindness
> And are master of all things,
> *Who remembers* the deeds of lovingkindness
> Performed by the fathers,
> And will bring a redeemer
> To their children's children
> For your name's sake in love.
> King, Helper, Savior and Shield!
> Blessed are you, Lord,
> Shield of Abraham.[47]

The second prayer of the Amidah continues by extoling God's works in the earth. The *Gevurot* states:

> *You are mighty* forever, Lord,
> You revive the dead,
> You are powerful to save.
> You make the wind blow
> And the rain fall.
> *You sustain the living* with loving kindness,
> *Revive the dead* in great compassion,
> *Support* the falling,
> *Heal* the sick,
> *Free* the captives,
> And keep faith with those who sleep in the dust.
> Who is like You,
> *Master* of mighty deeds,
> And who resembles you, King,
> You who kill and bring back to life.

---

47. Each of the following prayers are cited in Martin, *Prayer in Judaism*, 113, 117, 121, 124–26 (emphasis added).

And make salvation flourish?

Noteworthy are references to the power of God to revive deceased humanity and his apparent sovereignty over the natural world. This prayer moves from statements of praise to petitions concerning the falling, the sick, the captives, and those who have died. In explicit language, this prayer calls on God to compassionately act in behalf of his creatures on earth, most presumably through the act of resurrection (e.g., specific "results"). However, the theme of the *Kedusha* ("sanctification") directs the trajectory of the prayer from the low point on earth to highest heavens. The prayer states:

> We will sanctify your name in the world
> Even as they sanctify it *in the highest heavens*,
> As is written by your prophet:
> "And they called one unto the other and said:
> *Holy, holy, holy* is the Lord of hosts;
> The whole earth is filled with his glory."

Similar in content to Psalm 8, this prayer extols God's name. However, in contrast to Psalm 8:3, where the psalmist alone addresses God, the *Kedusha* employs inclusive/communal language that invites the participation of people on earth and the inhabitants of heaven (most presumably the angels). Following the language of Isaiah 6:3, this prayer raises the attribute of God's holiness (*qadosh*) to the superlative and declares that the earth is filled with God's glory.

Following the *Kedusha* are the thirteen benedictions containing the formula *baruch atta Adonai* ("Blessed are You, Lord"). DiSante says that these intermediate petitions (4–16) "may be regarded as the fundamental charter of Jewish values."[48] Such values include but are not limited to understanding, repentance, forgiveness, personal freedom, health, etc. These values are both practical and spiritual in nature and follow the acknowledgement and praise of God. As noted by Martin, "The first six of the Intermediate Benedictions of the Amidah are petitions for individual needs. As common to all men, however, they are couched in the plural. The next six are petitions for the collective needs of the Jewish people, and the final one is a plea that God may respond favorably to the prayers addressed to him."[49] A summary of the intermediate benedictions includes the following petitions in partial form: "Bring us back, our Father, to your Torah"; "Forgive us, our Father, for we have sinned"; "Look upon our affliction and take up our

---

48. DiSante, *Jewish Prayer*, 94.
49. Martin, *Prayer in Judaism*, 127.

cause"; "Heal us, Lord, and we will be healed"; "Bless for us, Lord our God, this year." The petitioners' confidence is summarized in the words, "*Blessed are You, Lord, who hears prayer.*"

Touching on the themes of hearing God, the oneness of God, love for God, the promise of divine blessing, the reminder to keep his commandments, and receiving the yoke of God's Kingdom, the Shema provided scriptural content for the praying community who addressed God twice daily in either private or communal settings. In particular, as a prayer, the Shema places the responsibility on the adult members of Jewish society to teach the commandments of God to their children and to construct visual reminders of God's words. The consequences, then, are practical in nature for any praying Jew. Remembering to do God's commandments results in blessing, whereas failure to do God's commandments results in punishment. As such, in contrast to prayers that implore God to hear, the language of the Shema is uniquely constructed to remind the one praying to hear. Thus, in seeking to be heard, the Shema reminds the one praying that God must also be heard and responded to in obedience.

Accordingly, the thrice-daily recitation of the Tefillah/Amidah, with its focus on the themes of the power of God and future redemption, provides a guide for praising, thanking, and petitioning God. As such, the Tefillah/Amidah is a thoroughly God-centered prayer that seeks for the name of God to be sanctified on earth by his people as it is in heaven by the angels. But this prayer is replete with requests that begin with the individual, yet extends to the needs of the community as a whole. It petitions God for the sick who are alive, but also petitions God to revive those who are dead. Thus the contextual trajectory of the Tefillah/Amidah is far-reaching, extending from earth to heaven, and makes request for life in the midst of death. It centers on the holiness of God but also assumes the fragility of man. The predicament of Israel notwithstanding, the Tefillah/Amidah confidently asserts that God hears prayer.

In summary, the Shema and Tefillah complement one another and provide instruction concerning how one may approach God and what one may expect from God in prayerful dialogue. As prayers, they assume the primacy of both the personal and communal aspects of prayer. They serve as reminders that one may pray in private, but the implications of prayer are necessarily public, extending from one's family to the nation of Israel as a whole. Therefore, the nature of these prayers precludes approaching the sacred space of prayer with mere self-interests in mind. Much like other OT prayers that center on the nature, name, and power of God, the assumption behind the Shema and Tefillah is that one may approach God in boldness and with confidence that his prayer will be heard and answered accordingly.

Questions

1. The Shema centers on love for God. How is love for God related to prayer to God in the Fourth Gospel?
2. The Shema places an emphasis on obedience to the commandments of God. How does keeping God's commandments and prayer relate in the Fourth Gospel?
3. The Shema emphasizes the necessity of remembering the words of God. Is this requirement emphasized in the Fourth Gospel? If so, how does it relate to prayer?
4. Are any prayers present in the Fourth Gospel that emphasize not only speaking to God but also listening to him?
5. The Amidah contains prayers that center on reviving the dead, healing the sick, and freeing the captives. How does this genre of prayer relate to prayer in the Fourth Gospel? According to the Fourth Gospel, what specific "result(s)" may one seek to obtain through prayer?
6. Both the Shema and Tefillah were prayed at certain times of the day. According to the Fourth Gospel, what time of day should prayer occur?

Prayers from Qumran

Of the eight hundred manuscripts from the Judean Desert, the Dead Sea Scrolls contain two hundred hymns, prayers, and psalms that provide important data concerning Jewish prayer in the Second Temple Era. The vast majority of the scrolls was discovered at Qumran, while a small percentage was discovered at other sites. Unknown before 1947, these documents provide information concerning a community that existed for approximately two hundred years (150 BCE to 68 CE).[50] Schuller says concerning the nature and content of this ancient discovery, "In addition to actual texts of prayers and psalms, there are explicit statements about praying, regulations regarding how and when to pray, and indirect references to the practice of prayer and other acts that were part of the worship (*avodah*) of God."[51] The literature of this time can be divided up into seven categories: (1) liturgies

---

50. Schuller remarks that the Essenes "seemed to have had little hesitation in putting their prayers and religious poetry into written form, in contrast to the practices of both Pharisaic and Rabbinic Judaism, where the setting down of prayers in writing was discouraged (cf. *Tosephta Shabbath* 13:4)" ("Prayer in the Dead Sea Scrolls," 69).

51. Schuller, "Prayer in the Dead Sea Scrolls," 66.

for fixed prayer time; (2) ceremonial liturgies; (3) eschatological prayers; (4) magical incantations; (5) psalmic collections; (6) Hodayot (or thanksgiving) hymns; and (7) prayers embedded in prose/narratives.[52] Thus, the scrolls provide a unique glimpse into prayers that would have otherwise been undocumented and, therefore, unknown.[53]

Scholars have sought to consistently maintain a distinction between the sectarian and non-sectarian writings of the Essene community.[54] The former writings are characterized by their cosmic dualism, determinism, and apocalyptic eschatology. The latter writings were produced earlier and were read more broadly in Second Temple Judaism.[55] Examples of sectarian prayers include the following: Thanksgiving Psalms or Hodayot (1QH^a; 4QH^{a-f}), the Blessings or Berakot (4Q286–290; 1QSb), and the Blessings of Purification (4Q512; 4Q414). Non-sectarian prayers include the following: Words of the Luminaries (4Q504) and the "apocryphal" psalms (11QPs^a; 4QPs^f). Penner says that this literary division provokes two important questions: (1) "What can the non-sectarian texts teach us about the broader landscape of Second Temple Judaism?"; (2) "What can the sectarian texts tell us about the distinct movement or community that is associated in some ways with the site of Qumran?"[56] The latter question inevitably seeks for answers that center on a smaller community of individuals whose religious experience was defined by its theological and eschatological outlook; thus the focus is more local in scope. The former question naturally centers on fixity of the liturgy in the era of the Essene in general and the Second Temple Era in particular; thus the focus is broader and more inclusive in scope.[57]

While these questions are important, perhaps the more relevant issue at hand centers less on the provenance of such prayers and more on their similarities with other Jewish prayer traditions. Sarason has shown rather convincingly the presence of overlap between Qumran and later rabbinic prayer materials in content, theme, prayer style, rhetoric, genre, vocabulary,

---

52. As noted in Chazon, "Hymns and Prayers in the Dead Sea Scrolls," 258.

53. For a work that considers the impact of the Dead Sea Scrolls on Johannine studies, see Coloe and Thatcher, *John, Qumran, and the Dead Sea Scrolls*.

54. Schuller identifies the Qumran group by the label "Essenes" or "the community" and thus avoids using the phrase "Qumran community" in order to orient the reader to all the members of the group—many of whom were married and lived among other towns and inhabitations. See Schuller, "Prayer in the Dead Sea Scrolls," 67.

55. Schuller, "Prayer in the Dead Sea Scrolls," 68.

56. Penner, *Patterns of Daily Prayer*, 40–41.

57. Penner remarks that documents such as *Words of the Luminaries*, *Festival Prayers*, and (perhaps) *Songs of the Sabbath Sacrifice* demonstrate that "the practice of fixed prayer was not a sectarian phenomenon, but was developing in more 'mainstream' forms of Second Tempe period Judaism" (*Patterns of Daily Prayer*, 42).

and idiom. How can such similarity be accounted for? He says that all the shared vocabulary "has a basis in biblical prayer language ... both communities self-consciously made use of the stock phrases, idioms, and words of biblical prayer."[58] Schuller says, "The very essence of prayer/hymnic discourse, whether sectarian or non-sectarian, is its dependence on a common stock of stereotypical and formulaic, biblically-based phraseology."[59] This is not to say that there are no differences in the social context, function, or application of such prayers. Such differences are evident and must be taken into consideration.[60] The main point is that the similarities in the prayer materials is likely due to a shared, common background or cultural horizon that is informed and shaped by biblical models.[61] And it is that model that in varying degrees served to shape the contours of prayer throughout Jewish history.

Schuller cites several important features of Qumranic prayer that are relevant to this analysis. First, the prayers of the Essenes must be viewed, in part, in light of the community's secession from the Jerusalem temple[62] and their view that prayer could replace sacrifice (though not ultimately). With this in mind, Schuller cites 1QS 9.5 as evidence that prayer, coupled with a way of life in obedience to the Torah ("as interpreted 'properly'") was like the sacrifices at the temple and could function as a means of atonement.[63] He explains further:

> This understanding of the cultic and atoning function that prayer could exercise seems to have developed largely as a

58. Sarason, "'Intersections' of Qumran and Rabbinic Judaism," 175. He points to Daniel 9, Nehemiah 9, and other writings, such as Judith 9 and 3 Maccabees 2. Sarason says, "The rabbinic *Yosher* benediction in the Genizah texts, in fact, is composed almost completely of a patchwork of biblical verses: Isa. 45:7, Ps. 104:24, and Ps. 136:7, which figure structurally in the Babylonian versions as well. The commonalities in the deployment of these themes between Qumran and the Rabbis undoubtedly reflects the shared background in the late Second Commonwealth" ("'Intersections' of Qumran and Rabbinic Judaism," 177).

59. Schuller, "Prayer, Hymnic, and Liturgical Texts," 170.

60. For a discussion of certain differences, see Penner, *Patterns of Daily Prayer*, 44–47.

61. Sarason "'Intersections' of Qumran and Rabbinic Judaism," 176.

62. Chazon and Bernstein note, "Prayer's function as a substitute for Temple worship and as the operative medium for contact with God led to the amassing of a large and rich corpus of liturgical and hymnic material by the Qumran group. The presence of biblical psalm in the corpus demonstrates that not all of the prayers were authored by the sect, and it is likely that many of the extra-biblical prayers which the Qumran sectarians copied and used were also not written by them" ("Introduction to Prayer at Qumran," 10).

63. Schuller, "Prayer in the Dead Sea Scrolls," 72.

> pragmatic response to the Essenes' conviction that the sacrifices in the present Jerusalem temple under the existing priesthood were being carried out according to misguided halakic practice ... and perhaps even more seriously—according to the wrong calendar, that is, a lunar calendar rather than the "proper" solar calendar. Thus the Essenes could not take part in the regular fixed daily, sabbath, and festival sacrifices. But in looking ahead to the final days of the great eschatological battle of the Sons of Light over the Sons of Darkness, the first stage of victory after seven years would involve the restoration of temple worship in Jerusalem (cf. 1QM 2.1–6).[64]

It is widely known that the Essene community believed that the Jerusalem priesthood was apostate and that the temple services were impure. Crump remarks, "Their remedy was to view their own community as a new spiritual temple replacing the old. They were assured that God heard their prayers because they were offered within the new human temple of the believing community."[65] Thus, in some respects, the praying Qumran community shared a common situation with other Jews, whether in the exilic or post-70 CE era; they had no access to the temple or its sacrificial system. As noted above, Jewish prayer originally consisted of spontaneous and personal outbursts of communication with God. While prayer did occur in connection to the temple, it also occurred apart from it. Thus, it is not hard to determine why the "offering" of prayer would be deemed a suitable substitute for the Qumran community.

Second, while the scrolls do contain spontaneous, personal words of devotion and petition (1QS 9.26), as indicated in the Rule of the Community (1QS 6.2–4), prayer was also a corporate activity in this ancient community. It is often assumed that the Essenes had specific places designated to pray, but Schuller says that there is little archaeological evidence for this assumption. Yet one passage in the Damascus Document refers to the "house of prostration" (*beth hishtahut*, CD 11.21–22). Some have viewed this phrase as referring to the Jerusalem temple or designated, local places of worship[66] away from the temple. Schuller notes, "For Essenes who lived at the site of Qumran, their place of prayer was probably the main dining hall. It is, in fact, on the basis of how many people could prostrate themselves in the community's dining room that Hartmut Stegemann argues that the group

---

64. Schuller, "Prayer in the Dead Sea Scrolls," 72.
65. Crump, *Knocking on Heaven's Door*, 30.
66. See Steudel, "Houses of Prostration," 49–68.

that lived there normally numbered only about 50 people."[67] As noted, in the eras that predate and postdate the Qumran community, prayer was offered at the temple, in the synagogue, at home, and in other places. Thus both the personal and communal nature of Essene prayer accords with, in some measure, what is seen in both the Old and New Testaments.

Third, there is notable evidence concerning the fixed times in which prayer was offered. Schuller cites 1QS 9.26–10.1 which states, "With the offering of his lips he will bless him [God] during the set times that he prescribed." Chazon and Bernstein thus observe that there were benedictions for the evening and the morning and for each day of the month (4Q503; cf. 4Q408).[68] Chazon also says that Daily Prayers (4QS503) consisted of morning and evening prayers that "praise God for the renewal of the heavenly lights at sunset and sunrise, and with each daily change in the moon's phases."[69] Chazon notes further, "4Q408 is another liturgy of morning and evening blessings which praises God's creation and daily renewal of light and darkness."[70] Bradshaw cites the following examples of fixed daily prayers that were likely repeated twice daily:[71]

1QS 10.1–3a		1QH 12.4–7
at the times which he has ordained,		at all times and season
(a)	at the beginning of the rule of light,	at the coming of light from [its dwelling],
(b)	at its turning-point,	at its turning-point in its ordered course, in accordance with the laws of the great luminary,
(c)	at its being gathered to the dwelling decreed for it,	at the turn of the evening and the departure of the light,

67. Schuller, "Prayer in the Dead Sea Scrolls," 73.

68. Chazon, "Hymns and Prayers," 259.

69. Following Hammerling (*History of Prayer*, 35), it is significant that the Qumran prayer text supports the existence of "liturgical alternative" to the temple sacrifices while the temple was still standing. The Qumran community practiced prayer at the rising and setting of the sun, which stands in contrast to the timing of prayer connected with sacrifices the temple.

70. Chazon, "Hymns and Prayers," 259.

71. Bradshaw, *Daily Prayer in the Early Church*, 4–5. For a critical discussion of these Dead Sea Scrolls documents, see Bradshaw, *Daily Prayer in the Early Church*, 4–7.

1QS 10.1–3a	1QH 12.4–7
(d) at the beginning of the watches of darkness when he opens his treasury and sets him above,	at the beginning of the rule of darkness,
(e) at its turning point,	in the season of the night, at its turning-point,
(f) at its being gathered from before the light,	at the turn of the morning and the time when it is gathered to its dwelling before the light,
(g) at the appearance of the luminaries from their holy realm,	at the departure of the night,
(h) and at their being gathered to the abode of glory;	and at the coming of the day;

Some have viewed 1QS 10.1–3 as containing six distinct times of prayer, but Schuller is right to say that this is "too literal of a reading of a poetic calendar."[72] He says further:

> From a combination of descriptive statements and actual prayer texts we can deduce at least some components of these daily time of prayer. "With the arrival of day and night I will enter the covenant of God, and at the exit of evening and morning I will speak of his laws" (1QS 10.10) probably alludes to the recitation of the Shema along with the Decalogue.[73]

Thus, the above examples are plausibly reflective of a twice-daily prayer pattern that was practiced in the Essene community. Yet as will be seen below, Essene prayer was not restricted to this model; rather the twice-daily recitation was one aspect of religious practice that fit within a broader spectrum of daily, annual, and festival prayers.

Accordingly, Words of the Luminaries (4Q504–6) are prayers for the days of the week, ending on the Sabbath. Chazon says, "All six weekday prayers open with a historical review and then petition for physical deliverance (Tuesday, Wednesday, Friday) or spiritual fortitude: knowledge of the Law, turning from sin and forgiveness (Sunday, Thursday; the Monday petition is unfortunately lost). Each petition is followed by a concluding

---

72. Schuller, "Prayer in the Dead Sea Scrolls," 74.
73. Schuller, "Prayer in the Dead Sea Scrolls," 74.

blessing and "Amen, Amen" response."[74] Songs of the Sabbath Sacrifice (4Q400–407; 11Q17) is best viewed as annual festival liturgy, which consists of thirteen Sabbath songs (of a sage) for the first quarter of the year. Chazon says, "The daring of these Sabbaths presumes a solar calendar of 364 days. This is an earthly liturgy in which human worshippers invite the angels to praise God and describe angelic worship in the heavenly temple."[75] Finally, Festival Prayers (1QS34–34bis; 4Q507–9) bear witness to prayer for annual festivals (The Prayer for the Day of Atonement) beginning with the New Year in Tishrei. Schuller cites the festivals of: the Day of Atonement, *Sukkot*, Passover, *Shavuot*, the beginning of each new month, the First Fruits of New Wine, Oil, and Wood (as specified in the Temple Scroll, 11Q19.11–25.2; and some of the calendrical texts, 4Q325, 327).[76]

Further, the Qumran documents also contained eschatological prayers that included prayers that were to be uttered in the final war. A brief summary of a few of these prayers begins with a discussion of War Scroll (1QM, 4QM$^{a, b, e}$). Chazon says:

> This operative plan for the eschatological war between the sons of light and the sons of darkness prescribes prayers for several stages of the campaign. The prayer before the battle (1QM 10:8– 12:18; 18:5–19:8) appeals to prophecies of salvation and divine deliverance of Israel in the past, while petitioning God to crush the nations and redeem his elect, holy people in the upcoming battle.[77]

Accordingly, the testimonies of War Rule (4Q285) and 11QBerakhot also relate to eschatological prayers. Chazon states concerning these works, "The overlapping portion of these scrolls is a blessing for Israel and the angels which reflect the sect's belief in its communion with angels. The blessing for rain, produce and physical well-being is based on Deuteronomic covenant blessings and curses (Deut 11:14; 28:12, 21–22; 31:20), with the biblical priestly blessing (Num 6:24) supplying the opening framework."[78] Moreover, Chazon and Bernstein note that Qumran documents also contain magical incantations (hymns) (4Q510–511; cf. 4Q444; 8Q5; 4Q560), collections of psalms (more than thirty biblical scrolls, non-canonical psalms, and several that compare biblical and non-biblical psalms), Hodayot hymns ("I thank you, Lord"; 1QH^a; 4QH$^{a, b}$), and embedded prose prayers

74. Chazon, "Hymns and Prayers," 259.
75. Chazon, "Hymns and Prayers," 259.
76. Schuller, "Prayer in the Dead Sea Scrolls," 77.
77. Chazon, "Hymns and Prayers," 262.
78. Chazon, "Hymns and Prayers," 262–63.

(pseudepigraphical prayers of Abraham [1QapGen ar], Levi [4QTLevi ar^b], and Joseph [4Q372]).[79]

In summary, the Qumran documents provide a unique, inside glimpse into the prayer life of (most probably) the Essene community. The above summary is not exhaustive but rather provides a brief outline of notable prayers from the Qumran community. In light of the data provided above, it is evident that the Essene community prayed both individually and communally, at different times, and on different occasions. This survey, then, demonstrates the presence of a supplementary stream of Qumranic tradition of prayer that, in varying degrees, was influenced by the biblical model and congruent with the praying Jewish community of the biblical tradition and the Second Temple Era. Most relevant to this analysis is the community's focus on prayer as a replacement for sacrifice. By seceding from the temple enterprise, the Essenes seem to indicate that although sacrifice was not unimportant, prayer could take place without it. But as indicated above, prayer was offered in the hope that true worship in the Jerusalem temple would be restored. By believing that the Jerusalem priesthood was apostate and that the temple services were unclean, the Essenes' remedy involved viewing their community as a new spiritual temple. Thus, by living in obedience to the Torah and right living, the Essenes believed themselves to function as a pure conduit or sounding board of prayer from earth to heaven. This conviction at least conceptually conveys the community's esteem for the temple as the place (or means) where true worship occurs. Yet in contrast to Solomon's account of the temple as the place of prayer, the Essene community itself was the "place" (of obedience and atonement) where prayers were channeled heavenward to God.

Questions

1. The Essenes were assured that God heard their prayers because they were offered within the new human temple of the believing community. On what grounds are prayers heard within the context of the Fourth Gospel?

2. As noted above, prayers coupled with a way of life in obedience to the Torah were like the sacrifices at the temple and could function as a means of atonement. Does the Fourth Gospel link prayer and obedience? If so, what is the practical outcome? Is prayer coupled with obedience more effective or potent?

79. Chazon and Bernstein, "Introduction to Prayer at Qumran," 11.

3. Various Qumran documents contain collections of hymns and psalms. Does the Fourth Gospel draw on psalmody in its articulation or prescription of prayer?

4. In what ways does the temple motif relate to the community of believers and prayer in the Fourth Gospel? How does prayer function in light of the abolition of temple worship?

CHAPTER 3

Greco-Roman Prayer

THE STUDY OF GRECO-ROMAN prayer is very complex and must be approached on its own terms.¹ While there is some overlap in theory with monotheistic religions, even a cursory survey of the pertinent ancient literature reveals a dynamic contrast in the context, form, and practice of prayer in comparison to Hebrew and Christian models. Of course, Greco-Roman religion stands in sharp contrast to the aforementioned Jewish religious presuppositions, practices, and attitudes in numerous ways. Most notably, the former is polytheistic and the latter is monotheistic. Jewish prayers centered on communication with one God. Greco-Romans prayers centered on communication with multiple gods. Whereas Jewish prayer involved communication between the "I" (human) and the "You" (God), Greco-Roman prayer involved the "I" and the "they" (gods).

Further, Jewish and Christian prayer presupposes the existence of sin and iniquity. The Greeks had no such concept. The Greeks prayed to heroes, but Jews prayed to the one God of Israel. Alderlink and Martin remark that Greco-Roman prayer was articulated in a standing posture with arms extended toward the deity being addressed, while Christian expressions often included prostrated stances of bowing and kneeling.² They also say that Greek and Roman prayers were usually verbalized orally (much like some Jewish prayers, 1 Sam 1:12) in public contexts. Pulleyn observes that the audible nature of prayer is consistent with the Greek's concept of gods who

---

1. For an extensive bibliography for Greco-Roman prayers, see Charlesworth with Harding and Kiley, *Lord's Prayer*, 239–47.

2. Alderlink and Martin, "Prayer in Greco-Roman Religions," 125. However, there are examples in both the Hebrew and Christian Scriptures where prayer was offered with raised hands (1 Kgs 8:22, 54; 2 Chr 6:13; 1 Tim 2:8). For a brief discussion of this matter, see Hvalvik, "Praying with Outstretched Hands," 82–84.

were not omnipresent and therefore whose attention could be sought by audible speech. The audible approach stands in slight contrast to Christian prayers, which were also (but not exclusively) private in nature and in some cases occurring at night (Mark 1:35; Luke 6:12; 22:41, 55).[3]

Yet Jewish, Christian, and Greek traditions converge at the point of viewing prayer as the means of communication by which one makes requests to a higher being(s) ("superior receiver"), in order to obtain favorable "results." And each tradition of prayer assumes that communication takes place in the space of prayer that is provided by a "superior" receiver. Accordingly, in a certain sense Jewish and Christian prayer resembles Greek prayer in that it is practical in nature, centering on the well-being of the individual and the entire community. Accordingly, it has been shown above that Jewish prayer also focused on spontaneous personal outbursts. In many instances the same may be said of prayer for the Greeks. Pulleyn says that "Greek prayers could in theory be made at any time of day or night as need arose. Large, public religious festivals might even involve staying up all night, the so-called παννυχίδες ('all-nighters'). There was no liturgy of the hours. None the less, prayer at dawn and dusk seemed to occupy a special place in the Greek world."[4] Accordingly, Greek prayers were personal expressions of dependence on gods who resembled humans in some respects but were more powerful. Heiler says, "The gods remain always personal, thinking, willing, and feeling beings, who, though they excel men in power and blessedness, are like them in their spiritual life. They are never dissolved into non-personal natural forces. Man can enter into relational space with the gods because they are like man."[5] Notwithstanding the similarities between the one praying and the one prayed to, the "superior/subordinate"[6] relationship remained a key distinction in religious practice.

The Precision of Prayer

In deciding which god to pray to, one must not approach the gods in a whimsical or arbitrary manner. While the worshipper must not approach the gods empty-handed (without a sacrifice), they must also be careful not to approach the gods empty-minded (without the correct words/name). Aune says concerning invocations:

---

3. Pulleyn, *Prayer in Greek Religion*, 188.
4. Pulleyn, *Prayer in Greek Religion*, 157.
5. Heiler, *Prayer*, 84.
6. Neyrey, *Give God the Glory*, 9.

In the polytheistic systems of both Greek and Roman religion, it was necessary to discover which deity one wanted to influence through invoking his or her name (cf. Varro in Augustine, *Civitate Dei* 4.22; Horace, *Odes* 1.2.25–26). Greek prayers used certain formulas that were intended to insure that the god addressed would not be offended by an incorrect invocation. In the hymn of Zeus in the *Agamemnon* of Aeschylus the formula "whoever he is" (*hostis poti estin*) occurs (Aeschylus, *Agamemnon* line 160). This is similar to the Roman liturgical formulas "whether a god or goddess" (*sive deus sive dea* or *si deus si dea*; cf. Livy 7.26.4; 8.26.4; Aulus Gellius, *Noctes Atticae* 2.28.3; Arnobius, *Adversus nationes* 3.8) and "by whatever name you want to be called" (*sive quo alio nomine te appellari volueris*; cf. Macrobius, *Saturn* 3.9.10; Vergil, *Aeneid* 2.351; Servius, *Commentary on Vergil's Aeneid* 2.351; Apuleius, *Metamorphoses* or *The Golden Ass* 11.2; Catullus 34.21–22).[7]

Further, although many prayers were bipartite, Alderlink and Martin argue that the typical structure of Greco-Roman prayers follows the tripartite structure.[8] This involves: (1) an invocation, (2) justification, and (3) request. For example, they cite the *Iliad* (16.233–48) as follows:

[INVOCATION]

High Zeus, lord of Dodona, Pelasgian, living afar off, brooding over wintry Dodona, your prophets about your living, the Selloi who sleep on the ground with feet unwashed. Hear me:

[JUSTIFICATION]

As one time before when I prayed to you, you listened and did me honour, and smote strongly the host of the Achaians, *so one more time* bring to pass the wish that I pray for.

[REQUEST]

For see, I myself am staying where the ships are assembled, but I send out my companions and many Myrmidons with him to fight. Let glory, Zeus of the wide brows, go forth with him to fight. *Make brave the heart inside his breast*, so that even Hektor will find out whether our henchman knows how to fight his

---

7. Aune, "Prayer in the Greco-Roman World," 34.
8. Alderlink and Martin, "Prayer in Greco-Roman Religions," 123.

battles by himself, or whether his hands range invincible only those times when I myself go into the grind of the war god.⁹

The tripartite prayer begins with a petition to a particular god, but it also includes a reasonable justification for the petition and then the actual request itself. If the request was the most common form of Greco-Roman prayer, then the one to whom the request was offered was of utmost importance. In fact, the precision by which the ancients approached the gods was inextricably linked to their view that their destiny hung in the balance. The polytheistic nature of Greek religion necessitated careful consideration of the one being prayed to since the options of gods abounded both in terms of worshippers' need and geographical location. Therefore, Greco-Roman prayer is not directed exclusively toward one particular deity[10] for all occasions but is directed toward a particular deity who is able to meet a certain need on a particular occasion.

While examples abound, a summary of the more popular gods will suffice.[11] For example, Zeus was the father of the gods and the Greek god of the sky (Acts 14:12–13; 2 Macc 6:2) who brought rain. Aphrodite was the god of reproduction/fertility. Demeter was the god who brought forth grain. Athena was the goddess of politics, war, and commerce. Dionysus was the god of wine and debauchery.[12] Jeffers remarks that the principal deity of the early days of Rome was Numa. He says that in addition to ancestor worship, "Gods specific to the household were popular in early Rome: the Genius, representing the life-blood of the family (and much later incorporated into the cult of the emperor); the Penates, or embodiment of the storehouse; Vesta, the spirit of the hearth; and Lar, the luck of the family. The *lares* were good spirits associated with certain localities and worshipped at crossroads."[13] Artemis, the goddess of fertility, is mentioned in Acts 19:35, and Acts 28:11 remarks that the ship on which the apostle Paul traveled contained the insignia of the twin patron gods of sailors, Castor and Pollux. Further, Roman gods/goddesses include but are not limited to Jupiter (the first official Roman state god), Mars (the god of war and hard labor), Saturn

---

9. Emphasis added.

10. Pulleyn says, however, "In Homer, it is interesting that the formula nearly always involves Zeus. It is as though the worshipper wanted to invoke all the gods, starting with Zeus and working downwards. He wants them all to be involved" (*Prayer in Greek Religion*, 111).

11. For an overview of the gods of nature and human life, see Nilsson, *History of Greek Religion*, 105–133.

12. For a fuller outline of the Greek and Roman gods and goddesses, see Jeffers, *Greco-Roman World*, 93.

13. Jeffers, *Greco-Roman World*, 95.

(the god of agriculture), Ceres (the goddess of fertility), Vulcan (the god of fire), etc.

Prayer and Magic

The topic of Greek and Roman magical prayer has received a generous amount of scholarly attention in the last century. A survey of this genre of prayer demonstrates that magic was interwoven in various strands of religious practice, took on various forms of expression, and was viewed in both negative and positive terms. Janowitz says that for the ancients, "'Magic' was not bad because it was fraudulent . . . in the main magic was dangerous because it *worked*."[14] In the present discussion of Greco-Roman prayer, "magic" relates primarily on the usage of words, sounds, and religious rhetoric in prayer that may be used to harness such powers. But Roman prayers did not merely consist of mere words recited in monotone fashion but also in hymns. Fowler notes:

> The oldest Roman prayers we possess are usually called hymns, because the Latin word for them was carmen. . . . The word carmen . . . was used by the old Romans for any kind of metrical formula, whether hymn, prayer, or spell. Pliny, when writing of magic and incantations, plainly includes prayer among them; and Dr. Jevons has recently pointed out that singing, and especially singing in a low voice or muttered tones, is a characteristic of magic not only in Greece and Rome, but in many parts of the world at the present day. The evidence of the word is thus strongly in favour of the view that these ancient carmina of Roman worship were really spells; and the Carmen Arvalium itself does not contradict it.[15]

While knowledge of the gods' names was important, it is unlikely that the usage of a name conferred or eventuated some special power of the god. Rather, Pulleyn states, "The enumeration of a god's names often had more to do with a desire to glorify that god by a rehearsal of his names and attributes. This fits in with what we saw of hymns, namely that they are a sort of χάρις intended to delight the god."[16] Nilsson says accordingly, "A magical rite has reference to 'power' in general, but 'power' may give place to 'the powers' or

---

14. Janowitz, *Magic in the Roman World*, 3.
15. Fowler, *Religious Experience of the Roman People*, 202–3.
16. Pulleyn, *Prayer in Greek Religion*, 115.

to a certain power, and we have here the first step towards the gods."[17] But what was the nature of this step? As noted, knowing a god's name and his corresponding ability was important. But such knowledge is only beginning since, as noted by Aune, the gods "were conceptualized as existing in space but not omnipresent, and therefore must 'come' in order to be present and actually hear the supplicant."[18] Thus, the worshipper's invocation involves the request for deity to come, but also to grant revelation in his coming. Aune cites the following example:

> O lord Apollo, come (*elthe*) with Paian.
> *Give answer* (*chēmatison*) *to my questions*, lord. O master
> *Leave* (*lipe*) Mount Parnassos and the Delphic Pytho
> Whene'er my priestly lips *voice secret words*,
> First angel of [the god], great Zeus, IAO
> And you, MICHAEL, who rule heaven's realm,
> *I call*, and you, archangel GABRIEL.
> Down from Olympos, ABRASAX, delighting
> In dawns, come gracious who view sunset from
> The dawn, ADONAI. Father of the world,
> All nature quakes in fear of you, PAKERBETH.
> I adjure (*horkizō*) God's head, which is Olympos;
> I adjure (*horkizō*) God's signet, which is vision;
> I adjure (*horkizō*) the right hand you held o'er the world. . . .
> They send (*pempson*) me the divine spirit and that it
> *Fulfill* what I have in my heart and soul.
> *Hear* (*kluthi*) blessed one, I call (*klēzō*) you who rule heav'n
> And earth and Chaos and Hades where dwell
> [Daimons of men who once gazed on the light].
> *Send* (*pempson*) me this daimon at my sacred chants,
> Who moves by night to orders 'neath your force,
> From whose own tend this comes, and let him tell (*phrasatō*) me
> In total truth all that my mind designs,
> *And send* him gentle, gracious, pondering
> No thoughts opposed to me. And may you not
> *Be angry* at my sacred chants (*epaoidais*). But guard
> That my whole body come to light intact,

17. Nilsson, *History of Greek Religion*, 106.
18. Aune, "Prayer in the Greco-Roman World," 32.

> For you yourself arranged these things among
> Mankind for them to learn. I call (*klēzō*) your name,
> In number equal to the Moirai themselves,
> ACHAIPHOTHOTHOAIEIAEIA
> AIEAIEIAOTHOTHOPHIACHA.
> (*Papyri Graecae Magicae* 1.296–327)[19]

Aside from the name of the god being addressed, the key words/phrases in this passage include, "Give answer to my questions," "leave," "voice secret words," "fulfill," "hear," etc. Aune is correct to note that, in many ways, this approach to prayer, namely invoking the presence of deity to come, stands in contrast to Hebrew and Christian prayer.[20] In the Greek and Roman magical paradigm of prayer, the gods must come near to be present and to impart revelation. In the Hebrew and Christian paradigm, God is omnipresent and thus near to the worshipper irrespective of invocation. However, the ubiquitous nature of the Christian God does not preclude the practice of prayer but rather provides justification for it. The Christian worshipper does not petition God for revelation per se, but petitions God on the basis of the revelation already imparted through the *Logos*.

In summary, in the laconic summary above I have provided a general profile of Greek prayer. Of course, the foundation of this genre of prayer was established hundreds of years before the Christian era. But what was the shape of Roman prayer in the first century CE? Ferguson says that the spirit of prayer in Rome was essentially Greek. He states, "Rome, with little of its own to give in the way of religion, filled its skeleton of religion with a Greek content; the old native forms continued in the various countries, but the spirit was Greek."[21] Thus, Greco-Roman prayer did not differ greatly from the Greek antecedents from which it sprung forth and grew.[22] How often did non-Jews pray? Where did they pray? To what extent were their

---

19. Aune, "Prayer in the Greco-Roman World," 39–40 (emphasis added).

20. In the OT, God came and made his name known to his people and on the temple. In the NT, the *Logos* came to his people as the temple of God and as the disclosure of God.

21. Ferguson, *Background of Early Christianity*, 173.

22. Aune insists that Greco-Roman prayer must be approached synchronically. He says, "While it is no doubt desirable to treat ancient prayer as a phenomenon that exhibited various changes through time, the fact is that there was a 'canonical' structure of prayer that exhibited remarkable stability throughout antiquity. In fact, some of the earliest literary evidence for prayer, the Homeric epics, continued to function as paradigms for prayer throughout antiquity. It is, of course, somewhat problematic to treat Greek and Roman prayer together. Yet it also needs to be noted that there are many common features between them" ("Prayer in the Greco-Roman World," 25).

prayers considered Greek in nature and practice? One can only draw general inferences from the surrounding religious traditions that shaped and influenced Roman culture. It is logical to assume that each person viewed prayer through his or her own religious upbringing and conviction, which likely consisted of a blend of Jewish and Greek thought and practice that had spiraled through the Mediterranean world in previous decades and centuries. Hence, the summary above provides credible and relevant suggestions concerning how a mid- to late first-century Greco-Roman citizen would have understood prayer in a general sense.

In a manner similar to the Jews, it has been shown that the Greeks and Romans maintained a worldview in which communication with the gods (or a god) is possible. The Greek gods were like humans in aspects ranging from their physical appearance to their ability to feel emotions and form relationships. Yet the Greek gods were viewed as superior to the humans who sought their aid and were dependent on the daily affairs of life. Yet in Greek prayer the need for metaphorical language is minimized given that the Greek gods, although greater than humans, are not omnipresent, transcendental beings who must condescend to human categories of speech in order to be understood. The nature of the Greek gods is more closely related to the nature of humankind than the nature of the Jewish God is to those who pray to him. Yet the omnipresent nature of the Jewish God means functional closeness between God and the one praying. This attribute does not preclude communication with the divine, but it provides justification for it as the worshippers are drawn into the relational space of prayer. Notwithstanding, the functional and relational distance between the Greek gods and humankind remains. As indicated above, this gap may be closed through the medium of prayer as the gods are summoned to come near and meet the needs of the one(s) praying.

Further, Greek prayer may be characterized as communication between a "subordinate" sender who submits his request to a "superior" receiver for the purpose of obtaining a favorable result and/or material blessing.[23] Thus, Greek prayer was offered in a cultural context in which spirituality and pragmatism coalesced. As such, prayer served as the means by which the practical needs of the worshipper could be met. Therefore, like other genres of prayer, it may be said that the purpose of Greek prayer is "to have some effect on the person with whom the prayer communicates; that is, it seeks results, which may for the time be classified as petitions for goods and services or as maintenance of relationships."[24] The pragmatic,

---

23. Neyrey, *Give God the Glory*, 9.
24. Neyrey, *Give God the Glory*, 9.

result-oriented nature of Greek prayer is evidenced by its association with magic. As noted, magic in the ancient world was not bad because it was fraudulent; it was dangerous because it proved effectual for harnessing the powers of the world for the good of the petitioner.[25] Thus, the employment of prayer in the Greco-Roman worldview demonstrates the heightened degree of dependency that humans maintained on the gods. Since the worshipper's destiny and well-being was directly linked to the gods, there was little room for self-reliance and autonomy.

While prayer was offered spontaneously, it was also offered in a twofold structure that includes an invocation and a short request. In some cases, the structure of prayer involved a tripartite structure that included an invocation, justification, and request. If the request was the most common form of Greco-Roman prayer, then the one to whom the request was offered was of utmost importance. Each word of prayer must be offered with precision and care in order that the request might be granted. As such, the polytheistic nature of Greek religion made prayer a calculated and risky task. Prayer must be addressed to the proper god, in the correct name and, in some cases, with a sacrifice that was offered as a gift or as a means to appease the gods. However, offering a petition to the wrong god could prove disastrous. Once the request was known, the god was addressed, and a favorable outcome was expected.

Questions

1. How does magical prayer in the name of the Greek gods differ from prayer in the name of Jesus?

2. Reciprocity maintained a key element in certain expressions of Greek prayer. Is this the case in Johannine prayer?

3. The Greeks' worldview precludes the Judeo-Christian concept of sin. As such, the relationship between the one praying and the one being prayed to was not dependent on correct behavior but rather on correct praying. What is the prerequisite to approaching the Johannine God in prayer?

4. In some cases, the Greeks sought to offer a sacrifice to sway the gods in their favor. According to the Fourth Gospel, how is divine favor obtained?

---

25. Janowitz, *Magic in the Roman World*, 3.

5. In Greco-Roman prayer, exactness of speech and precision of wording were essential when addressing the gods. Does the Fourth Gospel prescribe a formal approach of prayer according to certain words?

CHAPTER 4

Prayer in the Synoptics and Acts

IN THE PREVIOUS CHAPTERS we surveyed the Jewish and Greco-Roman prayer traditions. Now we will turn our attention to prayer in the Synoptic Gospels and Acts in order to better understand how prayer functioned in the life of Jesus and the early Christian communities. Of course, the scope of prayer in the NT is wide and deep. Accounts of prayer are seen in the Gospels, Acts, the Pauline and Johannine Epistles, and in other materials that are dated to the first century CE. But given the limitations of this book, the analysis below will focus exclusively on the most relevant narrative materials in order to arrive at a general conclusion concerning the nature of prayer as it occurred in the social atmosphere of the first-century Christian tradition. Specifically, the aim is to create a general profile of prayer from which the Fourth Gospel (as narrative material) may be compared and contrasted. An analysis of the Synoptic Gospels and the Fourth Gospel may naturally reveal points of similarity and dissimilarity. As will be shown, much like the Jewish and Greco-Roman traditions, the Christian tradition posits notable qualifications that must be met in order for prayer to be answered. Such qualifications enable the reader to discern how the larger Christian tradition compares with prayer in the Fourth Gospel.

The Posture of Prayer in the Synoptics

A cursory overview of the Synoptic Gospels reveals that prayer predominated the life of Jesus. As such, the Synoptic accounts reveal the variegated postures that Jesus assumed while praying. Examples of such postures include:

> Mark 7:34 says that before Jesus performed a miracle he *looked up toward heaven*, most presumably in an attitude of prayer.

Luke 22:41 states that he *knelt down* to pray.

In Matthew 26:39 it is said that Jesus *fell on his face* and prayed.[1]

Each example demonstrates Jesus' dependence upon and reverence for the Father in heaven.

The Timing and Place of Prayer

In addition to the posture of Jesus' prayers, the Synoptic accounts also indicate the general timing of his prayers. For example:

Mark 1:35 states that Jesus rose *very early in the morning* to pray.

Luke 6:12 states that before calling the twelve apostles Jesus went on the mountain and prayed *all night* to God.[2]

Furthermore, Jesus is seen praying not only early in the morning but also at other odd times:

Mark 6:46 and Luke 6:12 place Jesus *praying at nighttime*.

Matthew 14:23 says Jesus *prayed on a mountainside by himself*.

Luke 5:16 states that Jesus went to a *desolate place to pray* after cleansing a leper.

Mark 14:35; Matthew 26:36; and Luke 22:41 mention Jesus' *prayer in Gethsemane* (or the Mount of Olives, Luke 22:39) where *he withdrew from his disciples to pray*.[3]

At first glance, such episodes of prayer may not seem noteworthy since Jesus was a Jew who would pray as other Jews prayed. Jeremias says that Jesus participated in the "liturgical heritage of his people" that likely included three hours of prayer.[4] This heritage has roots in the efforts of Ezra, the scribe, and the 120 men of the great assembly who composed an outline of prayers and designated the times for their recitation in the fifth century BCE. Jeremias sees this threefold ritual of prayer as fitting in the custom of the day ("as his custom was," Luke 4:16) insofar as Sabbath worship was concerned. In this view, the morning prayers consisted of reciting the Shema

---

1. Emphasis added.
2. Emphasis added.
3. Emphasis added.
4. Jeremias, *Prayers of Jesus*, 73.

and praying the Tefillah together; in the afternoon the Tefillah was uttered; finally, the Shema was recited and the Tefillah was prayed at evening.

However, Marshall points out, "Because Jesus did everything that was normal for a Jew and more, it should not be considered startling that references to his prayers in the Synoptic Gospels are not more abundant. When prayer by Jesus is highlighted by the Synoptic Evangelists, it must be for special reasons, and we are entitled to ask in each case why."[5] To the question of why, Marshall says, "Prayer in the very early morning hours of the day may have been part of the pattern of Jesus's life—which would suggest that he was more pious than other Jews. And this is probably why such an early time for prayer is mentioned by Mark."[6] But the emphasis on prayerful conversations "very early morning" (Mark 1:35) and "all night" (Luke 6:12) most plausibly reflects Jesus' pious desire for solitude with God. It is the secret place where Jesus meets with the Father to speak to him in quietness and intimacy.

As demonstrated in the Synoptic accounts, Jesus modeled an intimate life of prayerful solitude with the Father. As such, Jesus' piety reflects his utter and extraordinary dependence on God, especially at crucially important times in his life that extended beyond early in the morning and late at night. For example:

> Luke 3:21 says that Jesus prayed *at his baptism*.[7]
>
> Luke 6:12 says that Jesus prayed all night *before choosing the twelve apostles*.
>
> Mark 6:41 says that Jesus gave thanks for the loaves and fish *before he fed the 5,000*.[8]
>
> Mark 8:6–7 says that Jesus gave thanks for the loaves and fish *before he fed the 4,000*.
>
> Mark 14:22–23 indicates that Jesus gave thanks *at the institution of the Lord's Supper*.

---

5. Marshall, "Jesus," 116.

6. Marshall, "Jesus," 116.

7. It should be no surprise that Jesus prayed on this occasion. Johnson remarks that "prayer is a constant motif in Luke-Acts, and the critical moments of Jesus' ministry are punctuated by prayer (3:21; 5:16; 6:12; 9:18, 28–29; 11:1; 22:41, 44–45; 23:46)" (*Among the Gentiles*, 69).

8. Marshall says that in regard to the feeding miracles, the "miracle was not specifically connected with the prayer." He notes that by giving thanks, Jesus did what was expected of a pious Jew who was head of his house ("Jesus," 119).

Mark 15:34 states that Jesus cried out (prayed) *from the cross*, "My God, my God, why have you forsaken me?"⁹

In Mark 14:36 Jesus addresses the Father as "Abba, Father." What, if anything, is unique about the term *Abba*?¹⁰ Wright says that there is a broad consensus concerning this term that states:

> (1) that Jesus indeed used this word in prayer, and (2) that the notion of God's fatherhood—though, of course, known also in Judaism—took central place in his attitude to God in a distinctive way. So when the prayer given to his followers begins with "Father" (Luke 11:2) or "Our Father" (Matt 6:9; cf. *Didache* 8:2–3, which also begins "Our Father"), we must understand that Jesus wants them to see themselves as sharing his own characteristic spirituality—that is, his own intimate, familial approach to the Creator.¹¹

Such a familial approach is elucidated in the Son's prayer in Mark 14:36 (ESV) where he says to his father, "Remove this cup from me. Yet not what I will, but what you will." Kebler remarks:

> This fear of death drives him into solitary prayer which in its direct and indirect form aims at the elimination of suffering from his Messianic ministry. To be sure, the prayer allows for the possible ultimate consent to the divine plan of passion. . . . But the request for the passing of the hour and the removal of the cup has every indication of a desire to bypass the cross.¹²

But the form of address itself demonstrates that Jesus viewed himself in close relationship to God and felt the liberty to address him forthrightly in the impending hour of suffering. And this form of address would have didactic value for Jesus' followers who would later find themselves in a variety of

---

9. Emphasis added.

10. See Jeremias's discussion of this term (*Prayers of Jesus*, 11–65). He concludes that Jesus' uniqueness in praying to the Father is seen in his usage of the term *abba*. Jeremias says, "To the Jewish mind, it would have been disrespectful and therefore inconceivable to address God with this familiar word. For Jesus to venture to take this step was something new and unheard of" (*Prayers of Jesus*, 62). In response to Jeremias, Crump is right to suggest that his work has not stood the test of time and reexamination (*Knocking on Heaven's Door*, 98–99). See Fitzmyer, "Abba and Jesus' Relationship to God," 15–38; Barr, "'*Abbā* Isn't 'Daddy,'" 28–47; Sanders, "Defending the Indefensible," 463–77.

11. Wright, "Lord's Prayer as a Paradigm," 134.

12. Kebler, *Passion in Mark*, 43.

desperate situations that necessitated closeness and intimacy with God.[13] As noted by Cullmann, "Daß Jesus es in dieser Familiarität auf Gott in seinen Gebeten anwandte, muß aufgrund seiner persönlichen Gebetserfahrung einer Absicht entsprochen haben, und so muß es auch von seinen Jüngern empfunden worden sein."[14] Furthermore, as will be discussed below, the term *Abba* was later used by Paul in Galatians 4:6 and Romans 8:15 in the context of Christian prayer.

As seen above, the Synoptics portray the outworking of Jesus' eternal relationship with the Father as he prays to him at various times and in various places. This relational model finds relevance in the life of a praying disciple who, on the basis of his prior relationship with God, may pray at any time and at any place for the purpose of experiencing ongoing intimacy with and help from his or her heavenly Father. As such, the Synoptics indicate that Jesus' closeness to God resulted in his effectiveness in prayer to God.

Prayer as Petition

The examples below demonstrate the axiomatic but (often) unstated rationale of prayer, namely: believers pray because they assume that it will produce a certain result. Marshall notes that Jesus offered prayers of petition for Peter (Luke 22:31–32) and for those who crucified him (Luke 22:32). The disciples were commanded to pray for those who persecute them (Matt 5:44), but they were also commanded to pray for themselves (in the face of temptation and danger: cf. Mark 13:18; 14:38 Luke 21:36).[15] Furthermore, both Matthew 7:7–11 and Luke 11:5–13 are concerned with asking or petitioning God. Jesus states:

> 7 Αἰτεῖτε καὶ δοθήσεται ὑμῖν, ζητεῖτε καὶ εὑρήσετε, κρούετε καὶ ἀνοιγήσεται ὑμῖν· 8 πᾶς γὰρ ὁ αἰτῶν λαμβάνει καὶ ὁ ζητῶν εὑρίσκει καὶ τῷ κρούοντι ἀνοιγήσεται. 9 ἢ τίς ἐστιν ἐξ ὑμῶν ἄνθρωπος, ὃν αἰτήσει ὁ υἱὸς αὐτοῦ ἄρτον, μὴ λίθον ἐπιδώσει αὐτῷ; 10 ἢ καὶ ἰχθὺν αἰτήσει, μὴ ὄφιν ἐπιδώσει αὐτῷ; 11 εἰ οὖν ὑμεῖς πονηροὶ ὄντες οἴδατε δόματα ἀγαθὰ διδόναι τοῖς τέκνοις ὑμῶν, πόσῳ μᾶλλον ὁ πατὴρ ὑμῶν ὁ ἐν τοῖς οὐρανοῖς δώσει ἀγαθὰ τοῖς αἰτοῦσιν αὐτόν. (Matt 7:7–11)

---

13. See Hurtado, "Place of Jesus," 38–44.
14. Cullmann, *Das Gebet im Neuen Testament*, 57.
15. Marshall, "Jesus," 120.

But certain Synoptic episodes reveal that petitionary prayer must take place with a disposition of confidence.[16] One must enter into the space of prayer with a posture of faith, not unbelief. This is indicated in Mark 11:22–24, where Jesus states:

> 22 καὶ ἀποκριθεὶς ὁ Ἰησοῦς λέγει αὐτοῖς· ἔχετε πίστιν θεοῦ. 23 ἀμὴν λέγω ὑμῖν ὅτι ὃς ἂν εἴπῃ τῷ ὄρει τούτῳ· ἄρθητι καὶ βλήθητι εἰς τὴν θάλασσαν, καὶ μὴ διακριθῇ ἐν τῇ καρδίᾳ αὐτοῦ ἀλλὰ πιστεύῃ ὅτι ὃ λαλεῖ γίνεται, ἔσται αὐτῷ. 24 διὰ τοῦτο λέγω ὑμῖν, πάντα ὅσα προσεύχεσθε καὶ αἰτεῖσθε, πιστεύετε ὅτι ἐλάβετε, καὶ ἔσται ὑμῖν.

The essence of this short instruction is encapsulated in the phrase ἔχετε πίστιν θεοῦ. In spite of the enormity of the problem or the nature of the requests, Jesus commands his disciples to believe that God is able to grant their requests. As one approaches God in this manner, one can be assured that he will have what he asked for.

Accordingly, in Luke 18:1–8, Jesus shares a parable concerning a persistent widow who kept requesting justice against her adversary. The judge responded by saying,

> 4 καὶ οὐκ ἤθελεν ἐπὶ χρόνον. μετὰ δὲ ταῦτα εἶπεν ἐν ἑαυτῷ· εἰ καὶ τὸν θεὸν οὐ φοβοῦμαι οὐδὲ ἄνθρωπον ἐντρέπομαι, 5 διά γε τὸ παρέχειν μοι κόπον τὴν χήραν ταύτην ἐκδικήσω αὐτήν, ἵνα μὴ εἰς τέλος ἐρχομένη ὑπωπιάζῃ με. (18:4–5)

Jesus notes that this is the same posture of faith and persistence that believers are to portray in their prayers to God.

A Model Prayer

In Matthew 6 Jesus provides several instructions on the nature and practice of prayer. In 6:5 he says that one must not be like the "hypocrites" who like to be seen in the open (ἐν ταῖς συναγωγαῖς καὶ ἐν ταῖς γωνίαις), but rather, one must seek to pray in secret (εἴσελθε εἰς τὸ ταμεῖόν σου καὶ κλείσας τὴν θύραν σου πρόσευξαι τῷ πατρί σου τῷ ἐν τῷ κρυπτῷ).[17] Keener says, "This text precludes not public prayer . . . but prayer to be seen and glorified by others."[18] Jesus says further, "And when you pray, do not heap up empty

---

16. See Marshall, "Jesus," 121.

17. For an analysis of the significance of the place of prayer, see Hvalvik, "Praying with Outstretched Hands," 58–63.

18. Keener, *Matthew*, 138.

phrases as the Gentiles do, for they think that they will be heard for their many words" (Matt 6:7). The reason for refraining from this type of prayer is founded on the fact that God already knows what one needs before one asks (6:8). In what is commonly known as the Lord's Prayer,[19] Jesus provides a model of prayer (6:9–13). He says:

> 9 Οὕτως οὖν προσεύχεσθε ὑμεῖς·
> Πάτερ ἡμῶν ὁ ἐν τοῖς οὐρανοῖς·
>   ἁγιασθήτω τὸ ὄνομά σου·
> 10 ἐλθέτω ἡ βασιλεία σου·
>   γενηθήτω τὸ θέλημά σου,
>   ὡς ἐν οὐρανῷ καὶ ἐπὶ γῆς·
> 11 τὸν ἄρτον ἡμῶν τὸν ἐπιούσιον δὸς ἡμῖν σήμερον·
> 12 καὶ ἄφες ἡμῖν τὰ ὀφειλήματα ἡμῶν,
>   ὡς καὶ ἡμεῖς ἀφήκαμεν τοῖς ὀφειλέταις ἡμῶν·
> 13 καὶ μὴ εἰσενέγκῃς ἡμᾶς εἰς πειρασμόν,
>   ἀλλὰ ῥῦσαι ἡμᾶς ἀπὸ τοῦ πονηροῦ.

Aside from Matthew's version, two other modified accounts appear in Luke 11:1–4, and in *Didache* 8.2. Crump says, "All of Luke's prayer is contained in Matthew's, making the first evangelist [Matthew] the more comprehensive of the two."[20] He says further that "Matthew augmented the received tradition to better serve the liturgical and theological purposes of his Gospel." But following Lohmeyer, France says "there is no improbability . . . that Jesus taught the prayer in different forms on two separate occasions."[21] It is possible that Jesus adapts an early form of what became a basic synagogue prayer, the Kaddish which began something like this:

> Exalted and hallowed be his great name
> in the world which he created according to his will
> May he let his kingdom rule

Absent from this prayer is what is present in both Matthew and Luke's versions, namely, "Our Father" (Matt 6:9) and "Father" (Luke 11:2), respectively. The former version entails a corporate dimension, whereas the latter version is more personal in emphasis. Yet Morris is right to say, "*Our* links the praying person to other believers; while the prayer may be used

---

19. For analysis of this prayer, see Lohmeyer, *Lord's Prayer*; Migliore, *Lord's Prayer*; Lochman, *Lord's Prayer*; Charlesworth et al., *Lord's Prayer*, 15–27; Lohse, *Vater Unser*.

20. Crump, *Knocking on Heaven's Door*, 97.

21. France, *Matthew*, 137.

in private it is meant to be prayed in community, which means that it may have had a liturgical use from the first."²² Notwithstanding, the form of address implies sonship, which is most clearly displayed and typified in Jesus' relationship with God. Cullmann says, "In diesem Gebet vernehmen wir Jesus selber."²³ In brief, as a son, Jesus teaches his followers how to approach his Father in the familial context of a previously established relationship of intimacy, honor, and love.²⁴

As such, the "Our Father" (Πάτερ ἡμῶν) phraseology conveys both familial and, by necessity, theological implications. God is portrayed as the public face of his family. As Jesus, the Son, approached the Father in relational space, so the disciples, as children, may also enter into this space. Yet the form of address reminds the disciples that while God is Father, he is in heaven and they are on earth. Crump notes, "To call God Father entailed several equally important components in the ancient world, namely: (1) *God is the Father-Creator*; (2) *God is the Father-King*; (3) *God is the Father-Redeemer*. When applied to God, these components naturally evoke a sense of "respectful dependence, and affectionate intimacy."²⁵

As such, the Lord's Prayer was issued by Jesus (the "subordinate" Son) as a model of how to pray to the Father (the "superior" receiver) within the context of a family relationship.²⁶ In this prayer the disciples are encouraged to pray that specific "results"²⁷ will be achieved, namely: that the Father's name will be hallowed, that the sphere and rule of heaven will become present on earth, that the Father's will will be done, that their needs will be met, that their sins will be forgiven, and that they will be preserved in the hour of testing (Matt 6:9–13). This precise model of this prayer is unique from the lips of Jesus, but thematic content has overlap with Jewish models of prayers such as the Tefillah.

---

22. Morris, *Gospel According to Matthew*, 144.
23. Cullmann, *Das Gebet im Neuen Testament*, 51.
24. Neyrey, *Give God the Glory*, 9.
25. Crump, *Knocking on Heaven's Door*, 99.
26. Neyrey, *Give God the Glory*, 9. By "subordinate" I am referring to Jesus' functional, earthly relationship with the Father (John 14:28). At the same time, Jesus was/is co-equal and co-eternal with the Father (1:1).
27. Neyrey, *Give God the Glory*, 9.

Prayer in Acts

Many scholars hold that the Gospel of Luke and Acts were written by the same author,[28] namely Luke and were composed as one volume. However, the present analysis will (for the most part) treat Acts separately in order to detect how prayer was said to have functioned in the post-resurrectional Christian community. But such treatment does not preclude highlighting the obvious parallels that exist between these documents. Accordingly, instead of analyzing prayer in Acts chronologically, the following analysis will analyze prayer categorically, that is, in categories that elucidate how prayer took place, when prayer took place, where it took place, and for what purpose it took place with special emphasis on the early Christian disciples. By filling in these categories the reader is therefore able to make general conclusions concerning the nature of prayer in the narrative material.

The Posture of Prayer

A review of Acts reveals much about the quantity of prayer, but much less about the posture that the early believers assumed when praying. Their posture in prayer was much like what was exemplified in the prayers of Jesus. A sample of these postures includes:

> Acts 7:60 states that Stephen *fell to his knees* and cried out with a loud voice.
>
> Acts 9:40 states that Peter *knelt down and prayed* before raising Tabitha from the dead.
>
> Acts 20:36 states that Paul *knelt down* with the Ephesian elders and prayed.
>
> Acts 13:3 states that believers *prayed and fasted* before laying hands.[29]

Each of these examples demonstrates that early Christian prayer was offered in a posture of humility and dependence on God the "superior" receiver.[30]

---

28. See Polhill, *Acts*, 23–27; Marshall, *Acts*, 46–48; Bock, *Theology of Luke and Acts*, 32–37.
29. Emphasis added.
30. Neyrey, *Give God the Glory*, 9.

The Place of Prayer

During the Second Temple Era, the temple and synagogue(s) maintained important roles in the lives of the Jewish community. That Jesus maintained high regard for the temple is not in dispute. He referred to it as his "Father's house" (Luke 2:49), and in Mark 11:17 Jesus refers to the temple as "a house of prayer for all the nations." In this latter episode he cleaned the temple likely because the money-changers were buying and selling in the court of the Gentiles and in doing so hindered Gentile worship. Yet there is no conclusive evidence that Jesus offered sacrifices in the temple. Martin says, "[Jesus] valued the Temple, but chiefly for the facilities it afforded for communion with God and for prayer more than for its sacrificial apparatus."[31] That the temple is a prominent place of worship is strongly emphasized in both Luke's Gospel and in Acts. Green says, "The Third Gospel emphasizes the function of the temple as a house of prayer (cf. Luke 1:8–23; 2:27–32, 36–38; 18:10–14; 19:46; 24:53), and the temple continues to serve this role in the book of Acts (cf. Acts 2:47; 3:1; 21:20–26; 22:17–21)."[32]

But how strong is the link between the Jewish custom (which includes high regard for worship connected to the temple and the synagogue) and early Christian prayer? Bradshaw says:

> Very many scholars have supposed that at first the Christians simply joined with others Jews in their daily worship and only began to hold their own services ... when they were eventually expelled from the synagogues and the *Birkath-ha-Minim* ... was incorporated with the *Shemoneh 'Esreh* in order to exclude them from participation in the services.[33]

It is clear that the believers regularly assembled in the temple (Acts 2:46; Luke 24:53) and in the synagogue (Acts 13:5, 14; 14:1; 16:13; 17:1, 10, 17; 18:4, 19; 19:8). Furthermore, Bradshaw says that the early believers may have formed a "distinct group within Judaism, like the Essenes and others, and to worship apart."[34] For evidence he cites: (1) the gathering to pray in the upper room (Acts 1:14); (2) the assembling at 9 a.m. on the day of Pentecost (Acts 2:1; cf. 2:15) presumably for worship in a private house; (3) the Jerusalem church meeting in the house of the mother of John Mark (Acts 12:5, 12); and (4) the believers congregating together in Solomon's

---

31. Martin, *Worship in the Early Church*, 22.
32. Green, "Persevering Together in Prayer," 186.
33. Bradshaw, *Daily Prayer in the Early Church*, 23–24.
34. Bradshaw, *Daily Prayer in the Early Church*, 24.

portico for teaching and likely for prayer.³⁵ In addition to the verses cited by Bradshaw, a further review of Acts reveals that the early believers prayed in various places at various times and in a wide variety of places. For example:

> Acts 3:1 indicates that Peter and John went up to *the temple at the ninth hour,* which was the hour of prayer.³⁶

> Acts 10:9 says Peter went *up on the housetop* about *the sixth* hour to pray.

> Acts 16:25 states that Paul and Silas prayed to God and sang hymns *in prison.*

If one assumes this profile is accurate, then Acts suggests that the believers did in fact meet regularly for prayer in a variety of places, both in and around the temple and synagogue, but also elsewhere! This profile is not completely different from models seen in Judaism since prayers were offered at the temple, in certain synagogues, at home, and other places. Thus, points of continuity are clear.

However, while the early patterns of Christian prayer may have followed the Jewish model initially, the primacy of the temple as a place of prayer dissipated gradually (and, of course, fully by 70 CE). Paul's prayer in the temple in Acts 22:17 is an example of the discontinuity that came to exist. The fuller context states:

> 17 Ἐγένετο δέ μοι ὑποστρέψαντι εἰς Ἰερουσαλὴμ καὶ προσευχομένου μου ἐν τῷ ἱερῷ γενέσθαι με ἐν ἐκστάσει 18 καὶ ἰδεῖν αὐτὸν λέγοντά μοι· σπεῦσον καὶ ἔξελθε ἐν τάχει ἐξ Ἰερουσαλήμ, διότι οὐ παραδέξονταί σου μαρτυρίαν περὶ ἐμοῦ. 19 κἀγὼ εἶπον· κύριε, αὐτοὶ ἐπίστανται ὅτι ἐγὼ ἤμην φυλακίζων καὶ δέρων κατὰ τὰς συναγωγὰς τοὺς πιστεύοντας ἐπὶ σέ, 20 καὶ ὅτε ἐξεχύννετο τὸ αἷμα Στεφάνου τοῦ μάρτυρός σου, καὶ αὐτὸς ἤμην ἐφεστὼς καὶ συνευδοκῶν καὶ φυλάσσων τὰ ἱμάτια τῶν ἀναιρούντων αὐτόν. 21 καὶ εἶπεν πρός με· πορεύου, ὅτι ἐγὼ εἰς ἔθνη μακρὰν ἐξαποστελῶ σε. (Acts 22:17–21)

Green says concerning this passage:

> Here is a fail-proof apologetic for Paul's mission. It was in the Jerusalem temple, while praying, that Paul received the divine

---

35. Bradshaw, *Daily Prayer in the Early Church*, 24.

36. Emphasis added. Peterson notes concerning Peter and John, "They wanted to be present for the service of public prayer that accompanied the evening sacrifice each day at three in the afternoon.... Even though Jesus had implied that he would replace the temple in the plan and purpose of God (cf. Matt 12:6; John 2:19–22; 4:21–24), his disciples did not immediately disengage themselves from the temple and separate themselves from the traditional practices of their religion" (*Acts of the Apostles*, 167).

mandate to take the gospel to the Gentile world. What is equally clear, though, is that this experience of prayer in the temple served to undermine for Paul the centrality of the temple for faith and life. Thus, a form of continuity with Judaism—has resulted in a divine mandate that subverts the central role of the temple for Jewish life.[37]

While Green may be correct, the lack of direct textual attestation concerning prayer "in" the temple in the Acts narrative serves as stronger evidence for *discontinuity*. Furthermore, Green's argument for discontinuity is further advanced by his focus on the Christological nature of certain early Christian prayers. Green says, "'God' is the object of prayer in a number of the reports of the church at prayer in Acts (e.g., 4:24–31; 10:2, 4; 12:5; 16:25), though more often the narrative does not specify to whom prayers were offered (e.g., 1:14; 2:42; 3:1; 6:4, 6; 9:11; 10:9). On several occasions, however, Luke specifically notes that prayers were offered to *Jesus—beginning with* the prayer regarding Matthias's replacement in 1:24–25."[38] The clearest examples he cites where prayer was offered to Jesus include the following:

59 καὶ ἐλιθοβόλουν τὸν Στέφανον ἐπικαλούμενον καὶ λέγοντα· κύριε Ἰησοῦ, δέξαι τὸ πνεῦμά μου. 60 θεὶς δὲ τὰ γόνατα ἔκραξεν φωνῇ μεγάλῃ· κύριε, μὴ στήσῃς αὐτοῖς ταύτην τὴν ἁμαρτίαν. καὶ τοῦτο εἰπὼν ἐκοιμήθη. (Acts 7:59–60)

10 Ην δέ τις μαθητὴς ἐν Δαμασκῷ ὀνόματι Ἀνανίας, καὶ εἶπεν πρὸς αὐτὸν ἐν ὁράματι ὁ κύριος· Ἀνανία. ὁ δὲ εἶπεν· ἰδοὺ ἐγώ, κύριε. 11 ὁ δὲ κύριος πρὸς αὐτόν· ἀναστὰς πορεύθητι ἐπὶ τὴν ῥύμην τὴν καλουμένην Εὐθεῖαν καὶ ζήτησον ἐν οἰκίᾳ Ἰούδα Σαῦλον ὀνόματι Ταρσέα· ἰδοὺ γὰρ προσεύχεται 12 καὶ εἶδεν ἄνδρα [ἐν ὁράματι] Ἀνανίαν ὀνόματι εἰσελθόντα καὶ ἐπιθέντα αὐτῷ [τὰς] χεῖρας ὅπως ἀναβλέψῃ. 13 ἀπεκρίθη δὲ Ἀνανίας· κύριε, ἤκουσα ἀπὸ πολλῶν περὶ τοῦ ἀνδρὸς τούτου ὅσα κακὰ τοῖς ἁγίοις σου ἐποίησεν ἐν Ἰερουσαλήμ· 14 καὶ ὧδε ἔχει ἐξουσίαν παρὰ τῶν ἀρχιερέων δῆσαι πάντας τοὺς ἐπικαλουμένους τὸ ὄνομά σου. 15 εἶπεν δὲ πρὸς αὐτὸν ὁ κύριος· πορεύου, ὅτι σκεῦος ἐκλογῆς ἐστίν μοι οὗτος τοῦ βαστάσαι τὸ ὄνομά μου ἐνώπιον ἐθνῶν τε καὶ βασιλέων υἱῶν τε Ἰσραήλ· 16 ἐγὼ γὰρ ὑποδείξω αὐτῷ ὅσα δεῖ αὐτὸν ὑπὲρ τοῦ ὀνόματός μου παθεῖν. 17 Ἀπῆλθεν δὲ Ἀνανίας καὶ εἰσῆλθεν εἰς τὴν οἰκίαν καὶ ἐπιθεὶς ἐπ' αὐτὸν τὰς χεῖρας εἶπεν· Σαοὺλ ἀδελφέ,

---

37. Green, "Persevering Together in Prayer," 187.
38. Green, "Persevering Together in Prayer," 187.

ὁ κύριος ἀπέσταλκέν με, Ἰησοῦς ὁ ὀφθείς σοι ἐν τῇ ὁδῷ ᾗ ἤρχου, ὅπως ἀναβλέψῃς καὶ πλησθῇς πνεύματος ἁγίου. (Acts 9:10–17)

Green notes, moreover, "So routine, in fact, is Christocentric prayer to the identity of the early Christians that they can be known as 'those who call upon the name of the Jesus' (cf. 2:21; 7:59; 9:14, 21; 22:16)." Therefore, he concludes, "The prayer practices of the early church, therefore, highlight the important Christological affirmations that move beyond what is characteristic of Judaism."[39]

Another Model Prayer?

The longest and the most content-enriched prayer appears in Acts 4:24–30. As seen in chapter 4, Peter and John are arrested and ordered to cease preaching in the name of Jesus (4:18). On their release they gave a report concerning what the chief priests and elders said (4:23). The response of their friends is to offer a proclamation of praise concerning God's sovereign rule over all things (4:24, δέσποτα, σὺ ὁ ποιήσας τὸν οὐρανὸν καὶ τὴν γῆν καὶ τὴν θάλασσαν καὶ πάντα τὰ ἐν αὐτοῖς). The prayer (4:25–26) then borrows from Psalm 2 in order to reiterate the futility of the plans of the people, kings, and rulers of the world. Verses 27–28 state the divinely ordained conspiracy and actions against Jesus. In verses 29–30 the believers make this petition:

> 29 καὶ τὰ νῦν, κύριε, ἔπιδε ἐπὶ τὰς ἀπειλὰς αὐτῶν καὶ δὸς τοῖς δούλοις σου μετὰ παρρησίας πάσης λαλεῖν τὸν λόγον σου, 30 ἐν τῷ τὴν χεῖρά [σου] ἐκτείνειν σε εἰς ἴασιν καὶ σημεῖα καὶ τέρατα γίνεσθαι διὰ τοῦ ὀνόματος τοῦ ἁγίου παιδός σου Ἰησοῦ.

The petitionary nature of verses 29–30 is made clear by the verbs ἔπιδε ἐπὶ and δὸς. Yet the nature of the requests do not mention the abolition of threats or persecution but rather that God would grant them the ability to speak the word, μετὰ παρρησίας. But the prayer not only asks God to "look upon" and "grant," but also asks for God to "stretch out" his "hand" to act (ἐν τῷ τὴν χεῖρά [σου] ἐκτείνειν σε εἰς ἴασιν καὶ σημεῖα καὶ τέρατα γίνεσθαι). But such actions are to be performed διὰ τοῦ ὀνόματος τοῦ ἁγίου παιδός σου Ἰησοῦ. Neyrey notes the following chiastic structure of verses 29–30 (Neyrey's translation):

---

39. Green, "Persevering Together in Prayer," 188.

"And now, Lord, look upon their threats,
- A. with all boldness
  - B. grant to your servants to speak your word,
    - C. while you stretch out your hand to heal, and signs and wonders are performed
      - D. through the name of your holy servant Jesus."
    - C'. And when they had prayed, the place in which they were gathered together was shaken.
  - B'. and they were all filled with the Holy Spirit and spoke the word of God.
- A'. with boldness.[40]

As seen above, the trajectory of this prayer initiates with praise/thanksgiving to God (as δέσποτα) and states the conspiracy against Jesus. But then the prayer moves to petition that healings and signs and wonders be performed "through the name of your holy servant Jesus." This phrase parallels with 3:6 (ESV) where Peter said to the lame beggar, "I have no silver and gold, but what I do have I give to you. In the name of Jesus Christ of Nazareth, rise up and walk!" Thus, while the thrust of the prayer is petitionary in nature, it seeks to highlight the power and rule of God (δέσποτα, but also κύριε in verse 29) through the name of his son (Ἰησοῦ Χριστοῦ τοῦ Ναζωραίου). Ironically, the very one who was conspired against (Jesus) will, through the granting of the believers' request, be shown as powerful (4:30). As such, this prayer may serve as a model in that it parallels some aspects of the Lord's Prayer by centering on the exaltation of God and highlighting his ("superior") sovereign rule over all things. The difference is seen in the absence of the phrase/concept "through the name of your holy servant Jesus" in the Lord's Prayer. But the prayer in Acts 4 states in explicit terms what is now possible in light of the death and resurrection of Jesus.[41] In other words, it highlights how certain "results" are achieved through Christo-centric praying. With the aid of Synoptic terms, one might say that the Father's (God) kingdom is manifest through his Son (Jesus) both in the words spoken by the believers and by miracles and signs and wonders performed. Hence, both prayers draw the one praying into the prayer in order to participate in God's salvific activities in the earth.

---

40. Neyrey, *Give God the Glory*, 82.

41. As Peter notes in Acts 2:36, ἀσφαλῶς οὖν γινωσκέτω πᾶς οἶκος Ἰσραὴλ ὅτι καὶ κύριον αὐτὸν καὶ χριστὸν ἐποίησεν ὁ θεός, τοῦτον τὸν Ἰησοῦν ὃν ὑμεῖς ἐσταυρώσατε.

Prayer and the Holy Spirit

The theme of the work of the Holy Spirit is prevalent throughout Luke-Acts. Bock says, "There are sixteen direct mentions of the Holy Spirit in Luke's gospel plus a few other passages where he is the topic through a figure of speech (such as a reference to power). . . . In Acts, there are at least fifty-seven references to the Spirit."[42] Yet an examination of the Lukan material reveals that the Spirit and prayer are often located together in the same context. Specifically, Helen and Leonard Doohan note that prayer of intercession is closely connected with the Holy Spirit and with the Kingdom. They cite the following examples:

> The annunciation, the episode of Zechariah, the birth and baptism of Christ, Peter's confession at Caesarea Philippi, the transfiguration, the sending of the seventy disciples on mission, Jesus' prayer at Gethsemane, the crucifixion, Pentecost, the election of Matthias, the description of the life of the early Church, the election of the seven deacons, the apostles' visit to Samaria, and Paul's farewell to the elders at Miletus. There remained in the church's thinking a close connection between prayer and the Spirit's presence and power (4:31).[43]

They conclude that based on this evidence,

> The general thrust of Luke's approach seems to be that in petitionary prayer the believer channels the activity of the Holy Spirit for the spreading of the kingdom. One of the characteristic features of Luke's teaching is his insistence on prayer as a way of tapping the dynamic energy of the Spirit.

Notwithstanding, Luke says the Spirit may be asked for (αἰτοῦσιν). In Matthew 7:11 "good things/gifts" are given to the disciples who ask, whereas in Luke 11:13 "the Spirit" is the "good gift" given upon the disciples' request. Thus, in Lukan theology, the Spirit is the good gift, but according to Jesus, the Spirit can be asked for. The language of verses 9–10 indicates that one may ask and seek, but verse 13 clarifies the nature of one's request, namely: "If you then, who are evil, know how to give good gifts to your children, how much more will the heavenly Father give the Holy Spirit to those who ask him!"

Accordingly, in Acts 2:1 Luke says that believers were gathered in one place and were subsequently "filled with the Holy Spirit." Acts 4:31 says

---

42. Bock, *Theology of Luke and Acts*, 211.
43. Doohan and Doohan, *Prayer in the New Testament*, 61.

that just after the believers prayed, "The place in which they were gathered together was shaken, and they were all filled with the Holy Spirit and continued to speak the word of God with boldness." Perhaps the clearest link to prayer and the Spirit is seen in the context of the conversion of the Samaritans. Acts 8:14–17 states:

> 14 Ἀκούσαντες δὲ οἱ ἐν Ἱεροσολύμοις ἀπόστολοι ὅτι δέδεκται ἡ Σαμάρεια τὸν λόγον τοῦ θεοῦ, ἀπέστειλαν πρὸς αὐτοὺς Πέτρον καὶ Ἰωάννην, 15 οἵτινες καταβάντες προσηύξαντο περὶ αὐτῶν ὅπως λάβωσιν πνεῦμα ἅγιον· 16 οὐδέπω γὰρ ἦν ἐπ' οὐδενὶ αὐτῶν ἐπιπεπτωκός, μόνον δὲ βεβαπτισμένοι ὑπῆρχον εἰς τὸ ὄνομα τοῦ κυρίου Ἰησοῦ. 17 τότε ἐπετίθεσαν τὰς χεῖρας ἐπ' αὐτοὺς καὶ ἐλάμβανον πνεῦμα ἅγιον.

Numerous suggestions have been offered concerning the reason behind the sending of Peter and John to Samaria so that the new believers could receive the Spirit.[44] Regardless, the most pertinent point in the present analysis is that they prayed for the Samaritans to receive the Holy Spirit. While prayer and the coming of the Spirit are not mentioned in Acts 10:44–45 or 19:1–7, they are linked in 8:15. In the final analysis, a review of the Luke-Acts materials demonstrates that prayer and the Spirit are often located in the same context. In certain cases, prayer is directly linked to the Spirit, whereas in the other cases there is an indirect link. Notwithstanding, the evidence above demonstrates that children of the kingdom may ask their Father for good things/gifts and he will in return grant their requests.

Questions

Based on the analysis above, it is not clear what the relationship is between narrative materials and the Fourth Gospel. To what extent the Johannine community was influenced by the narrative accounts is difficult to state with any degree of certainty. However, at the very least, one can say that the Synoptic Gospels, Acts, and the Fourth Gospel share a similar cultural and religious space, and that space is characterized by complementary expressions of prayer. Thus, having established the general setting of prayer in the early church, there are several relevant questions that can be set forth:

1. Does the Fourth Gospel provide a model of how one should pray?

---

44. See Marshall, *Acts*, 166–67; Bruce, *Book of the Acts*, 169–70; Twelftree, *People of the Spirit*, 87–88; Dunn, *Baptism in the Holy Spirit*, 59–68; Horton, *Acts*, 166.

2. The Lord's Prayer includes familial language that conveys theological implications for prayer. How does the Lord's Prayer relate to prayer in the Fourth Gospel?

3. The Synoptic Gospels omit Jesus' statement from the cross, "It is finished" (John 19:30) Is this statement a prayer? If so, what is the meaning of Jesus' words?

4. In light of the destruction of the temple and the abolition of sacrifice, would Jews and early Christians say along with Jesus, God always hears me?

5. While Luke-Acts shows the close relationship between the Spirit and prayer, Luke does not provide detailed, explicit information concerning how the Spirit equips the believer to pray. How does the Fourth Gospel enhance one's understanding of the Holy Spirit's role in prayer?

CHAPTER 5

A House of Prayer

Analysis of John 14

THE PREVIOUS THREE CHAPTERS provide an analysis of the Jewish, Greco-Roman, and Christian religious backdrop that should be considered when analyzing prayer in the Fourth Gospel. The length and depth of the previous analysis demonstrates that the Fourth Gospel was produced in a dense religious and theological context in which other streams of influence were present. However, it is not altogether clear to what extent these religious traditions influenced the practice of prayer as it is defined in the Fourth Gospel. By drawing from the various questions posed in the previous chapter, the present analysis will elucidate to some extent how Johannine prayer compares with prayer in the aforementioned religious traditions.[1] Further, the primary aim of the present chapter centers on examining John 14 on its own terms in order to gain a clearer understanding concerning how it contributes to the Johannine profile of prayer and how it provides the reader with a clearer understanding of the nature, purpose, and qualifications of prayer.

---

1. However, the main focus of this chapter does not involve juxtaposing the various religious traditions of prayers. Rather, comparisons and contrasts will be offered at various, relevant points throughout the present analysis that elucidate points of similarity and dissimilarity.

The Prerequisites to Prayer: John 14:1

As noted in the previous chapter, prayer involves communication between a sender and receiver in a "subordinate/superior" relationship.[2] This is the relational paradigm displayed in Jewish and Christian prayer traditions, as well as the one portrayed in the Fourth Gospel. As such, the basic assumption(s) of prayer is that God hears and responds to the subordinate's prayer request(s). The pertinent question at this point is as follows: according to chapter 14 of the Farewell Discourse, what prerequisites, if any, must be fulfilled in order for prayer to be answered? The analysis that follows below will seek to answer this question by examining the content of John 14.

In 14:1 Jesus says to his disciples, μὴ ταρασσέσθω ὑμῶν ἡ καρδία (also seen in 14:27). The term ταρασσέσθω ("be troubled") appears in several cases to indicate Jesus' troubled emotional state (11:33; 12:27; 13:21). In the immediate context of 14:1, this term centers on the disciples' emotional state that was influenced by several factors including: predictions of betrayal and denial, as well as the fact of Jesus' departure. With this term (ταρασσέσθω) in mind, Beutler sees Psalm 42–43 (41–42 [LXX]) as the common background tradition.[3] He says, "The [double] psalm is constructed symmetrically: at the end of each of the three strophes, after four or five verses, respectively, there occurs a refrain: 'Why are you cast down, O my soul, and why are you so disquieted within me? Hope in God; for I shall again praise him, my help and my God' (Ps 42:6, 12; 43:5)." He justifies the usage of this tradition due to obvious similarities of theme and content with John 14. In 14:1 the nature of the disciples' troubled hearts most notably centers on the news of Jesus' departure. In light of this impending crisis, the sentiment of Psalm 41:6, 12 and 42:5 (LXX) comes to bear: ἔλπισον ἐπὶ τὸν θεόν. Beutler says further:

> Here too, of course, John has not taken over his source word for word: "trust in God" becomes "believe in God and believe in me." Why? Just as the substantive ἐλπίς ("trust," "hope") is absent from the Fourth Gospel (and indeed from the first three), so also the verb is scarcely encountered.... Otherwise it is the verb πιστεύειν ("believe") that dominates the vocabulary and the thought of the evangelist. In the fourth gospel, it is focused throughout on Jesus and his mission in connection with which

---

2. Neyrey, *Give God the Glory*, 9.

3. Beutler, *Do Not Be Afraid*, 26. Beutler discusses this topic in his commentary on the Fourth Gospel, *Das Johannesevangelium*, and in his examination of the first Farewell Discourse, *Do Not Be Afraid*. I have quoted the latter from the English edition since the German was not available. See the German edition for a more thorough examination of the topic at hand.

the predominant construction is πιστεύειν εἰς ("believe in"). Precisely for this reason the evangelist had to change his pretext into πιστεύετε εἰς τὸν θεὸν καὶ εἰς ἐμὲ πιστεύετε ("believe in God and believe in me").[4]

Thus, the disciples could theoretically express their troubled emotional state in terms similar to what is stated in Psalm 41–42 (LXX). And much like the psalmist, the disciples are required to place their hope in God. In the language of the Fourth Gospel, the disciples are commanded to believe in Jesus (in particular) in the midst of their troubled circumstances just as they believe in God. As will be discussed below, belief/faith in God finds its most appropriate expression through prayer to the Father in Jesus' name. In fact, a review of the Fourth Gospel reveals that the Evangelist records numerous examples of so-called faith/belief in Jesus. Understanding the nature of such belief is vitally important, largely because genuine faith in God/Jesus is the prerequisite to effectual prayer in 14:12–14.

Van der Watt is right to say, "Faith is not defined in a single verse in the Gospel, but its full extent is gradually developed throughout the Gospel.... Not all faith is salvific faith, for instance, the 'believers' in 6:60–66 or 8:31 (see 8:44) are apparently not saved."[5] Concerning the nature of faith/belief in Jesus, he lists two contexts where faith does not lead to salvation:

> (a) *Faith for the wrong reasons*: Faith that accepts Jesus, but for the wrong reasons and without an adequate change in one's attitude toward oneself or towards Jesus does not seem to be salvific, even though a positive attitude towards Jesus is expressed.[6]

For example, in 2:23 the signs that Jesus performed resulted in belief in Jesus' name. Yet verse 24 indicates that such belief was rather superficial since Jesus "would not entrust himself to them, for he knew all men." Van der Watt says, "It seems that the inadequacy of faith based on signs alone is emphasized. Although this positive attitude of faith might be the 'first step' toward Jesus, it does not ensure salvation yet."[7] The second example is as follows:

---

4. Beutler, *Do Not Be Afraid*, 29.
5. Van der Watt, *Introduction*, 53.
6. Van der Watt, *Introduction*, 53–54.
7. As will be shown, there are instances in the Fourth Gospel where the narrative reveals the progressive nature of faith. In some cases, the movement of one's expression of faith is positive and forward but inauthentic. In other cases, the movement is positive, forward, and authentic.

(b) *Faith that is not expressed in deeds*: Jesus's argument in 8:30–47 emphasizes that faith without resulting deeds is inadequate. According to 8:30 many put their faith in him, even as he spoke (8:30). Jesus explains to *these believers* (8:31) that being a child of God should become apparent in their behavior (8:39–42). Although these people "believe" (8:31), their deeds deny such belief, proving them to belong to the family of Satan (8:44).[8]

In 8:31 Jesus implies that the true, authentic mark of a disciple is that he or she abides in his word with the result of knowing the truth and being set free by the truth (καὶ γνώσεσθε τὴν ἀλήθειαν, καὶ ἡ ἀλήθεια ἐλευθερώσει ὑμᾶς).

Finally, Van der Watt says about the nature of true, salvific faith:

(c) True faith involves acceptance and deeds.[9]

He goes on to cite the episode of the man born blind as an example where true, authentic faith is demonstrated. He says concerning this man:

> This blind man concludes that Jesus must be from God (9:27–33), and defends his conviction to the point of losing everything (9:34). But there is a twist in the story. Even though the man is willing to lose everything in defending Jesus, he is not saved yet, not before he also accepts Jesus for who he really is, the Lord, the Son of Man (9:35–38).[10]

The evidence for the authenticity is seen when the blind man's positive confession in 9:30–33, which moves to a full expression of belief after he was cast out. He says in verse 38, πιστεύω, κύριε. Curiously, the man born blind not only gained his physical sight, but also believed to the point of seeing and knowing who Jesus really is. Dodd says that "faith is a form of vision."[11] He says, "In the first place, there is a form of vision, simple physical vision, which may exist without faith. Many of the contemporaries of Jesus saw Him in this sense, but without any saving effects. But when simple vision is accompanied by faith, it leads to vision in a deeper sense." Culpepper remarks, "With delightful subtlety, the narrator shows us the man's insight and exposes the Pharisees' blindness":

---

8. Van der Watt, *Introduction*, 54.
9. Van der Watt, *Introduction*, 54.
10. Van der Watt, *Introduction*, 54–55.
11. Dodd, *Interpretation of the Fourth Gospel*, 185–86.

Contrasting Reponses in John 9	
The Blind Man	The Pharisees
"I do not know" (v. 12).	"This man is not from God" (v. 16).
"I do not know whether he is a sinner" (v. 25).	"We know that this man is a sinner" (v. 24).
"One thing I do know, that though I was blind, now I see" (v. 25).	"We know that God has spoken to Moses, but as for this man, we do not know where he comes from" (v. 29).[12]

In this case, the man born blind truly believed in Jesus in a manner that elucidated the full acceptance of his person and work (vv. 31–33). And the one who has faith and sees will thus act according to what he sees, and thus Jesus' work becomes the believer's work.

With this example in mind, it is important to define the nature of authentic faith. Van der Watt remarks:

> In a nutshell: salvific faith is a self-sacrificing, intellectual, and existential acceptance of the message and person of Jesus to the extent that it completely transforms a person's thoughts and deeds in accordance with Jesus' message and leads to an obedient life of doing what a child should do.[13]

Thus, these passages indicate that verbal profession of belief and/or faith is insufficient for salvation. True faith is intellectually adhering to the person and work of Jesus to the point that the course of one's life, in thought, word, and deed, is visibly altered. Such faith not only unites a man to Jesus at the moment of salvation but also is required throughout the duration of one's relationship with Jesus.[14] Furthermore, faith in God does not merely mean believing that God exists, but it also involves trusting God as the "superior" receiver. Trusting God translates into trusting Jesus. As trust is placed in Jesus, the trajectory of one's life is patterned after the will, mission, and commandments of God. It is in the context of this genre of faith where the individual looks away from trusting in his own (or anyone else's) resources and trusts in "God alone." As such, faith in God is the prerequisite for effectual prayer and provides the remedy for the disciples' troubled hearts.

---

12. Culpepper, *Gospel and Letters of John*, 177.
13. Van der Watt, *Introduction*, 55.
14. Carson, *Gospel According to John*, 347–48.

A House Prepared for Prayer: John 14:2–11

What follows in John 14:2–3 is Jesus' statement concerning the Father's house (οἰκίᾳ), its many rooms (μοναὶ πολλαί), and his promise to prepare (ἑτοιμάσαι) a place (τόπον) for his disciples. In light of Jesus' ministry and mission, such a "house" (John 2:19–21) cannot be physical (John 4:20–24) and therefore must be interpreted in a metaphorical sense as the place where God dwells. But what is the nature of this place? The exact meaning of Jesus' words has provoked much scholarly debate. Many assert without reservation that the Father's house is heaven, which contains "rooms" (ESV), "mansions" (KJV), "dwelling places" (NASB). Further, the promise, καὶ ἐὰν πορευθῶ καὶ ἑτοιμάσω τόπον ὑμῖν, πάλιν ἔρχομαι καὶ παραλήμψομαι ὑμᾶς πρὸς ἐμαυτόν, ἵνα ὅπου εἰμὶ ἐγὼ καὶ ὑμεῖς ἦτε (14:3), has also provoked lengthy scholarly discussions, especially concerning its relationship to the *parousia*. As seen earlier in John (5:25–29; 6:35–40, 44–48), the tension between a consummative and realized eschatology is elucidated. Some scholars view Jesus' coming as a straightforward statement concerning his second advent. The phrases πάλιν ἔρχομαι (present tense) and καὶ παραλήμψομαι ὑμᾶς (future tense), coupled with the ἵνα clause, ὅπου εἰμὶ ἐγὼ καὶ ὑμεῖς ἦτε suggest a future outlook for Jesus' return that involves him taking the disciples to the place where he is (presumably heaven).

In a different vein of thought, some scholars see Jesus' statement as a reference to his coming at the hour of the disciples' death, and thus, according to Brown, this statement (14:3) serves as "a reinterpretation of the *parousia* theme when it was realized that the *parousia* had not occurred soon after the death of Jesus and when the disciples began to die."[15] Dodd, who views chapter 14 as the Johannine reinterpretation of the church's current belief concerning the departure and return of Christ, interprets Jesus' statement about "coming again" in the sense that: (a) Christ will continue his mighty works in the disciples (14:12); (b) the Paraclete will dwell in them (14:15–17); (c) they will live by virtue of the living Christ (14:19); and (d) they will continue in personal interchange of agape with him (14:21).[16] It is possible that the language of verses 2–3 is intentionally open ended, allowing both a near and future coming of Jesus. As such, any interpretation that relegates these verses to either an end-of-life or end-of-the-age paradigm may overlook John's nuanced eschatology and the overall context of chapter 14. But the unfolding themes of the sending of the Spirit and the

---

15. Brown, *Gospel According to John (XIII–XXI)*, 626.
16. Dodd, *Interpretation of the Fourth Gospel*, 395.

mutual indwelling of the Father and Son in the believer elucidate, in some measure, the nature of Jesus' promise, πάλιν ἔρχομαι.

Thus, it is accurate to say that the Father dwells in heaven and that "my Father's house" would convey the idea of heaven against a Jewish background, but Coloe argues that "in the Hebrew Scriptures, 'my father's house' always means the group of people who make up the household [or home], such as the family and servants, or even the future descendants."[17] For example, "So Joseph said to his brothers and to his father's house, 'I will go and tell Pharaoh and say to him, My brothers and my father's house have come to me'" (Gen 46:31). In light of this reality, she admits that Jesus' use of the phrase "my Father's house" (2:16) to refer to a building is "quite strange," but suggests that the Evangelist was moving his readers from the notion of the temple as a building to something more relational (as seen in 2:21). She sees the notable shift from the word "house" (*oikos*, as in chapter 2) to "household" (*oikiai*, as in 14:2) as providing evidence in favor of this assertion. She observes that in the Fourth Gospel the term *oikos* is used only with the sense of a building, namely, the temple building (2:16, 17) and the house at Bethany (11:20). But the term *oikiai* is used with a more fluid range of meanings: it can mean a physical building (11:31; 12:3—both references to the house at Bethany), but it can also mean the household ("the father believed and all his household" [4:53]; "the slave does not continue in the household forever" [8:35]).[18]

Notwithstanding the disciples' culturally conditioned understanding (which was both revelational and geographical in nature),[19] the context of 14:2–3 indicates that Jesus was referring to heavenly relationships that begin on earth and are characterized as being permanent, rather than transient "dwelling places." The term μοναί occurs twice in the NT—in 14:2 and 23. In its verbal form, *meno* means "to remain." In the present context, the term conveys the notion of remaining in a permanent "dwelling place" that is consonant not only with Jewish thought[20] but also, and more importantly, with other NT passages that speak of the eternal state, such as 2 Corinthians 5:1 ("a building from God") and Hebrews 12:22 ("the city of the living God, the heavenly Jerusalem"). More relevantly, Coloe points out that "the emphasis of 14:2 is not the believers coming to dwell in God's heavenly abode,

---

17. Coloe, "Temple Imagery in John," 375.

18. Coloe, "Temple Imagery in John," 375.

19. Köstenberger notes, "The image used by Jesus may also have conjured up notions of a luxurious Greco-Roman village, replete with numerous terraces and buildings, situated among shady gardens with an abundance of tress and flowing water" (*Encountering John*, 152).

20. 1 Enoch 39:3–7. See Kysar, *John*, 220–21; Keener, *Gospel of John*, 932–39.

but the Father, the Paraclete, and Jesus coming to dwell with the believers."[21] As such, the "place" is relational in nature and begins on earth. She cites evidence from select verses throughout chapter 14 that, in her view, precludes interpreting 14:2 as a reference to a mere heavenly dwelling. For example:

a. the Father who dwells (*menon*) in Jesus (v. 10)
b. the Paraclete who dwells (*menei*) with believers, and in the future will be in them (v. 17)
c. the Father and Jesus who will make their dwelling (*monen*) with the believer (v. 23)
d. Jesus dwells (*menon*) with the disciples (v. 25)

The repetitive mention of "dwelling" and "remaining" as seen in chapters 14–15 provides support for her view. However, the fact that the Father, Jesus, and the Paraclete are said to dwell within the disciples on earth should not force one to relegate the language and reality of permanent dwellings to one space/locale. It seems that the textual evidence may assume a twofold dwelling: one that would eventually involve the disciples with God in heaven (14:2–3), and one that would more immediately center on the Father, Son, and the Paraclete residing within the disciples while they were on earth (14:17, 23, 25).

Moreover, Neyrey says that the phrase "in my Father's house . . . suggests an intimate kinship relationship, such as Father and Son, God and the disciples, and perhaps other Christians yet to be brought in—'many rooms.'"[22] Thus, in this view the focus on 14:2 is not exclusively or primarily on heaven but on heavenly relationships that occur on the earth because of Jesus' preparatory work on the believer's behalf. This work takes place in a manner similar to a patron-client relationship where relational exchange occurs between parties of unequal status. And the vital link between these two parties is the broker. But how does Jesus function in this role? Following Albert Oepke, Neyrey says:

> When the New Testament calls Jesus a broker, it shades the term into many meanings: he is the unique mediator . . . between the one God and humankind (1 Tim 2:5), the mediator of the new covenant (Heb 8:6; 9:15; 12:24), and "priest . . . according to the order of Melchizedek" (Heb 5:6; 6:20; 7:17). In contrast to Levitical priesthood, Jesus' priesthood/brokerage is vastly superior because Jesus "is able for all time to save those who approach

---

21. Coloe, "Temple Imagery in John," 376.
22. Neyrey, *Give God the Glory*, 194.

God through him, since he always lives to make intercession for them."²³

But as a mediator/broker, Jesus' interests centered not only on loyalty to the Father but also on securing a place for his clientele. And that place was not physical locale but rather a spiritual relationship. Neyrey remarks:

> Jesus next states that he goes away and comes back—he goes to "prepare a place for you" and then says "he will come again and will take you to myself." He states as his purpose that "where I am you may be also." After brokering his relationship with the Father, he returns to solidify his relationship with God's clients. He does not say that he will take the disciples to the "Father's house," but rather that he will facilitate his brokerage by maintaining a favored relationship with the disciples. Thus, I would extend the sense of "relationship" to the "place" Jesus prepares.²⁴

Further, it is in the context of offering a way to this relational place that Jesus issues the statement, ἐγώ εἰμι ἡ ὁδὸς καὶ ἡ ἀλήθεια καὶ ἡ ζωή· οὐδεὶς ἔρχεται πρὸς τὸν πατέρα εἰ μὴ δι' ἐμοῦ (14:6). As indicated, the only way to come to the Father is through the "way" or brokerage of the Son.²⁵ The term ὁδός can refer to a literal or figurative path or highway. Yet its placement alongside ἀλήθεια καὶ ἡ ζωή precludes a literal, physical meaning. As the way and the truth and the life, Jesus represents the Father by his words and works. As the Father's works unfold in Jesus, the Father is thus revealed. Accordingly, the work of the patron (Father) will be recapitulated in his clients (disciples) who have been relationally prepared by the broker (Jesus). Since the patron and broker are one, it may be said that the client carries on their works as evidenced by contractual relationship forged on the basis of faith.

Moreover, it is in this relationship that the Father is present through the Son. For example, travel of any significant distance often necessitated banding together in groups to avoid danger. Jeremias notes concerning travel to Jerusalem, "The traveller's preparations . . . included finding company for the journey, since the prevalent brigandage . . . made it hazardous for anyone to travel alone for any great distance."²⁶ He also says that the traveller's journey was made on foot, but also by donkey, which enabled one to travel more quickly. Notwithstanding, given the nature of travel in the first

---

23. Neyrey, *Give God the Glory*, 200.
24. Neyrey, *Give God the Glory*, 194.
25. For a discussion of Jesus as intercessor/advocate, see Hurtado, "Place of Jesus," 36–38.
26. Jeremias, *Jerusalem in the Time of Jesus*, 59.

century, it is plausible to suggest that in certain cases friendships would be established between certain individuals along the way to a destination. As such, the actions and words of the individuals would serve to form a profile of their identity. In a similar manner, the disciples traveled (presumably) on foot with Jesus, witnessed a variety of his works and deeds, and heard his words. Therefore in 14:7 Jesus claims that the disciples, by virtue of knowing him along their travels, have seen the Father. Yet Philip still wanted to see the Father (14:8). Jesus says in verse 9, τοσούτῳ χρόνῳ μεθ' ὑμῶν εἰμι καὶ οὐκ ἔγνωκάς με, Φίλιππε; ὁ ἑωρακὼς ἐμὲ ἑώρακεν τὸν πατέρα·πῶς σὺ λέγεις·δεῖξον ἡμῖν τὸν πατέρα; During the duration of the time that Jesus was with his disciples, the Father was functionally present to them. Thus, there was no need for further revelation of the Father since he was manifest to the disciples through Jesus, the Way.

As noted above, Beutler sees a thematic connection between the disciples' "troubled" hearts in 14:1 and the suffering righteous person spoken of in Psalm 41:6, 12; 42:5 (LXX).[27] But he also reads the departing language of 14:4–6 in light of Psalm 42, which speaks of the worshipper who is far away from the sanctuary of God. Verse 3 states, ἐξαπόστειλον τὸ φῶς σου καὶ τὴν ἀλήθειάν σου· αὐτά με ὡδήγησαν καὶ ἤγαγόν με εἰς ὄρος ἅγιόν σου καὶ εἰς τὰ σκηνώματά σου. Insofar as the present discussion is concerned, the relevant themes/terms involve the truth (ἀλήθειάν) that leads (ὡδήγησαν) the psalmist to God's tabernacles (τὰ σκηνώματά).[28] Beutler says, "Die 'Zelte' dürften die in 14,2 genannten 'Wohnungen' sein." He notes further, "Thema könnte aus diesem Psalm stammen, zumal es mit dem Thema der 'Wahrheit' verbunden erscheint."[29] Following Beutler's interpretation, Jesus is the fulfillment of the one who leads people via the way of "truth" (14:6) to the dwelling place(s) of God. As will be discussed in greater detail below, Jesus is not only the *locus* of God's revelation/truth, but he is also the one who opens the "way" to God through prayer in his name (14:13–14; 15:7, 16; 16:23–24). Such access, then, becomes the practical solution to the disciples' troubled hearts. Finally, in the face of the world's hatred and opposition (15:18–25; 16:2–4), the disciples will be led by truth (via the Paraclete) and have perdurable access to God.

---

27. Beutler, *Do Not Be Afraid*, 26–30.
28. Beutler, *Das Johannesevangelium*, 376–79.
29. Beutler, *Das Johannesevangelium*, 379.

Believing for Greater Works: John 14:12

In John 14:12 the Evangelist turns his attention to the corollary of believing in Jesus. He indicates that the one who believes in Jesus may enter into relational space with God (14:2–3). As the disciple occupies this space by faith, he may imitate Jesus by doing the works that Jesus did, and even greater works. Jesus says in 14:12:

Ἀμὴν λέγω ὑμῖν,

ὁ πιστεύων εἰς ἐμὲ τὰ ἔργα

ἃ ἐγὼ ποιῶ

κἀκεῖνος ποιήσει

καὶ μείζονα τούτων ποιήσει,

ὅτι ἐγὼ πρὸς τὸν πατέρα πορεύομαι

The promises of verses 12–14, which involve doing the works of Jesus and the granting of requests made in his name, are preceded by the double-amen saying (ἀμὴν, ἀμὴν). This term is translated as "in truth, in very truth" (NEB); "amen, amen" (ESV); "truly, truly" (NASB); "verily, verily" (KJV); "most assuredly" (NKJV); and "very truly I tell you" (NIV). The phrase "amen, amen, I say to you" appears twenty-five times in the Fourth Gospel; in twenty occurrences the "you" is plural; in the other five it is singular. Ἀμὴν is used thirty-one times (in single format) in Matthew, thirteen times in Mark, and six times in Luke (though the latter also uses ἀληθῶς at 9:27; 12:44; 21:3; and ἐπ' ἀληθείας at 4:25).

The background of Jesus' usage of the term is rooted in the monotheistic nature of Israelite worship and proclamation. Schlier notes, "The OT uses the term in relation to both individuals and the community (1) to confirm the acceptance of tasks whose performance depends on God's will (1 Kgs 1:36); (2) to confirm the application of divine threats or curses (Num 5:22); and (3) to attest the praise of God in response to doxology (1 Chr 16:36). In every case acknowledgment of what is valid or binding is implied."[30]

The Fourth Gospel presents Jesus as absorbing ἀμὴν into his own ministry and applying it consistently throughout the Fourth Gospel. For example, Jesus used this term (in double) when speaking to Nathanael (1:51), Nicodemus (3:3, 5, 11), the Jews (5:19, 24, 25; 6:26, 32, 47, 52; 8:34, 51, 58; 10:1, 7; 12:24), and in his final words to the disciples (13:16, 20–21, 38; 14:12; 16:20, 23; 21:18). In contradistinction to the usage of "amen" (in single format) to conclude a prayer and statements of doxology, on certain

---

30. Schlier, "amén," *TDNT* 53.

occasions Jesus used "amen, amen" to introduce specific authoritative pronouncements (as in 3:3; 10:1). However, the double-amen saying also serves to validate antecedent words, phrases, and sentences. For example, in 1:51 a double-amen statement modifies Jesus' words, "You will see heaven opened, and the angels of God ascending and descending on the Son of Man." In this instance, the announcement concerning Jesus is the link between heaven and earth and the means by which the realities of heaven and earth are brought down to earth. It is the prophetic explanation of what it means to see "greater things" (1:50); but this announcement also serves as the end of chapter 1. Thus, by virtue of its placement in verse 51, the double-amen saying serves as an authoritative conclusion concerning the mission of the Son of Man. The same placement and application of the double-amen statements is seen in 8:58 where Jesus defended himself against the Jews with the statement, "Truly, truly, I say to you, before Abraham was, I am."

Similarly, in 14:12 the double-amen statement and the phrases that follow are not to be divorced from the preceding verses but are rather the outcome of them. The authority of Jesus' words is established not only by virtue of his identity as "the way, and the truth, and the life" (14:6) but also in light of the works he performed (14:10–11). Hence Jesus did not demand that his audience deem his words as both true and trustworthy without qualification, but rather as the natural corollary of his relationship with the Father (5:19; 10:30). Moreover, in the case of 14:12, ἀμὴν modifies λέγω and is thus followed by the participle ὁ πιστεύων. Following Schnackenburg, Jesus' usage of this term justified and strengthened the demand of faith.[31] In light of the double-amen statements, Jesus' disciples could have firm assurance that Jesus was telling the truth and would grant exactly what he promised: the believing one(s) will do the works Jesus did and even greater works. Additionally, as will be demonstrated below, the double-amen statement provided the disciples with assurance that they would perform greater works than Jesus performed and that prayers offered in Jesus' name would be answered.

The condition to performing such works is belief/faith in Jesus. In this instance, Jesus simply stated that the object of one's belief must be in him (ὁ πιστεύων εἰς ἐμὲ). However, in 14:12 the corollary of belief is not eternal life (although that is certainly included), but performing greater works than Jesus ("the works that I do, he will do also; and greater *works* than these he will do; because I go to the Father"). But in verse 12, the one who believes included Jesus' immediate disciples and those who will come to believe (the general participle "whoever believes" or the "believing one").

---

31. Schnackenburg, *Gospel According to St. John*, 70.

The theme of works is introduced in 14:10 (ὁ δὲ πατὴρ ἐν ἐμοὶ μένων ποιεῖ τὰ ἔργα αὐτοῦ) and 14:11 (εἰ δὲ μή, διὰ τὰ ἔργα αὐτὰ πιστεύετε). In verse 12 Jesus stated that the believing one will do τὰ ἔργα ἃ ἐγὼ ποιῶ. The term ἔργα occurs 176 times in the NT; AV translates it as "work" 152 times, "deed" 22 times, "doing" once, and "labour" once. In 3:19-20 and 7:7 the concept of *works* is presented in the context of human agency, specifically as the evil deeds performed by those who love darkness; such works, however, stand in contrast to those performed in the light and in God (3:21). Yet, in the majority of cases throughout the Fourth Gospel, ἔργα is used in relation to the acts and deeds of Jesus. Much of the background for understanding the works of Jesus is located in the OT where Yahweh's power is manifested and his authority made known, particularly in Psalm 104:24 (which assumes Genesis chapter 1) where God's work in creation is given special attention. The OT presents the works of God as extending to his interaction with and deliverance of the people of Israel (e.g., Ps 77:11-20; 46:8-10). The works of Jesus may be rightly viewed as originating with Yahweh since John presents Jesus as the Logos who came from God as God (1:1). As noted, the term *works* is used in the context of ethical deeds. Most pertinent, however, is the term's appearance in the context of specific miraculous deeds performed by Jesus (John 5:17, 36; 10:25, 32).

As noted, in the context of John 14 the term *works* appears in verse 10 where Jesus stated, τὰ ῥήματα ἃ ἐγὼ λέγω ὑμῖν ἀπ' ἐμαυτοῦ οὐ λαλῶ, ὁ δὲ πατὴρ ἐν ἐμοὶ μένων ποιεῖ τὰ ἔργα αὐτοῦ. In this instance, Jesus presented his words as consonant with works that originated with his Father. But 14:12a indicates that belief in Jesus will result in such works being reproduced in and through the disciples. In 14:12b, Jesus stated that the believer will perform "greater works" in light of his departure to the Father. The question that is naturally provoked concerns the nature and meaning of the term *greater* in relation to *works*. Believers will do works μείζονα τούτων, that is, greater than those performed antecedently because of his departure to the Father. While Jesus' departure is mentioned in 14:2-3 (for the preparation of "rooms" or "dwelling places" for the disciples and his subsequent return to take them to himself) and 14:28 (to provoke rejoicing among the disciples), the focus of verse 12 centers on the temporal consequences of his absence. Jesus' departure to the Father, which involves his crucifixion, resurrection, and subsequent glorification, provides the framework for both the promise and the occurrence of "greater works." Such works are not merely greater in intensity per se, rather they are greater because they are, as Carson notes, constrained by "salvation-historical realities."[32] He says

---

32. Carson, *Gospel According to John*, 496.

further, "In the wake of his [Jesus'] glorification, his followers will know and make known all that Jesus is and does and their every word and deed will belong to the new eschatological age that will then have dawned."[33] Culpepper notes, "The future works will be greater not because they will be better or more spectacular, but because they will be more extensive (the mission and spread of the church)."[34]

Although the foundation of the performance of such works is Jesus' departure to the Father, the phrase "whoever believes in me will also do the works that I do" seems to imply that the notion imitation, or *mimesis*, may loom in the cultural backdrop.[35]

> ### Excursus: Imitating Jesus (Mimesis)
>
> Although the term *mimesis* is not employed in the Fourth Gospel, the concept is implied in various instances. Jesus, the Logos, not only came from God but also is God (1:1). Because the Father and the Son are presented as perfectly unified (10:30; 17:11, 21, 23), Jesus does nothing out of his own will (5:30) but only does what the Father is doing (5:19; 10:25, 37–38; 14:10, 31) and speaks only what he hears from the Father (12:49). Hence, the Son's imitation of the Father flows forth from intimacy of relationship and oneness in function. Yet the fundamental expression of Jesus' imitation of the Father also manifests horizontally in his deeds and commands. Van der Watt correctly notes, "Jesus's ethical behaviour cannot be separated from who he is and what he offers. Christology and ethics are interrelated in the sense that ethics is embedded in but also flows out of Christology."[36] That the behavior of Jesus is to be imitated in the lives of his disciples is implied in 12:26 where Jesus states, "If anyone serves me, he must follow me; and where I am, there will my servant be also" (ὅπου εἰμὶ ἐγὼ ἐκεῖ καὶ ὁ διάκονος ὁ ἐμὸς ἔσται). Fundamentally, the meaning of Jesus' command to follow him is seen in light of verse 24, which speaks of a grain of wheat falling to the earth and dying. Thus, Jesus uses metaphorical language that points to his

---

33. Carson, *Gospel According to John*, 496.

34. Culpepper, *Gospel and Letters of John*, 211.

35. The concept of *mimesis* is also seen in the Pauline letters, in which Paul refers to imitation of himself, Christ, God, or other churches (1 Cor 4:10–14, 16; 11:1; Phil 2:5; 3:17; Eph 5:1; 1 Thess 1:6; 2:14; 2 Thess 3:7). See also Matt 5:48 (to be perfect as your heavenly Father); Heb 13:7 (to imitate one's faith).

36. Van der Watt, "Mimesis or Imitation in Ethical Dynamics."

literal cross-death to convey the notion of denying or dying to one's own desires. Van der Watt explains:

> Those who love their lives more than Jesus are not regarded as followers of Jesus. This implies imitation, walking in the footsteps of Jesus, which means doing what Jesus did. Hating or losing one's life means that one will keep it for eternal life (obviously signifying the fruit) and *vice versa*. The application of the death to the disciples should be noted. Hating their physical lives (ψυχὴν) is equaled to the death of the seed. This is identified with following Jesus like a servant and indeed serving Him (12:26).[37]

Accordingly, the practical illustration of Jesus' ethical behavior and teaching is seen in the foot-washing episode of chapter 13. This episode not only reveals Jesus' love for his disciples but also demonstrates how the disciples are to love one another. Specifically, Jesus' words in 13:15, "For I have given you an example, that you also should do just as I have done to you" (ὑπόδειγμα γὰρ ἔδωκα ὑμῖν ἵνα καθὼς ἐγὼ ἐποίησα ὑμῖν καὶ ὑμεῖς ποιῆτε) are an implicit reference to the concept of *mimesis*. The preceding verse ("If I then, your Lord and Teacher, have washed your feet, you also ought to wash one another's feet") elucidates the practical expression of Jesus' love, but it also reiterates the teacher/student, lord/servant paradigm alluded to in 12:26. As the Father is greater than Jesus, so Jesus is greater than his students/servants. Yet the authenticating mark that one is truly Jesus' disciple lay in his willingness to follow him and imitate his behavior, even to death. Noteworthy is that the relational framework that exists between Jesus and his disciples is established and preserved on the basis of love. And this love has a particular genre of expression. Jesus states in John 15:13, "Greater love has no one than this, that someone lay down his life for his friends." Although Jesus is the forerunner of this genre of love, the same is expected of the disciples (15:18–16:4). In this sense, then, Jesus provides an example of the nature of self-sacrifice that he requires for his disciples to follow.

Yet in 14:12 there is no mention of death to self or losing one's life; rather the emphasis rests on the works that are possible in those who have faith in Jesus. But as noted above, mere verbal profession of belief and/or faith is insufficient for both salvation and an ongoing discipleship relationship with Jesus. Instead, true

---

37. Van der Watt, *Introduction to the Johannine Gospels and Letters*.

> faith involves adhering to the person and work of Jesus to the point that the course of one's life, in thought, word, and deed, is visibly altered. Specifically, true faith looks away from self and looks to Jesus for salvation, teaching, guidance, and so forth. By its very nature, salvific faith requires the heart conviction and verbal concession that one's own resources are woefully insufficient and wholly inadequate to fulfill the demands of Jesus. Thus, one may read into 14:12 in the following manner: The one who truly believes in Jesus and has forfeited his rights and desires for Jesus may do the same works that Jesus performed. The believer will speak as Jesus spoke and act as he acted. While not all believers will raise the dead, heal the sick, or open the eyes of the blind, the deeds they perform will be consonant with Jesus' ethical character and eschatological mission. If Jesus' mission involved making the Father known and doing his will, then the believer's mission involves imitating Jesus in the same endeavor. In the end, the corollary of imitation involves manifesting the character, will, and mission of the absent Jesus to the world.

How Prayer "Works" in the Context of John 14:13–14

At this juncture of the analysis it is pertinent to address how the works of Jesus (and greater works) are produced in the life of the believer. Thus, the question that undergirds the following analysis is as follows: How will greater works be practically carried out in light of Jesus' absence? As will be demonstrated below, the disciples' "working" is made possible by their "asking" in Jesus' name. Once petitioned according to this qualification, Jesus states that he himself will "do it."

Jesus says in John 14:13–14:

καὶ ὅ τι ἂν αἰτήσητε ἐν τῷ ὀνόματί μου
τοῦτο ποιήσω,
ἵνα δοξασθῇ ὁ πατὴρ ἐν τῷ υἱῷ.
ἐάν τι αἰτήσητέ με ἐν τῷ ὀνόματί μου
ἐγὼ ποιήσω.

Verse 13 begins with the copulative conjunction καὶ, which links the clause that follows to the one that precedes it. The relative clause ὅ τι ἂν αἰτήσητε may be viewed as a continuation of the former clause and dependent on ὅτι ἐγὼ πρὸς τὸν πατέρα πορεύομαι or an independent clause intended to advance the thought further;³⁸ the latter being most preferable. On one hand, Jesus' promise that the disciples will perform greater works is the direct corollary of his departure to the Father, hence the ὅτι phrase. On the other hand, the grounds of the performance of greater works also involve the disciples' requests in Jesus' name. Thus, verse 13 elucidates the nature and scope (τι ἂν αἰτήσητε), condition (ἐν τῷ ὀνόματί μου), and corollary (ἐγὼ ποιήσω) of the disciples' request-making.

Noteworthy is the absence of an object to the verb αἰτήσητε (v. 13). In fact, all witnesses omit a "me" that is substantially attested to in verse 14. Thus, it is not altogether clear whether prayer is to be offered to Jesus or to the Father. Bultmann sees the clause ὅτι ἐγὼ πρὸς τὸν πατέρα πορεύομαι as strictly substantiating what had gone before, while at the same time closely connecting the ὅτι-clause with ὅ τι ἄν.³⁹ Nevertheless, both 13b and 14b emphasize the centrality of Jesus' response to the prayer in his name, τοῦτο ποιήσω and ἐγὼ ποιήσω. Therefore, two explanations are possible: (1) prayer is directed to Jesus, who in turn grants the requests, or (2) prayer is directed to the Father, but requests are granted by Jesus. Whichever antecedent one chooses (Jesus or the Father), the outcome is the same: Jesus will answer the prayer (he will do whatever is requested).

A Demarcation of Prayer?

As seen in 14:13–14, the believing disciple may approach his superior in order to verbalize and ask "whatever" or "anything" he wishes. With this in mind, one may ask, is there a particular terminology of prayer ("asking") that reflects the uniqueness of and the distinctions within the Father-Son-disciple(s) relationship? There are two important terms that directly relate to this question. As seen in 14:13–14 the Evangelist employs the term αἰτήσητε in relation to prayer. This term appears several times in the Fourth Gospel in both horizontal and vertical fashions, namely, in the context of the Samaritan woman asking Jesus for a drink (4:9), Martha's assurance that God will give Jesus whatever he asks for (11:22), and, as noted, in the context of the believers' prayer to God (14:13–14; 15:7, 16; 16:24, 26). The term ἐρωτάω is also relevant to the present discussion. Insofar as the Fourth Gospel is concerned, the Evangelist's use of ἐρωτάω carries the meaning of "to ask a question" in numerous instances (see 1:19, 21, 25; 9:2, 19, 21; 16:5, 19, 30). In other instances, the term carries the meaning of "to ask for" something (4:31, 40, 47; 14:16; 16:26; 17:9). While some argue that ἐρωτάω and αἰτέω

38. Westcott, *Gospel According to St. John*, # 174.
39. Bultmann, *Gospel of John*, 611.

are virtually synonymous,⁴⁰ Ostmeyer nonetheless views them as indicating the demarcation of prayer in the Fourth Gospel. He says:

> Jesus is the only person to use the verb ἐρωτάω as a form of address to God. While ἐρωτάω never appears in the communication of the disciples with God, αἰτέω is likewise not used by Jesus. Only Jesus prays directly to God. If the disciples turn to God or Jesus, "αἰτέω in the name of Jesus" is employed. Ἐρωτάω, used by Jesus, corresponds to αἰτέω in the name of Jesus, which the disciples are expected to do—the terms are not exchangeable. Different relationships with God are expressed by different terms of prayer.⁴¹

If Ostmeyer is correct, it may be plausible to suggest that, insofar as prayer is concerned, the Evangelist's usage of the terms αἰτέω and ἐρωτάω elucidate the distinctions that exist between the subordinate disciples and the superior Father. Following Ostmeyer, on one hand, the disciples could not pray directly to the Father (hence, his usage of ἐρωτάω). Yet, on the other hand, the new way of praying introduced in 14:13-14 (in Jesus' name) provided the basis upon which they could ask God (αἰτέω) while allowing positional distinctions to remain in place. In this understanding, Jesus brokers access to the Father and therefore makes effectual prayer possible. By virtue of their belief in Jesus and the use of his name in prayer, the disciples are afforded the privilege of "asking" the Father for "anything" or "whatever."

Yet what is the nature of "whatever"? Are there boundaries that limit the range of one's requests, or may requests be offered without qualification and/or limitation? In 14:13a, the phrase ὅ τι ἄν, best translated as "whatever" or "anyhow," is followed by the verb αἰτήσητε. Thus ὅ τι ἄν αἰτήσητε is translated, "whatever, anyhow you ask." The concept of asking for "whatever" may appear open-ended and undetermined. However, in the case of 14:13-14 in particular, the nature and content of one's request/asking is linked to the preceding verse (v. 12) where the theme of works is highlighted. Therefore, Jesus permitted one to ask/pray for "whatever" "greater works" one wishes, that is, provided that the works are congruent with his

---

40. Carson says concerning these terms (in relation to John 16:23), "Although in classical Greek the verb 'to ask' (*erotao*) means 'to ask a question' rather than 'to ask for [something]' ... in the Greek of the New Testament period *erotao* can have either force." He continues, "If the two verbs [αἰτέω and ἐρωτάω] are roughly synonymous, with meaning 'to ask for [something],' then the only contrast in the verse is between the disciples asking Jesus for things during the period of his public ministry, and their asking the Father for things after Jesus has risen" (*Gospel According to John*, 545).

41. Ostmeyer, "Prayer as Demarcation," 246.

mission and his name. The analysis that follows directly below will explore in detail the meaning and application of Jesus' name.

Praying in Jesus' Name

As indicated in 14:13–14, the condition to effectual prayer is that one must pray according to Jesus' name. But what is the significance of prayer in a particular name?[42] Malina says that in the Mediterranean world one's name and reputation are "the most valuable of assets."[43] Dodd notes, "The name of a person is the symbol of his personal identity, his status, and character; and so, for the Hebrew monotheist, the Name of God stands as a symbol for His sole deity, His glory, and His character as righteous and holy."[44] Crump remarks, "To believe in Jesus' name is to confess his true identity as the Son sent from the Father now offering us eternal life. Confessing Jesus' name is equivalent to surrendering to his lordship as the savior."[45]

But what is the meaning of Jesus' name? One must first turn to the OT background that the Johannine story must be read against. Bietenhard says concerning the name of God in the OT:

> *The Name Yahweh.* Knowing the name of God is important in the OT (Gen 32:30). God reveals his name to Abraham (Gen 17:1) and Moses (Exod 6:2). Invocation of his name is common, but incantation is forbidden (Exod 20:7). God promises to hear when properly called upon, but his name is a gift of revelation, not an instrument of magic. Yet invocation of his name implies faith in his power, as in swearing (1 Sam 20:42), cursing (2 Kgs 2:24), or blessing in his name (2 Sam 6:18). The name may indeed stand for the person (Lev 18:21; [Amos] 2:7). If the name is in the angel of Exod 23:21, this means that God himself is present in revelatory action. While he himself is in heaven, he chooses a place for his name to dwell (Deut 12:11; 2 Sam 7:13; 1 Kgs 3:2). This is the pledge of his saving presence. It assures a high estimation for the temple and yet also a low estimation, for God is not tied to the temple by causing his name to dwell

---

42. The term ὀνόματί is seen throughout the Fourth Gospel in relation to John the Baptist (1:6), Malchus (18:10), believers (10:3), and the Father and the Son. Jesus states, "I have come in my Father's name, and you do not receive me" (5:36). Accordingly, Jesus makes the request, "Father, glorify your name" (12:28), and later declares, "I have manifested your name to the people" (17:6).

43. Malina, *New Testament World*, 37.

44. Dodd, *Interpretation of the Fourth Gospel*, 93.

45. Crump, *Knocking on Heaven's Door*, 159.

there. After the exile, the name often denotes the glory of God. A common idea is that God will be gracious to Israel so that his name may not be dishonored among the nations. Much more frequently, however, the name now stands for the person, and this leads to the hypostatizing of the name whereby it stands alongside God as an acting subject or an instrument in his hand (cf. Ps 20:1; Prov 18:10; Mal 1:11).[46]

The Fourth Gospel presents that "person" or "acting subject" in God's "hand" as the Logos who came from God as God (1:14) to reveal the Father (14:6–10; 17:25–26). With this background in mind, a proper definition of Jesus' name may be stated as follows: the name of Jesus encapsulates his nature and earthly mission, which involved performing the works of the Father, offering salvation to all who believe, and bringing glory to the Father. There are seven "I am" (ἐγώ εἰμι) statements (with predicates) littered throughout the Fourth Gospel that expound the nature and identity of Jesus. These include the following: I am the bread of life (6:35, 48, 51); I am the light of the world (8:12; 9:5); I am the door of the sheep (10:7, 9); I am the good shepherd (10:11, 14); I am the resurrection and the life (11:25); I am the way, and the truth, and the life (14:6); I am the true vine (15:1). Van der Watt says, "Usually these sayings . . . are linked to either Exod 3:14, Deut 32:39, or to the 'I am'-sayings in Deutero-Isaiah (for instance, Isa 43;10, 25; 45:18–19; 46:4; 48:12, 17; 52:6). Jesus is thus identified as the Lord of history and savior of Israel."[47] Van der Watt sees these statements as allusions to Jesus' divine nature and thus divine authority. But he further sees another aspect that relates to Jesus' mission as an envoy: "The way in which envoys made themselves known at their destinations was to identify themselves with the words 'I am so and so.' On questions like 'who are you' this would also have been the way to answer. Jesus also identifies himself in this world by saying 'I am.'"[48] Therefore, in this view, Jesus appears to the world as the divine savior who announces his identity in a manner that would naturally be understood when read against the backdrop of the divine name and nature of Yahweh revealed in the OT.

Thus, Jesus' mission is relational and revelational in nature. By using the phraseology, "I am," Jesus connects his person and work to Yahweh of the OT. By performing signs, Jesus revealed his power and glory (2:11; 4:46–54; 5:1–15; 6:5–14; etc.). In the incarnation, Jesus revealed his identity as the only Son who has always existed with the Father (1:1, 14, 34; 8:28, 58; 17:5,

---

46. Bietenhard, "ónoma," TDNT 696.
47. Van der Watt, Introduction, 42.
48. Van der Watt, Introduction, 2.

24). By taking on the role of rabbi (1:38, 49), Jesus revealed his intention to instruct. By laying down his life on a cross (10:15; 19:30), Jesus revealed his role as a good shepherd. Therefore, in light of the coming of Logos, the world is not left in darkness concerning the Johannine God. Simply, Jesus' mission involved bringing clarity rather than confusion. Jesus came to elucidate, not obscure. He came to reveal, not conceal. So when a "subordinate" prays in Jesus' name, he is praying in the "superior" authority of what that name symbolizes or represents, namely God's person, his authority, and his mission. The same God who spoke in the burning bush and through the prophets will answer those who approach him on the basis of the name that has been revealed in the Son.

Excursus on the Use of the Concept of "Name" in Greek Prayer

Unlike some participants in Greek religion, Jesus' disciples are not left without a proper name and form of address in prayer. It has been noted that Greek prayer often involved prayer to deities whose names were unknown. Aune says, "In numerous magical texts the deity addressed is said to have a 'secret name,' which is often followed by a sequence of incomprehensible 'magical words' (*voces magicae*)—as, for example, the following from a *Papyri Graecae Magicae*:

> Invocation: Yes, lord, because I call upon (*epikaloumai*) your secret name which reaches from the firmament to the earth, ATHEZOPHOIM ZADEAGEOBEPHIATHEAA AMBRAMI ABRAAM THALCHILTHOE ELKOTHOOEE ACHTHONON SA ISAK CHOEIOURTHASIO IOOSIA IICHEMOOOOAOAEI.[49]

Aune continues:

Not only must a divinity be addressed with precision and courtesy, but such invocation must also be accompanied by formal titles, powers, and attributes of the deity if he or she is to hear the prayer. The following poem by the first-century CE poet Catullus follows the conventions of an invocation directed to Diana (the Latin name for Artemis), who is identified by her divine parents, Latona and Jove, as well as by her aliases, including Juno Lucinia, Trivia, and Moon:

> O Child of Latona, great offspring of greatest Jove,

---

49. Aune, "Prayer in the Greco-Roman World," 34–35.

> whom your mother bore by the Delian olive tree,
>
> that you might be the lady of mountains and green woods,
>
> and secluded glens and sounding rivers;
>
> you are called Juno Lucina by mothers in birth pains,
>
> you are called mighty Trivia and Moon with counterfeit light.
>
> You, goddess, measure out by monthly course the circuit of the year,
>
> You fill full with goodly fruits the country home of the farmer.
>
> Be thou sanctified by whatever name you wish (*sis quocumque tibi placet sancta nomine*); and as of old you were accustomed, with good help keep safe the race of Romulus. (Catullus)[50]
>
> In light of these examples, prayer in Jesus' name is utterly simple. Johannine prayer is explicitly monotheistic, whereas Greco-Roman prayer is polytheistic. The former asserts the existence of one God, but the latter asserts the existence of many gods. While it is true that Jesus has many titles ("Son of God," "Rabbi," etc.), he prescribes prayer in one name. Finally, instead of praying to an unnamed god, or to the wide variety of known gods (whether Zeus, Aphrodite, Demeter, Athena, Dionysus, Numa, etc.) who must be petitioned according to their availability and ability, the Johannine believer may pray in the one known name that effectually eventuates the will and power of the one true God (17:3).

The Name and Place of Prayer

Two further questions were raised in chapter 2 of this book that relate to the temple and God's name. For example:

> (1) In light of 1 Kings 8, Jewish prayer could be offered toward the temple that bore God's name. How does God's name relate to prayer in the Fourth Gospel? (2) The emphasis in 1 Kings centers on the temple being a place of prayer. What emphasis does the Fourth Gospel place on the temple? Does it connect prayer to the temple? How does prayer in the temple change in light of Jesus?

As noted, the Jerusalem temple was the place where the name of God dwelt (1 Kgs 8:16–20, 29; see also 1 Chr 22:10, 19; 2 Chr 6:7–10, 20; etc.).

---

50. Aune, "Prayer in the Greco-Roman World," 36.

According to Solomon's prayer of dedication for the temple, whenever the people sinned and were defeated by their enemies, they were to acknowledge God's name and pray in the temple. Solomon's request centered on God hearing their prayer and forgiving their sin (1 Kgs 8:33–34). Similarly, if the heavens were shut up because of sin, the people were to pray toward the temple and acknowledge God's name in the hope that he would forgive them (1 Kgs 8:35–36). If a foreigner (who hears of God's great name) prays toward the temple, then Solomon requests that God would hear and answer in response to his name (1 Kgs 8:41–43). Thus, as the earthly dwelling place of God, the temple that bore God's name may be viewed as a sounding board from which prayers are channeled heavenward to God. As the metaphorical space of prayer, the temple represents the localized presence of God with his people.

It is possible that a first-century believer who was familiar with the Jewish prayer tradition might naturally connect the temple/name motif in 1 Kgs 8 and 2 Chr 6 with John 14:13–14. In contrast to Solomon dedicating the temple as the dwelling place for the name of the LORD, the Fourth Gospel presents Jesus as the new place of worship/prayer. As such, God's name would no longer dwell in a physical structure but with disciples who believe in Jesus. In light of Jesus' replacement of the temple (John 2:21), prayers are no longer directed toward the physical temple as the metaphorical dwelling place of God but are instead offered in the name of Logos made flesh (John 1:14), who was with God and is God (John 1:1). Since the claims of Jesus ("I am") and the name of Jesus is associated with the object of Solomon's address (the name, the "LORD," 8:22–23, 25–26, 28, etc.), prayer in Jesus (as the new temple), then, is likened to prayer in the name of Yahweh, with all that his name represents. Jesus, then, might naturally be viewed as the one who brings prayer in the temple and personal prayer together. Since Jesus will dwell in the disciples, they have no need to participate in the physical temple. Free outpouring of the heart may continue to God apart from the physical temple, but not apart from Jesus, the new temple. He is the conduit through which prayer is offered heavenward to the Father.

Therefore, Jesus' original audience (pre-70 CE) could have conceivably interpreted Jesus' cross-death and glorification as the necessary abolishment of the cultic worship. Thus, in this view, the physical temple would become obsolete even before its destruction. The audience addressed by the author of the Fourth Gospel (post-70 CE) would have viewed the destruction of the temple, or the Father's house, as inconsequential insofar as sacrifice and prayer were concerned since both atonement for sin and accessibility to God through prayer were made available through Jesus. In light of his death as a sacrificial substitute, prayer would no longer be offered toward a physical structure that bore God's name, but instead it would be directed toward the Father in the name of Jesus (John 14:13–14; 15:16). Much like the physical structure of the temple, Jesus' physical body would no longer be present after his ascension; yet believers could approach God through the name of Jesus. Thus, the worshipper is said to have direct access to the space of prayer before God and to have his prayers heard by virtue of Jesus' atoning sacrifice.

Therefore, much like the people of Judah were without a physical temple after its destruction in 586 BCE, the disciples found themselves without Jesus' physical presence after his departure. Yet much like the exiles, the disciples possessed a name through which prayer could be offered. But in contradistinction to the exiles, the disciples were given the specific name Ἰησοῦς to pray in light of his departure. As members of the household of God who were indwelt by the Spirit and equipped with Jesus' name, the disciples could approach the Father freely without physical or spiritual limitations. Thus, Jesus' name may be likened not only to the "title deed" of prayer but also to the sounding board from which the disciples' prayers are channeled to the Father. Any "result" asked for in his name will be heard and granted.

Prayer for the Father's Honor/Glory

In 14:13 Jesus says that he will do whatever is requested for a very distinct purpose, namely, ἵνα δοξασθῇ ὁ πατὴρ ἐν τῷ υἱῷ. This ἵνα-clause necessarily demands an examination of two key terms that relate to prayer: δοξασθῇ and πατήρ. The latter term (πατέρ) is seen throughout the Farewell Discourse, appearing twenty-three times in chapter 14 alone. Specifically, Jesus speaks of the Father's house (14:2), knowing the Father (v. 7), seeing the Father (v. 9), the work of the Father (v. 10), his departure to the Father (v. 12), the glory of the Father (v. 13), and so forth. The chart below serves to outline further the nature of the Father's relationship to the Son (and vice versa) as it is seen throughout the Fourth Gospel.[51]

Passage	Father/Son Dynamic
1:1–2	The Son was with God (the Father) in the beginning
1:18	The Son was at the Father's side in the beginning

---

51. For an analysis of Johannine symbolism within the lens of Jesus' relationship with the Father, see Akala, *Son-Father Relationship*.

3:35	The Father loves the Son and has given all things into his hands
3:36	The wrath of God remains on those who reject the Son
5:22	The Father has given all judgment to the Son
8:12–20	The Father bears witness to/about the Son
8:54	The Father glorifies/honors the Son
10:30	The Father and Son are one
12:49–50	The Son speaks by the Father's authority
14:6	The Son provides the way to the Father
14:10	The Son is in the Father and the Father is in the Son
14:13	The Father is glorified in the Son
6:11; 11:41–2; 12:27–28; 17; 19:28, 30	The Son prays to the Father
20:1–10	The Father vindicates the Son

The actions of giving, speaking, granting, and glorifying, along with the realities of the Father and Son being "with" and "in" one another, elucidates the relational intimacy and functional harmony that occurs between them. Whatever one does is for the good of and in harmony with the other. Neither the Father nor the Son acts in isolation but rather with consideration for each other. Perhaps the Son's desire for his Father's glory is most aptly summarized in 17:1 where Jesus says, Πάτερ, ἐλήλυθεν ἡ ὥρα· δόξασόν σου τὸν υἱόν, ἵνα ὁ υἱὸς δοξάσῃ σέ. The Father-Son relationship is somewhat comparable with cultural models in the first century CE. It has been pointed out by scholars that Jesus lived in a cultural context in which collectivism, rather than individualism, was practiced. In Malina's view, personal/individual introspection and psychoanalysis were foreign practices to the first-century world. This is not to say that ancient persons were void of a sense of individualistic awareness. Rather, it is to say that one's self-awareness was bound to the larger cultural framework in which he lived. Malina remarks that the first-century Mediterranean world "consisted of persons who considered themselves in terms of the group(s) in which they experienced themselves as inextricably embedded."[52] In this view, collectivism is best seen as a network of brothers and sisters, men and women, and/or human personalities who shared a distinct common heritage. To know one

---

52. Malina, *New Testament World*, 62.

member who operates within the framework of the shared convictions and assumptions of the others is to know the entire group identity.[53]

This model is not only replicated in the Father-Son relationship and first-century culture but also seen in the Father-Son-disciple relationship. In particular, the concept of collectivism establishes a precedent of prayer for the disciples who enter into the familial relational space with God.[54] As children of God, believers enter into the space of prayer where concern for the Father and the family is top priority. Thus, one will not seek to pray with merely his own interests or "results" in mind but will pray according to the interests of the family and for the "maintenance of relationships" within the family.[55] If the Father's house is to be viewed in terms of disciples who are in familial relationship with God, then disciples are to pray that the rooms of the Father's house become occupied on the basis of the brokerage of the Son. Such prayer may also involve a concern for the fruitfulness of those who take up residence in the household of God (John 15:1–7). As prayers are answered, relational space is occupied, fruitfulness is cultivated, and the Father receives glory. In John 11:41–42, for the benefit of those listening, Jesus gives thanks to the Father and does so, namely so they may believe that the Father sent him (ἐγὼ δὲ ᾔδειν ὅτι πάντοτέ μου ἀκούεις, ἀλλὰ διὰ τὸν ὄχλον τὸν περιεστῶτα εἶπον, ἵνα πιστεύσωσιν ὅτι σύ με ἀπέστειλας). While the immediate audience is not family per se, it is Jesus' stated desire that they become so through his prayer. On believing in Jesus, individuals become children of God and members of the family of God (1:12). Therefore, Van der Watt is right to say:

> Members of the family should also defend and enhance the honour of the family. The Son defends the honour of his Father's home (2:16–17). He does what the Father requires of him in order to glorify the Father. The Father again glorifies his Son and his other children (12:26). The children should bear fruit to the glory of the Father. They are a unity—like the Father and Son are one, the children are one. Jesus and the Father will be in them and they will be in the Son. This expresses the unity, which exists in the family as group and this unity is constituted and expressed through common love, knowledge, will, actions, honour and purpose. What belongs to the family belongs to all of them, and they will not be left as orphans who are without hope or protection, but the Father and Son will care for them.[56]

---

53. Malina, *New Testament World*, 63.
54. As evidenced in John 1:12–13 and implied in 3:3.
55. Neyrey, *Give God the Glory*, 9.
56. Van der Watt, *Family of the King*, 316.

Based on their previously established relationship with God, the subordinate disciples may approach God freely and openly in prayer to make their requests known. In return, the Father always hears their prayers and answers them, that is, when prayers are issued for his glory. The promise of such "hearing" is noted in 11:42 where it is said that the Father always hears Jesus when he spoke/prayed. That the Father both heard and answered Jesus is evident by Lazarus's resurrection from death (11:43–44). The Lord's Prayer assumes the attentiveness of God, who may be approached as a "Father" (Matt 6:9, Πάτερ ἡμῶν) who provides for his children and protects them (6:11–13). Most notably, the assumption of the Lord's Prayer is that disciples may enter into the space of prayer freely without fear of being rejected or shamed. As Jesus depended on the Father, so the disciples may depend on Jesus to answer prayer as they issue it in his name.

Moreover, the disciples are commissioned to pray in a collective mindset that takes into account their identity as children of God who are members of the family of God. Neyrey and Stewart note, "In antiquity a person is primarily known as the 'son of So-and-So' or the 'daughter of So-and-So.' Identity and honor derive in large part from membership in a family or clan. ... To know a person, ancient peoples thought it essential to know that person's bloodlines (see Cicero, *Inv.* 1.24.34–35; Quintilian, *Inst.* 3.7.10–11)."[57] Hence, what unites believers in the family of God is not blood but rather their common faith in Jesus (not their bloodline, but their belief-line). And their faith expressed through prayer is the means by which the head of the family is glorified and honored. As a son, Jesus brought glory to the Father. As children of God, believers also share in this privilege as they make their requests known in Jesus' good name. But in the Johannine model, praying in Jesus' name leads to "working" for the Father's glory. Jesus indicates that he "will do" whatever is asked for in his name, which indicates that Jesus' work of glorifying the Father continues even after his earthly ministry ceased. In the case of John 14:13, the self-manifestation of the Father's glory is seen in the Son as he answers prayers on behalf of believers. Thus, God's glory originates with the Father but is inextricably bound to, embedded in, and manifested through the work of the Son that continues through his praying children.

The Paraclete and Prayer

While the departing nature of chapter 14 is clear enough, the question remains concerning the extent to which one can justifiably label this chapter

---

57. Neyrey and Stewart, *Social World of the New Testament*, 89–90.

(and the entirety of the Farewell Discourse) *farewell genre*. In their attempt to determine the nature and background of this discourse in general and Jesus' departing words in particular, select scholars[58] have located similarities between the literary form of John's discourse and other "farewell discourses" or "testaments" of famous heroes from antiquity.[59] However, Witherington points out that certain events reported in the Farewell Discourse provide a portrayal of a first-century Greco-Roman banquet[60] (with a closing *symposium*) rather than a Passover meal.[61] Particularly, Jesus is portrayed as sharing a final meal with the disciples (13:1–30), which is followed by a farewell speech (13:31–16:33). He says that a Greco-Roman banquet began with a meal followed by a *symposium* (teaching, dialogue, or entertainment period following the meal but during the drinking party). This event was male-only, with women excusing themselves before the *symposium*. Witherington remarks that a transition was made between the meal and the drinking party (or *symposium*) by a wine ceremony where wine was poured out to the god. After the transition (cf. Plato, *Symp.* 176A), a hymn or chant would be offered to the god, perhaps a calling on a god as savior (cf. Athenaeus, *Deipn.* 15.67b–c). Finally, the drinking party would continue with entertainment or, for some, conversation on topics ranging from history to philosophy.[62]

With this profile in mind, Witherington provides an in-depth analysis of chapters 13–17, where Greco-Roman elements are brought forth uniquely through Jesus' actions and words.[63] In particular, he says, "Jesus is portrayed as not just any kind of great teacher in the discourse but as a Jewish sage (16:25–27) who speaks parabolically and explains his figures of speech to his disciples in this sort of setting."[64] Thus Jesus is depicted as Wisdom (Prov 9:5–6) who summons his disciples to "hear and heed" the voice of wisdom. But Witherington notes moreover, "The reason that Jesus's last meal with his disciples is portrayed as a Greco-Roman banquet, instead of bringing out its association with the Jewish Passover meal, is that this material is now a part

---

58. Keener, *Gospel of John*, 896–98; Ashton, *Understanding the Fourth Gospel*, 470–78.

59. For an outline of the scholarly attention paid toward the current farewell and others found in Old and New Testaments and in extrabiblical Jewish sources, see Hwang, "Presence of the Risen Jesus," 111–13.

60. See Bennema, *Excavating John's Gospel*, 140. For a definitive analysis of the banquet in the early Christian world, see Smith, *From Symposium to Eucharist*, 13–46.

61. Witherington, *John's Wisdom*, 231.

62. Witherington, *John's Wisdom*, 232.

63. Witherington, *John's Wisdom*, 233–34.

64. Witherington, *John's Wisdom*, 233.

of a missionary document."⁶⁵ As such, the more universal aspects of Jesus' character, mission, and ministry are highlighted. Therefore, the last meal might naturally appeal to Gentiles and to some Diaspora Jews.

Furthermore, the Farewell Discourse centers not only on Jesus "going" (14:3) but also on his "coming," (14:3), "doing" (14:13–14), and "dwelling" (14:17, 23) in the disciples. In this model, Jesus' promises involve the continuation of his mission to both the Jew and non-Jew through his disciples. Furthermore, the progression of the Farewell Discourse (and Brown's outline above) culminates with the theme of a successor being sent in Jesus' absence, the Paraclete. Although the parallel is not precise, Jesus' words in 14:25–26 may indicate that the Paraclete would be sent to officiate a teaching symposium in Jesus' absence. As will be discussed below, as the Paraclete continues to educate the disciples, they would in turn be equipped to continue their conversation with God through the medium of prayer. The corollary of such prayerful conversation centers on Jesus coming "to do" (14:13–14) whatever is requested, thus fulfilling his mission through his disciples.

The Paraclete's role in chapter 14 centers on his identity as an abiding successor to Jesus, who will teach the disciples and remind them of his words. In light of the Evangelist's emphasis on Jesus' departure and prayer in his name, this writer is left with the impression that the symposium that began in the Farewell Discourse will be carried forth in the form of a conversation (or prayerful dialogue) between the believer and God. Even in Jesus' absence, God will continue to communicate truth to believers through the Paraclete and believers will continue to communicate with God through prayer. The analysis below will explore the possibilities of how the Paraclete equips the believers in this regard.

The Paraclete as Educator and Prophet

The following questions were raised earlier and will be answered below: (1) "Luke-Acts shows the close relationship between the Spirit and prayer, yet Luke does not provide detailed, explicit information concerning how the Spirit equips the believer to pray. How does the Fourth Gospel enhance one's understanding of the Holy Spirit's role in prayer?"; (2) "The synagogue served as a place of education and learning. In what manner does instruction take place in light of Jesus' departure to the Father? In what ways is education linked to prayer?"

---

65. Witherington, *John's Wisdom*, 233.

In light of Jesus' departure, the Paraclete will function much like a symposium teacher who will equip the disciples to offer prayers that are congruent with Jesus' teaching and mission. While it is true that disciples will not be orphaned, as children of God (1:12–13) they will require continuing education in Jesus' absence. And part and parcel of such education involves both the "teaching" and "reminding" (14:26) of the truth initially revealed though Jesus. As Jesus prepared to depart, he indicated that the Paraclete would be sent to educate the disciples in an ongoing *symposium*. And part and parcel of the Paraclete's identity is that he is the Spirit of Truth (14:16–17). The term ἀλήθεια is used throughout the Fourth Gospel in a variety of contexts (4:23–24; 8:40, 45; 14:6; 17:17, 19; 18:37). But Bultmann says, "*alḗtheia* is 'authenticity,' 'divine reality,' 'revelation,' especially in John, where this reality, as a possibility of human existence, is out of reach through the fall but is granted to faith through revelation by the word (cf. John 8:44; 1 John 1:8; 2:4)."[66]

In the context of 14:17, the Evangelist connects *truth* to the Spirit, hence, τὸ πνεῦμα τῆς ἀληθείας. Carson says that in contrast to the dualistic usage of this phrase in first-century Judaism ("spirit of perversity," the two spirits referring to two "inclinations" that battle it out in every human being), the Fourth Gospel presents a different reality.[67] Following the trajectory of Jesus' ministry (14:6), the Paraclete carries forth the truth revealed in and through Jesus to the disciples.[68] Carson notes, "Judging by the description of his work, the Paraclete is the Spirit of Truth primarily because he communicates the truth."[69] This, according to 16:13, means that he, being the truth in person, guides his people into that realm of truth which is embodied in Christ and in his redemption." Malina and Rohrbaugh say that the Advocate (the Paraclete) "facilitates the continued presence of Jesus (vv. 12, 16), guarantees truthfulness in the antisociety (v. 17; 16:13), and reminds group members of the meaning of what Jesus said and did."[70] The disciples who have entered into the relational space with Jesus/Father have the ability to receive such truth (8:47; 10:3) as it is imparted through the Son and the Spirit/Paraclete in the Son's physical absence. Thus, prayer to the Father, then, will accord with the truth revealed by the Spirit, who is sent in Jesus' name (14:26) and will be consonant with his mission.

---

66. Bultmann, "*alḗtheia*," *TDNT* 39.
67. Carson, *Gospel According to John*, 500.
68. Köstenberger, *Encountering John*, 157.
69. Carson, *Gospel According to John*, 500.
70. Malina and Rohrbaugh, *Social-Science Commentary*, 231.

Thus, the Paraclete is the Spirit of Truth who functions as a teacher or tutor. Van der Watt says concerning education in the Mediterranean world, "Education was ... the responsibility of the father, whether he undertook it himself, or whether he made use of another teacher."[71] He notes that the Father educated the Son (5:17–30) and the Son educated his disciples, but he also notes how such education continued through the Paraclete in Jesus' absence. Such education may be prophetic in nature. Neyrey presents a model of communication that includes the following. He says:

> A sender sends a message via some channel to a receiver to have an effect. In prayer the senders are the Johannine members who send a message via Jesus-as-channel to God; but in prophecy the process is reversed, as God speaks to mortals, not listens to them. In prophecy (1) God, the sender (2) sends a verbal message (3) through the channel of Jesus, the "Spirit of Truth," or a disciple-prophet, (4) to the receivers, the members of the Johannine group, (5) for the purpose of communicating to them special information.[72]

In many cases throughout the Fourth Gospel, the primary mode of communication takes place through Jesus. He came from "above" (8:23) to those who were "below" (1:14). Yet in light of Jesus' departure, the Paraclete assumes the role of the communicator/prophet, and, as noted by Neyrey, he functions as "a broker of special knowledge about Jesus."[73] After Jesus departed, the Paraclete, the Spirit of Truth, would further teach the disciples truth from "above." Thus, both Jesus and the Paraclete prophetically revealed aspects of what Van der Watt calls the "story behind the story."[74] Jesus came from *above* to his disciples, who are *below*. In doing so, the truth from above lifted his disciples from below into a realm of knowledge that provides a glimpse into the story behind the story. Although Jesus unpacked and revealed some of this story, there was more left to communicate. Thus, in Jesus' absence the Paraclete prophetically taught the disciples and reminded them of the words Jesus spoke. In doing so, the truth revealed by the Spirit was received by the disciples and then conceptualized and prayed back to the Father. Thus, there exists a circular model of communication of truth beginning with the Father, mediated through the Son, communicated/taught by the Spirit, received by the disciples, and finally prayed back to God in Jesus' name. The aim, then, was for the disciples to be acclimated

---

71. Van der Watt, *Family of the King*, 221.
72. Neyrey, *Give God the Glory*, 178.
73. Neyrey, *Give God the Glory*, 186.
74. Van der Watt, "Narrative and Ethics."

with God's story in order to make that story their reality through prayer. By praying in Jesus' name and on the basis of what is good and true[75] the disciples brought heaven (above) to the earth (below), thus actualizing the transcendental story.[76]

The Paraclete as Mediator and Broker

As the Helper, the Spirit is sent to aid and equip the disciples who would naturally feel alone and discouraged in light of Jesus' departure. But in addition to teaching and education, what other benefit(s) does the Paraclete bequeath? In verse 18 Jesus says, "I will not leave you as orphans; I will come to you" (ESV). Carson remarks, "Jesus consoles them: *I will not leave you as orphans*, children bereft of parents who would support them—though in secular Greek the word *orphans* is also used of children stripped of only one parent or of disciples stripped of their master."[77] Keener points out, "Although 'orphan' technically referred to the fatherless, it could also apply to other sorts of bereavement."[78] If this is the case, then the Paraclete functions in a consolatory role for the disciples who would be troubled over Jesus' absence. In 1 John, Jesus is presented as a heavenly, forensic helper (2:1, ἐάν τις ἁμάρτῃ παράκλητον ἔχομεν πρὸς τὸν πατέρα Ἰησοῦν Χριστὸν). In this particular instance, Jesus is clearly presented as the one who helps by "speaking" on the believer's behalf. In John 14:13–14, Jesus assumes the role of a helper who grants requests made in his name. But as Jesus' successor, the Paraclete functions as "another Helper" (14:16) to the disciples. As a helper, the Spirit opens a channel of divine communication through which the Father and Son are present to the believer. Far from being orphaned and oppressed, by virtue of the coming Paraclete, the disciples would be permanently indwelt by their Father and the Son in whose name they offer prayer.

Further, Tricia Brown provides a thorough analysis of the pre-Johannine usage of παράκλητος. She observes, "In the various occurrences of παράκλητος prior to the Gospel of John the term usually carries a connotation of 'mediator' or 'broker,' with the glaring exceptions being the passages

---

75. Van der Watt, "Narrative and Ethics."

76. Van der Watt says, "Believers are expected to mimic Jesus. As Jesus loved, they should love (13:34), as Jesus walked, they should walk (1 John 2:6), as he is pure, they should be pure (1 John 3:3), as he is righteous, they should be righteous (1 John 2:28). His narrative should become their narrative" ("Ethos of Being Like Jesus").

77. Carson, *Gospel According to John*, 501.

78. Keener, *Gospel of John*, 973.

in Job and Philo's *De Opificio Mundi*, sec. 23, where the terms bears the meaning of 'helper' or 'assistant.'"[79] She says further:

> In several of the texts, the παράκλητος stands in the gap between two parties, where one party possesses some sort of benefit to which the party needs access. And in most of the passages, the element of inequality between the two parties stands out. Furthermore, in these texts it is the function of the παράκλητος to bridge the divide between the more and less powerful, facilitating access to the benefits required by the less powerful party, while not disrupting the balance of the relationship between the two parties. The παράκλητος bridges the divide between them while still maintaining separateness.[80]

Brown points out that the Evangelist stresses the "insurmountable divide between God and humanity more than any other Evangelist."[81] Yet due to his origin, nature, and intimacy with God, Jesus alone provides humanity with access to God. He is the one who brokers a relationship between the patron-Father and the client-disciple(s) (14:6). She writes that "Jesus is the only one who provides access to the realm of God because he is the only one sent from that realm."[82] However, she points out that the Fourth Gospel provides a model where a broker may provide his clients with access to Jesus. As such, this model allows for a subordinate broker (Paraclete) who works in conjunction with the superior, exclusive broker (Jesus). In the context of 14:25–26, the Paraclete is said to "teach" the disciples "all things" and "bring to their remembrance" all that he said to them. As such, the Paraclete assumes an educational and prophetic role in and for the disciples. By virtue of the indwelling presence of the Spirit, believers have access to Jesus and therefore to the Father. Thus, according to the context of 14:17 and 14:23, such access does not primarily center on heaven but rather on the presence of God on earth. This concept/reality may be illustrated in the following manner (which assumes a post-glorification paradigm):

---

79. Brown, *Spirit in the Writings of John*, 180.
80. Brown, *Spirit in the Writings of John*, 180.
81. Brown, *Spirit in the Writings of John*, 197.
82. Brown, *Spirit in the Writings of John*, 195.

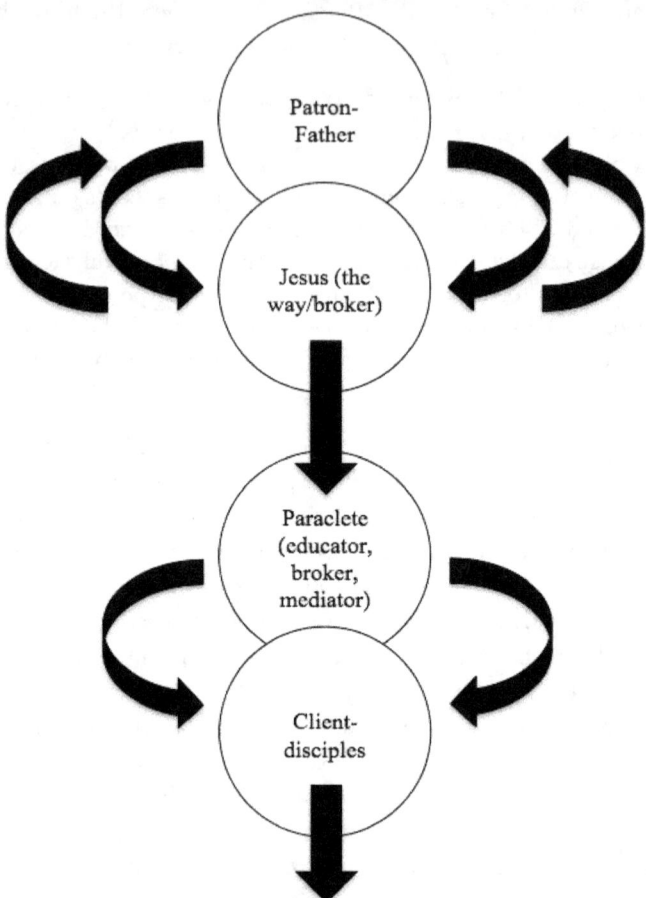

The disciples who have faith in Jesus and obey his commandments are:

1. indwelt by and in union with the Father, Son, and Spirit-Paraclete,
2. possessors of the name of Jesus,
3. educated and prophetically informed,
4. privileged to pray and have their prayers answered, and
5. able to perform greater works that glorify God.

In light of this reality, believers become the dwelling place of God on the earth; the space where heaven and earth intersect; the place where prayers are offered, answered, and fleshed out. As such, the indwelling Paraclete (the Spirit of Truth) eventuates prayer and worship devoid of ties to any particular geographical place (4:20–23). Just as a Paraclete-led symposium may occur wherever the disciples meet (since the Spirit dwells with them and in them), so the disciples may continue their conversation with God without concern for a physical locale (synagogue or temple) or physical person (Jesus). The disciples may enter into the relational space of prayer by faith and with the help of the Paraclete who teaches them and reminds them of the truth revealed through the Son (14:26). Therefore, in light of Jesus' coming and eventual departure, prayer/worship will no longer be tied to a physical temple. Rather, prayer will be offered in Jesus' name and will occur by the influence and indwelling presence of the Paraclete. Moreover, in contrast to the reality of prayer in the First and Second Temple Eras, the believer (14:2, 17, 23), not the physical temple (1 Kings 8:29), now possesses God's name and is indwelt by his Spirit. In contrast to Jewish prayer, Johannine prayer is not merely offered by a person (disciple), but it is offered through the name of a specific person (Jesus) with the help of the Spirit-Paraclete. But like Jewish prayer, Johannine prayer may be spontaneous; it may be spoken verbally; and it may occur at home, in the synagogue, or in any physical structure as long as it is offered in Jesus' name.

Moreover, the sending of the Paraclete at Jesus' request (14:16, 26) may serve to reassure the disciples of the efficacy of prayers offered in Jesus' name. In 14:13–14 the emphasis of making requests in Jesus' name assumes union with Jesus. The same assumption undergirds the promise of 14:26. Thus, 14:13–14 is thematically linked to 14:26 insofar as union with Jesus and the preeminence of making requests in Jesus' name are concerned. However, a distinction must be made between the scope and outcome of the promises made in 14:13–14 and 14:26; the former pertains to the disciples' requests, the latter pertains to Jesus' request. But the fulfillment of 14:26 (that is, the Father answering Jesus' request) would further encourage the disciples to ask in Jesus' name. If the Father sent the Spirit at Jesus' request and in his name, he would certainly answer the disciples' prayers that are issued in the name of their earthly host, Jesus.

CHAPTER 6

Prayer that Produces

Analysis of John 15

THE FOCUS OF THE last chapter centered on an exegesis of John 14 for the purpose of detecting how the materials within this section of the Farewell Discourse contribute to the Johannine profile of prayer. The aim of this chapter involves analyzing how John 15 contributes to one's understanding of the theme of prayer in light of the metaphorical imagery of the vine/branch imagery, the concept of remaining in Jesus, love for Jesus, friendship with Jesus, and the role of the Paraclete. Accordingly, the conclusions of the previous chapters will be taken into consideration at various points in order to gain a fuller understanding of how the Evangelist's audience understood Jesus' remarks about prayer and the efficacy thereof. The aim, then, is to gain a clearer understanding of the nature, purpose, and qualifications of prayer. In light of Jesus' farewell, this chapter addresses the basic qualifications that must be met in order for prayer to be answered.

The Prerequisites to Answered Prayer

As noted in previous chapters, prayer occurs in the relational space where humanity and divinity intersect. It is the space where a "subordinate" sender communicates with a "superior" receiver. In chapter 14 the Evangelist presents faith as the prerequisite for entering into relational space with God in general but also promotes faith in Jesus as the prerequisite to answered prayer in particular. Those who believe in Jesus become dwelling places for the Paraclete, who mediates the presence of the Father and Son to believers.

Such disciples are not only indwelt by God's presence but are also equipped with Jesus' name. As they offer prayer in his name, Jesus says he will do whatever they request. In chapter 15 "asking" God (in prayer) is not explicitly discussed until verse 7. As will be discussed below, the placement of prayer at this point is likely due to the fact that the Evangelist seeks to stress the prerequisite of prayer a second time, only this time in different terminology. Further, the promise is made in chapter 14 that Jesus will make his home in believers.

However, in chapter 15 Jesus places a demand on the disciples to remain in him, which implies the necessity of continuing faith in Jesus. The necessity of remaining in Jesus becomes especially pertinent in the face of the "hard times" predicted by Jesus. The disciples must remain in relational space with him (as the vine) if they desire to be fruitful and bring glory to the Father (the gardener). As they remain in the vine, the disciples can have the assurance that they may ask for anything they wish in prayer and it will be done for them. Thus, the immediate discussion below centers on examining the viticultural language that is employed to communicate the nature of the disciples' relationship to Jesus and the work of the Father in Jesus'/the disciples' behalf.

The True Vine: John 15:1a

In attempting to analyze prayer within the context of John chapter 15, one must have a grasp on the literary features employed in the first eight verses. Pertinent questions include the following: What is the nature of language used? What do the images represent or stand for? More specifically, what does a vine and a vinedresser and branches and pruning have to do with prayer? How do these images apply to the disciples? As chapter 15 begins, the imagery shifts from God dwelling within the believer to the believer remaining in Jesus, the vine. As such, the imagery of a prepared "house" fades as viticultural imagery predominates (15:1–8). Verse 1 begins with the last occurrence of the Ἐγώ εἰμι statements of the Fourth Gospel. This statement is modified by the clause, ἡ ἄμπελος ἡ ἀληθινὴ. Jesus identifies his father in the predicate clause that follows, ὁ πατήρ μου ὁ γεωργός ἐστιν. The Evangelist's unique identification of Jesus and the Father provides a foundation for the imagery and implications that follow.

A metaphor is necessitated when the literal meaning of a word in the sentence is incongruent with reality. However, such incongruency must be established on the basis of the context in which the words in question appear. For example, the phrase ὁ πατήρ μου ὁ γεωργός ἐστιν may in fact be a truthful literal statement. As this phrase stands on its own, its contents are not incongruent with literal realities. Yet, given the present context, Jesus identified his father, a transcendent reality, in a manner that is incongruent with experience and reality. The same may be said of the statement, Ἐγώ εἰμι ἡ ἄμπελος ἡ ἀληθινή. Logically, the Ἐγώ εἰμι clause assumes and explicitly conveys human identity and awareness, whereas ἡ ἄμπελος assumes and explicitly conveys agrarian identity and function.[1] Thus, the vine imagery may be viewed in metaphorical and symbolic terms. As such, Jesus is not merely presented as the vine, but the "true" vine (ἡ ἄμπελος ἡ ἀληθινή), that is, he (symbolically) stands and functions in place of that which is false and that which has failed.

There is some scholarly disagreement over the meaning and application of ἀληθινή in relation to the vine. For example, Brown is not persuaded that John sought to polemicize by presenting Jesus in this manner. He writes, "It does not seem that in claiming to be the real vine Jesus is polemicizing against a false vine; rather he is emphasizing that he is the source of 'real' life, a life that can come only from above and from the Father."[2] He continues, "'Real' here is the language of Johannine dualism distinguishing what is below from what is above."[3] Notwithstanding, the most likely background for the vine imagery is seen in the OT[4] portrayal of Israel as a vine, most particularly in negative rather than positive terms.

Concerning the vine symbol, Culpepper says, "The vine was so widely recognized as a symbol for Israel that it is frequently found on coins from the Maccabean period on.... In the praise of Wisdom in Sirach 24, Wisdom likens herself to a vine:

> Like the vine I bud forth delights,
>
> and my blossoms become glorious and abundant fruit.
>
> Come to me, you who desire me,
>
> and eat your fill of my fruits."[5]

---

1. Van der Watt clarifies further, "The figurative use of semantically related words like vine, branches, pruning, fruit indicates that a single, nevertheless complex facet of reality (i.e., single = vine farming; complex = different aspects taken from the semantic field of vine farming—vine, branches, fruit, etc.—are used) is presented, more or less within one textual locality" (*Family of the King*, 28).

2. Brown, *Gospel According to John (XIII–XXI)*, 674.

3. Brown, *Gospel According to John (XIII–XXI)*, 674.

4. While there is no explicit OT link to Jesus as the true vine, Brown is right to suggest that the "OT and Judaism supplied the raw material from which this *mashal* [material] was composed, even as they supplied the raw material for the *mashal* of the sheepgate and the shepherd (29:397–98)" (*Gospel According to John [XIII–XXI]*, 672).

5. Culpepper, *Gospel and Letters of John*, 214.

The OT employs the vineyard theme/metaphor on certain occasions, particularly in the context of the people of Israel. For example, certain passages speak about the reality of (Hos 10:1), the rejoicing over (Isa 27:2), and the positive expectation for the fruitfulness of a vineyard (Isa 5:3–4). Other passages speak about a vine in the context of disappointment (Jer 2:21) and judgment (Jer 8:13; Ezek 15:1). Further, both a mother (Ezek 19:10) and a wife (Ps 128:3) are compared to a fruitful vine. Accordingly, the OT devotes attention to the failures of Israel, thereby providing some justification for viewing Israel as the false vine and Jesus as the true vine. Beasley-Murray remarks, "It is striking that in every instance when Israel in its historical life is depicted in the OT as a vine or vineyard, the nation is set under the judgment of God for its corruption, sometimes explicitly for its corruption, sometimes explicitly for its failure to produce good fruit (Isa 5:1–7; Jer 2:21)."[6] Perhaps the clearest and most important OT passage that relates to the topic of the vineyard is Psalm 80:8-18, which brings together the themes of the vine and the son of man.[7]

This passage clearly identifies God as the gardener of the vine, the nation of Israel (vv. 7–8). The psalmist thus portrays Israel as being transported from slavery into a favorable environment (vv. 9–11) where it thrived for a season (v. 10). Yet God (the gardener) permitted its plundering (vv. 12–13). Accordingly, the psalmist's plea centers on God showing regard once again for the vine he planted (vv. 14–15). What follows is the psalmist's mention of the "son of man." While it is possible that the title "son of man" may be a reference to Israel, it is more likely a reference to the hope of the Davidic King who would come to rule. Van der Watt notes, "For a person familiar with Ps 79 (LXX), the similarity between Jesus as Son and the son mentioned in the Psalm, would be apparent."[8] Moreover, Streett remarks that the Evangelist may not be contrasting Jesus' self-designation as "the true vine" with a failed Israel / vine since the psalmist does not condemn Israel for failure.[9] Streett, following Köstenberger, notes, "Instead, it may simply mean that 'Jesus, the Messiah and Son of God, fulfills Israel's destiny as the true vine of God' (Ps 80:14–17)."[10] Thus, the connection between Psalm 80 and John 15 is the fulfillment of messianic destiny. As the true vine, Jesus fulfills the destiny that the psalmist pleads for in chapter 80.

6. Beasley-Murray, *John*, 272.

7. For further discussion of the relationship between Psalm 80 and John 15, see Morris, *Gospel According to John*, 669; Van der Watt, *Family of the King*, 52.

8. Van der Watt, *Family of the King*, 46.

9. Streett, *Vine and the Son of Man*, 215–16.

10. Streett, *Vine and the Son of Man*, 215–16.

Moreover, Witherington notes, "The primary issue [in chapter 15] here is not *where* is the true people of God (in Jesus now, in Israel before) but rather *how* can the true people of God remain faithful and continue to function properly despite a hostile environment."[11] While this statement is correct, it must be pointed out that the *how* can only be answered in light of the *where*. The *where* has always been in the context of relational space with God. Israel failed largely due to its deviation from Yahweh and his commandments. If they had remained faithful, they would have been fruitful. As such, one's relationship with God, not identification with or being a member of Israel, was the means by which one could produce fruit. As will be argued below, the thrust of chapter 15 centers on the disciples remaining in the vine Jesus (*where*) as the means to bear fruit for God (*how*). Since Jesus is the locus of God's revelation, the disciples must remain united to him and be obedient to him in order to bear fruit. While Israel was fruitless, Jesus proved fruitful in his earthly ministry and subsequently on his departure through the disciples/branches who remain in him. As such, the disciples who are in union with the vine are guaranteed success as they pray. In short, since Jesus will not fail, the disciples who remain in relational space with Jesus [*where*] may be assured that their prayers, which are issued in Jesus' name [*how*], will not fail.

The Gardener's Identity: John 15:1b

John chapter 15, verse 1b indicates that Jesus is not alone in the fruit-producing enterprise, καὶ ὁ πατήρ μου ὁ γεωργός ἐστιν. The vine is said to receive care from the "gardener" (ESV, NIV), "vine-dresser" (NASB, RSV), or "husbandman" (KJV). In ancient culture, vineyards demanded specialized care and attention. Without a gardener the vineyard would eventually become unfruitful and die. Therefore, the life of the vine was inextricably linked to the attention of the gardener. The Evangelist designates an identity to the gardener (ὁ πατήρ μου) but then identifies the gardener's role in verses 2 and 6. Verse 1 presents an analogy of sorts that illustrates the roles of both Jesus and the Father and how they function together. Van der Watt remarks, "These phrases [I am the vine, the Father is the gardener, you are the branches] indicate to the reader that there are indeed two interpretative levels (literal and figurative), and that on the figurative level vine, gardener or branch can and should for instance be replaced with Jesus, Father and disciples, respectively."[12] As such, Van der Watt says that the relationship

---

11. Witherington, *John's Wisdom*, 255.
12. Van der Watt, *Family of the King*, 33.

between Jesus and the Father is analogous to the relationship between a vine and the gardener.[13]

While Jesus is clearly presented as the vine, according to 15:2 the Father functions as the gardener/vine-dresser (ὁ γεωργός) who takes away branches that do not bear fruit (πᾶν κλῆμα ἐν ἐμοὶ μὴ φέρον καρπὸν αἴρει αὐτό) and prunes those that are fruitful (πᾶν τὸ καρπὸν φέρον καθαίρει αὐτὸ ἵνα καρπὸν πλείονα φέρῃ). Following the figurative-from-literal paradigm of verse 1, John introduces a new character category in verse 2 with the phrase πᾶν κλῆμα ἐν ἐμοί. Here the preposition ἐν and the pronoun ἐμοί serve to identify the nature of the term κλῆμα. In keeping with the metaphorical language of the opening verse, this term (not used elsewhere in the NT) is a reference to Jesus' disciples (as in chapter 14) who derive their life from the vine. This is implied in verse 2 but becomes clearer in verse 5, where John expands the discussion beyond the Father and himself to those who are in some genre of relationship with him or "in" him (ἐγώ εἰμι ἡ ἄμπελος, ὑμεῖς τὰ κλήματα). Once again, if Jesus is the vine who supplies nutrients to the branches, then it follows that the branches are Jesus' disciples who received his life-giving nourishment. Or to state it another way, the qualities of the vine (Jesus) are transferred only to true disciples who adhere to Jesus' teaching and remain in union with him.

The Gardener's Work: John 15:2

In light of the analysis above (see chapter 3), the Fourth Gospel indicates that not all professing disciples were true, fruitful disciples. As indicated by John 15:2, while certain branches/disciples proved to be fruitful, others proved to be fruitless. In verse 2 Jesus states the course of action that is taken to remove the unfruitful branch/disciple, but he also enunciates the care that is provided for the fruitful branch/disciple. In the immediate context, the gardener's actions are portrayed by the terms αἴρε and καθαιρει. The former term pertains to the action performed on the fruitless branch, whereas the latter term pertains to the action performed on the fruitful branch.

Outside the context of John 15, καθαιρει appears at least once in the context of viticulture. Inside the context of chapter 15 the term may be naturally translated as "prunes" or "cleanse." The immediate context of chapter 15 does not provide any viticultural explanation concerning how this action takes place. What is emphasized, however, is the logical goal of such pruning, namely fruitfulness. Of particular importance is the relationship between Jesus' word as a mechanism of the disciples' initial cleansing/

---

13. Van der Watt, *Family of the King*, 32.

pruning and its function as an antecedent and precondition to bearing fruit and having one's prayers answered. Jesus states in 15:3, ἤδη ὑμεῖς καθαροί ἐστε διὰ τὸν λόγον ὃν λελάληκα ὑμῖν. The only other instance (in the Fourth Gospel) where the term καθαροί is used in reference to the disciples is 13:10, where it is said that the disciples are clean. In this instance, the saving work of Jesus is in view. The clause καὶ ὑμεῖς καθαροί ἐστε refers to the action of foot washing that foreshadows Jesus' death. Beasley-Murray notes, "The action of Jesus is parabolic of the greater cleansing that he is about to achieve through his redemptive death, by which his disciples ... will be granted not only remission of guilt, but a part with him in the eternal kingdom."[14] Brown notes concerning the connection between 13:10 and 15:3, "Jesus's word may be said to make them clean already because they have received his word and they are in the context of 'the hour' which will make the working of that word possible."[15] Hence Jesus' word (15:3) and actions (13:10) are not incongruent but rather work harmoniously. In the case of 15:3, it is not that Jesus' word is actual pruning shears; rather it can be said that the disciples were clean already through the antecedent work of Jesus' word, which encapsulates all that Jesus is and does.[16]

Moreover, Brown understands the adjective καθαροί as referring to Jesus' reassurance that the disciples have no need of being "trimmed clean" by the Father.[17] He sees being "clean" not in reference to sin but from "all that prevents fruit-bearing." Schnackenburg remarks similarly, "In its present context, this sentence [15:3] can only be understood in the following sense: God, the vine-dresser, does not need to clean or purify the disciples, because they are clean already and can therefore bear abundant fruit so long as they abide in Christ."[18] This connection is justifiable in light of the phrase καὶ πᾶν τὸ καρπὸν φέρον καθαίρει αὐτὸ ἵνα καρπὸν πλείονα φέρῃ (v. 2). But while Jesus' word was the precondition to the disciples' cleanness, abiding in his word is the precondition to the disciples' ongoing fruitfulness, especially as it will relate to having their prayers answered. As will be demonstrated below, cleanness through Jesus' word and closeness with Jesus and his word (or remaining in Jesus) results in fruitfulness for God.

The term αἴρω is employed twenty-three times in the Fourth Gospel. In eight places it could be translated "take up" or "lift up" (5:8–12; 8:59;

---

14. Beasley-Murray, *John*, 234.
15. Brown, *Gospel According to John (XIII–XXI)*, 677.
16. Carson, *Gospel According to John*, 515.
17. Brown, *Gospel According to John (XIII–XXI)*, 676. OT references to pruning include Lev 25:3–4; Song 2:12; Isa 2:4; 5:6; 18:5; Joel 3:10; Mic 4:3.
18. Schnackenburg, *Gospel According to St. John*, 98.

10:18, 24). In thirteen places the term is best translated as "take away" or "remove" (11:39, 41, 48; 16:22; 17:15; 19:15, 31, 38 [2x]; 20:1–2, 13, 15). The NKJV/NASB and KJV render αἴρει as "takes away" or "taketh away," respectively. The ESV translates the term as "removes." The NIV renders it as "cuts off." Whichever translation one chooses, the employment of this term in chapter 15 is clearly figurative. As the gardener of the vine, the Father removes branches/disciples that fail to bear fruit. However, some scholars have suggested that in contrast to being removed, the fruitless branches are "lifted up" so that they can receive exposure to the sun and produce abundant fruit. Laney summarizes the rationale behind this interpretation, "It is reported that during their nonproductive season, the stalks of the grapevine are down on the ground. But when the time comes for the stalks to bear fruit, the vinedressers begin to lift them off the ground. Rocks are used to support the stalks until they are in a position for fruit-bearing. This 'lifting' process reportedly exposes the grapes to the sun."[19] Derickson says further,

> When Jesus gave the analogy of the vine and the branches, He based it on the cultural practice of His day, which was to clean up only the fruit-bearing branches and tidy up the rows during the early spring growth following blooming. Severe pruning and removal of branches did not occur until the grapes were harvested and dormancy was being induced.[20]

Therefore, in his view, καθαίρει should inform the meaning of αἴρει. The removal of branches goes hand in hand with the action of cleaning/pruning. The removal of nonfruitful branches took place in anticipation of later growth and the pruning of fruitful branches took place for more immediate, unhindered growth of existing fruitful branches. Derickson goes on to say:

> Certain non-fruiting branches were tied to the trellises along with the fruiting branches while the side shoots of the fruiting branches were being "cleaned up." The non-fruiting branches were allowed to grow with full vigor and without the removal of any side growth or leaves, since the more extensive their growth the greater the diameter of their stem where it connected to the vine, giving greater ability to produce more fruit the following season. Removing the non-fruiting branches from the ground and placing them on the trellis would allow the rows of plants to

---

19. Laney, "Abiding Is Believing," 59.
20. Derickson, "Viticulture and John," 51–52.

benefit from unhindered aeration, considered an essential element to proper fruit development.[21]

While a presentation of the Father as a loving gardener who removes unfruitful branches with the anticipation of future growth and fruitfulness is certainly congruent with the nature of the Father in Johannine literature, the language of verse 2 (and verse 6) points to the permanent removal of branches that possessed no life within. Furthermore, scholarly opinion ranges from viewing the unfruitful branch of verse 2a as: (1) true believers who forfeited their salvation, (2) professing believers who were never truly in Jesus, or (3) true believers who, because of some unidentified reason, have failed to bear fruit but retain their salvation. The second view is the most likely meaning that John had in view. As indicated above, the Fourth Gospel speaks of disciples/branches who were in fellowship with Jesus and received wisdom from him but did not possess a salvific relationship with him. Such disciples walked with Jesus and kept company with Jesus but proved they were not truly "in" him. For example, in chapter 6 the conditional phrases "come to me" (v. 44), "feeds on my" (vv. 54, 58), "drinks" (v. 54), and "remains in me" (v. 56) are employed to convey the necessity of perdurable faith in Christ. And true faith results in salvific fellowship that stands in contrast to a mere, empty profession of faith that leads to temporary fellowship and eventual severing from the vine.

Finally, some have raised the question concerning whether the removal of unfruitful branches in verse 2a has any connection with the branches in verse 6 that are gathered, thrown into the fire, and burned. Derickson suggests that these verses must be interpreted separately since the actions of pruning and removing occur at different times of the year (spring/fall).[22] In his view, the emphasis of verse 2 rests on usefulness, not divine judgment. While it is possible that John addressed two separate actions that take place at different times of the year, the immediate context leaves the reader with no definitive conclusion. Further, there is no syntactical evidence that would force a seasonal dichotomy between these verses; thus, Derickson's assertion must be defended on other grounds. The similarity of consequence ("removal" and "thrown away") links verses 2 and 6 together in a harmonious manner.[23] Carson sees verse 2 as preparing the way for verse 6. In verse 2a the branch is said to be unfruitful. In verse 6a the branch that is thrown away and burned is the one that is withered, and a withered branch is an

---

21. Derickson, "Viticulture and John," 49.
22. Derickson, "Viticulture and John," 50–51.
23. Van der Watt, *Family of the King*, 41.

unfruitful branch.[24] Thus, the concept of uselessness and deadness is implied in both verses. In short, such branches are good for nothing. Thus, read together, verses 2 and 6 provide justification for verses 4, 5, and 7, where the condition for bearing fruit is established. Therefore, only those who remain in Jesus (the vine) will bear fruit. Those who fail to remain will be fruitless and will be permanently removed.

The Prerequisites to Answered Prayer: John 15:7

At this textual juncture, the topic of prayer returns to the Farewell Discourse. Yet once again, the Evangelist notes the condition that must be fulfilled in order to make prayer effectual. Specifically, in John 14:1 and 12 the necessity of belief in Jesus is highlighted. But in 15:3–7 the Evangelist highlights the necessity of remaining in Jesus and Jesus' words remaining in the disciple. He states in 15:7:

> ἐὰν μείνητε ἐν ἐμοὶ
> > καὶ τὰ ῥήματά μου ἐν ὑμῖν μείνῃ,
> ὃ ἐὰν θέλητε
> αἰτήσασθε,
> καὶ γενήσεται ὑμῖν.

As the discourse expands, a subtle shift occurs in this verse where the discourse transitions from the third person (v. 6) to the second person plural where the disciples are addressed directly. Another textual shift also occurs in verse 7 as the bulk of vineyard imagery fades into the background; however, such imagery does not completely disappear but selectively reappears as the discourse recapitulates and expands the theme of the consequence of remaining in Jesus (καρπὸν, vv. 8, 16). Jesus has already stated, ὁ μένων ἐν ἐμοὶ κἀγὼ ἐν αὐτῷ οὗτος φέρει καρπὸν πολύν, ὅτι χωρὶς ἐμοῦ οὐ δύνασθε ποιεῖν οὐδέν (15:5). In 15:7 he states the same positive reality by reiterating the necessity of remaining in him. Here μείνητε is used as a second person plural, aorist, active, subjunctive verb. In verse 7a the term is used with ἐὰν to form a subordinate conditional clause. The disciples are to remain in Jesus, but Jesus' words must also remain in the disciples.

The verb μένω occurs forty times in the Fourth Gospel. It is used in reference to remaining in a physical place such as in 1:38, 39; 4:40; 7:9; 10:40; and 11:6, 54. It is also used in reference to the perdurability of God's wrath (3:36) and sin (9:41) on/in an individual. However, John's usage of μένω

---

24. Carson, *Gospel According to John*, 518.

(in relationship to Jesus) is not employed in the context of a physical place in general but in the context of a relational space in particular. The Spirit (1:32-33) and the Father (14:10) are both said to dwell/remain in Jesus, and the Spirit (14:17) and Jesus (15:4) are said to abide/remain in believers.

In the case of 15:4, the opening clause, μείνατε ἐν ἐμοί, κἀγὼ ἐν ὑμῖν, may be understood in three ways: (1) Conditional: "If you remain in me, I will remain in you." This particular reading credits the believer as the "cause" of Jesus remaining in the believer. (2) Comparison: "Remain in me, as I remain in you."[25] Newman and Nida rightly note, "If the clause is interpreted as a comparison, then the first clause is most appropriately understood as an imperative, for example, 'continue to be a part of me even as I am a part of you' or 'continue to be joined to me even as I will remain joined to you.' (3) Mutual imperative: 'Let us both remain in each other'; 'Let there be mutual indwelling.'"[26] The most appropriate reading that fits best with the overall context of 15:1-7, where absolute dependence on Jesus is key in the fruit-bearing enterprise, is the first reading with some modification. Thus, the imperative places responsibility on those who claim to be "in him" (v. 2) to remain "in him." And such remaining occurs through the dynamic activity of faith in Jesus and belief in his word. In turn, Jesus promises to "remain in" the believer.

As will be discussed further below, it is squarely within this relational context where divine life is received, relational intimacy is experienced, and effectual prayer to the Father is offered. Remaining in Jesus (the vine) is equivalent to remaining in relationship[27] with him and being granted access to the space of prayer. As such, since the believer has constant access to Jesus, he therefore has constant access to the Father through prayer in Jesus' name. Thus, the concept of abiding in chapter 15 is congruent with the theme of asking in Jesus' name (14:13-14), since both assume union with Jesus. Therefore, whether one is said to remain in Jesus (and his words remain in the disciple) or to pray in Jesus' name, one may expect to have his prayers answered since he granted the "power of attorney."[28] Thus, expulsion from the synagogue and/or the destruction of the temple would have no practical impact on the Johannine believer who prays while united to the vine. By virtue of his faith in Jesus, he is no longer "in" the temple or synagogue but rather in Christ, the vine. It is this relational context (14:1-3,

---

25. As outlined in Carson, *Gospel According to John*, 516.

26. Newman and Nida, *Handbook on the Gospel of John*, 481.

27. Neyrey writes, "'Abide' refers not to geographical space but to social relationships and group adhesion" (*Gospel of John*, 254).

28. Aune, "Prayer in the Greco-Roman World," 176.

12–14; 15:1–5) where the practical outcome of remaining in Jesus and prayer are elucidated.

In chapter 15, Jesus communicates the message of the necessity of remaining in Jesus to the disciples (later the Johannine group) for the effect of provoking loyalty to Jesus in the midst of their sorrow (14:1) and impending persecution (15:18–16:4). As seen in chapter 15, the call to abide/remain in Jesus appears numerous times in verses 4–7. Each exhortation builds on the other to reinforce and expound the vine/branch imagery stated in 15:1–2. Although chapter 15 describes this relational space in agrarian (15:1–2) rather than household terminology (14:2–3, 23), the implication is the same. As such, the call to remain is not a static end but rather a dynamic means to the end of a relationship with the Son characterized by communication via prayer. In the context of 15:7, abiding in Jesus and his words gives rise to the promise that the disciples may ask for whatever they wish and it will be done for them. But like 14:13–14, one must keep the condition in mind. If the same word that cleansed the disciples (13:10; cf. 15:3) remains in them, they may ask (imperative, αἰτήσασθε) whatever they wish and it will be done (γενήσεται ὑμῖν). Or in other terms, loyalty begets loyalty. As the disciples are loyal to Jesus, God will be loyal to them, for God will answer their prayers.

Accordingly, the demand for loyalty/obedience to Yahweh's words/commandments is present throughout the OT. In particular, the concept of God's words remaining in the believer is seen in the Shema (Deut 6:4–9; 11:13–21; Num 15:37–41). As noted in the first passage, the worshipper was to talk of the commandments of God when he sat in his house, and when he walked by the way, and when he lay down, and when he rose up. He was to bind the commandments as a sign on his hand, and they were to be as frontlets between his eyes. He was to write them on the doorposts of his house and on his gates (6:7–9). According to the Talmud, worshippers were to wear the *tefillin*, which contain Torah passages that were written down on parchment slips and inserted in boxes made of hard leather. Steinsaltz says, "The name *Tefillin*—from the word *Tefillah*, prayer—apparently derived from this custom of wearing them during prayer services. In the Torah, they are known by the unique term *Totafot*, as well as by the more general words for 'sign' and 'reminder.'"[29] Hence, this external sign would serve to remind the people of God about the necessity of walking in obedience and not forgetting God and his words/commandments.

> Accordingly, in Numbers 15:37–39 the author commands the people of Israel to make tassels on the corners of their garments

---

29. Steinsaltz, *Guide to Jewish Prayer*, 350.

and to put a cord of blue on the tassel of each corner. The tassels were to remind the people of the commandments of the LORD and the necessity of obedience to them. Hammer explains, "The fringes contained a thread of deep blue . . . a symbol of divine royalty, comparable to the purpose of Roman nobility. Seeing them reminds us of how we are supposed to live in the sight of God."[30] Therefore, the apparel reminds the people of God of what they have heard and how they are to respond in lifestyle and practice. As they are obedient to God's commandments, they will experience blessing in the land (Deut 11:13–15).

It is debatable whether or not the Evangelist's audience would have made the connection between the requirements of the Shema and remaining in Jesus' words, but the concepts of binding God's word on the worshipper and Jesus' words remaining in the believer are conceptually congruent in nature and highlight the necessity of loyalty/obedience to God. In one sense, the Johannine disciple must "bind" Jesus' words to his heart and life in such a manner as to influence and determine the nature of his thinking, speaking, acting, and praying. As noted in the previous chapter of the present work, the Spirit-Paraclete will "bring to remembrance all that Jesus said" to the disciples (14:26). The corollary is that prayer is answered, fruit is brought forth, and God is glorified (15:7–8).

Returning to 15:7, when the condition of loyalty to remain/dwell in is met, the corollary of answered prayer is guaranteed since Jesus is present when his words are present (and vice versa).[31] Van der Watt explains further, "Words in the Gospel are not something which is spoken and then disappear. They have a permanent quality in the sense that the message being communicated by the words remains. If the effect of what was said remains, it is said that the words remain in a person (see 15:7)."[32] As noted, the one who loves Jesus and keeps his commandments is granted the privilege of the helping presence of the Spirit (14:15–17), who works in Jesus' absence to ensure that the effect of his words remain (and do not disappear) both in times of peace and in times of persecution (14:26; 15:20). Notwithstanding, the lasting effects of his words are educational and revelational in nature, that is, Jesus' words do not merely inform, they also transform the disciples'

---

30. Hammer, *Entering Jewish Prayer*, 128.

31. Van der Watt notes, "The way in which Jesus is present in the disciples is *inter alia via* his words" (*Family of the King*, 42). He says elsewhere, "Remaining in the words of Jesus is an expression indicating full acceptance of the message to the extent that it becomes one's own ideas that determine one's life and actions" ("Salvation," 121).

32. Van der Watt, *Family of the King*, 77.

way of thinking when abided by and adhered to.³³ The vine (Jesus) provides nourishment (the word) to the disciple who remains in him so that, as noted by Brodie, the word may "sink in ever more deeply."³⁴ Therefore, much like disciples who pray in Jesus' name (14:13–14), which means praying with all that his name represents, a disciple educated by the words of Jesus will pray in a specific manner that is congruent with his education.

Therefore, the aim is for the nourishing words from the vine to transfer to the hearts and minds of the disciples. As this occurs, the disciples' word-informed prayers are offered to the Father-gardener, who hears and responds. Thus, the sender (the Father), the messenger (Jesus), and the receiver (the disciples) display what Brodie calls "the picture of profound union, of blending of wills."³⁵ As such, the disciples' unity with and loyalty to Jesus and his words elucidates a social orientation where honor for others is esteemed.³⁶ In this model, Jesus' will becomes the disciples' will. Honor for God is established when this blending occurs and when one offers requests that are congruent with his will. By allowing Jesus' words to remain within, the disciples collectively share a group-oriented language (via the words of Jesus) that esteems, rather than diminishes, the wishes of their master. Thus, as one approaches God in prayer, he does not merely ask for his own good³⁷ but for the good of all. In short, the disciples are not commissioned to offer renegade prayers that center on their own interests. Rather, they are equipped to offer prayers that center on the "maintenance of relationships" within the gardener-vine-branch paradigm.³⁸ In the final analysis, one's union with the vine provides the relational scenario that accommodates one's asking in Jesus' name (14:13–14; 15:16) and the Father's granting of the request (15:7, 16).

The Consequence of Remaining: John 15:6–8

While the condition and corollary of John 15:7 is clear enough, the relevant question at this point in the present analysis centers on why the topic of

---

33. Newman and Nida remark, "Both Jesus and his words are the absolute revelation of God" (*Handbook on the Gospel of John*, 483).

34. Brodie, *Gospel According to John*, 481.

35. Brodie, *Gospel According to John*, 481.

36. For a complete discussion of "honor," see Malina, *New Testament World*, 30–52.

37. Haenchen says that prayer "emanating" from the "good life" in Jesus will be heard "because the ego does not dominate" (*Commentary on the Gospel of John Chapters 7–21*, 132).

38. Neyrey, *Give God the Glory*, 9.

prayer is located between the discussion of fire (v. 6) and fruitfulness (v. 8). As noted above, the branches that are removed represent disciples who professed faith in Jesus but were never in fact "in him." The consequence of failing to remain in Jesus is stated in verse 6, ἐὰν μή τις μένῃ ἐν ἐμοί, ἐβλήθη ἔξω ὡς τὸ κλῆμα καὶ ἐξηράνθη καὶ συνάγουσιν αὐτὰ καὶ εἰς τὸ πῦρ βάλλουσιν καὶ καίεται. At first glance, this consequence may seem to have little to do with prayer. However, this threat is issued just previous to the promise concerning prayer. Thus, the threat of verse 6 must be carried into the promise of verse 7. As such, the logic of flow of the narrative indicates that while remaining in Jesus ensures that one's prayers are answered, the converse is equally true, namely that failure to remain ensures that one's prayers will go unanswered. Verse 6 indicates that the branch that fails to remain is one that is withered and is one that will be gathered and burned.

Following the exegetical conclusions stated above, if a professing (but not authentic) disciple (branch) is removed from the vine (Jesus), then the natural corollary is that he no longer has access to the relational space in which eternal life is granted and effectual prayer is offered. To state things in a different manner, he no longer has contractual right to stand in relational space with Jesus in general or to pray in his name in particular. He then forfeits his ability to do the works of Jesus (14:12) and to receive the helping presence of the Spirit, who is sent to educate him in prayer. Furthermore, following the usage of the term ἐβλήθη in 15:6, the branch (disciple) is removed and burned, which implies that his prayers too will be thrown out. Although that one may wish to have his prayers heard, in the end they will fall on deaf ears. Thus, Jesus' words in 15:5 (ὅτι χωρὶς ἐμοῦ οὐ δύνασθε ποιεῖν οὐδέν.) take on practical significance. Neyrey remarks, "Because we observe an argument being made, not merely information being imparted, we consider 15:1–8 a crisp example of deliberative rhetoric, which places before the disciples the decision of 'remaining,' a deliberation richly rewarded or severely sanctioned."[39]

Moving from verse 6 to verse 8 is the positive corollary of remaining in Jesus and having one's prayers answered. The Evangelist states in verse 8:

ἐν τούτῳ ἐδοξάσθη ὁ πατήρ μου,
ἵνα καρπὸν πολὺν φέρητε
καὶ γένησθε ἐμοὶ μαθηταί.

Put simply, receiving Jesus' words, remaining in him, and prayer through him eventuates bearing fruit for the Father's glory. The corollary of such "remaining" is seen in the following statements: Physical fruit is bore

---

39. Neyrey, *Give God the Glory*, 184.

by abiding in a physical vine. Spiritual fruit is bore by abiding in Jesus, the vine. Verse 8 begins with the prepositional phrase, ἐν τούτῳ. In this case, the demonstrative pronoun τούτῳ functions adjectivally primarily in reference to bearing fruit, thus proving to be Jesus' disciples (γένησθε ἐμοὶ μαθηταί). Therefore, abiding in Jesus empowers believers not only to pray but also to bear much fruit through their praying. To the degree that Jesus' words and will are prayed, prayer is answered and fruit is brought forth through the disciples.

In 14:12 Jesus indicates that the disciples will perform "greater works" because of his departure to the Father. Similarly, 15:5 indicates that a true branch/disciple will not just bear fruit but will bear "much fruit" because of the gardener's care and attention (15:1–2). Apart from Jesus the disciples can do nothing (15:5). Thus, Jesus does not speak of mere fruit in isolation but rather of much fruit in demonstration, hence the attributive adjective πολὺν (15:8). To the extent that fruit is brought forth and discipleship is confirmed, the Father is glorified.

Further, the fruitfulness of the disciples is inextricably linked to their status as members of God's family. Malina defines one's status in society in terms of a social system. He says, "Status in the first-century Mediterranean world derived mainly from birth and was symbolized by the honor and prestige already accumulated and preserved by one's family."[40] Malina notes that most people in the Mediterranean world "worked to maintain their inherited status, not to get rich. The goal of life in a closed society such as theirs is contentment derived from preserving one's status, not acquisition or achievement. With such a goal in mind, it would be impossible to attempt to convince such people that they might improve their social standing with more work."[41] As believers in Jesus, the disciples received a new "status" as branches that maintained the privilege of being in union with the vine. By virtue of their belief in and union with Jesus they received the right to become "children of God" (1:12) who would become the dwelling place of God (14:17, 23), and they were recipients of the words of Jesus/God (15:7). Thus, in a similar manner as seen in the broader Mediterranean culture, the disciples could not improve their status by doing more "work." Rather, the onus was on them to maintain their status by simply remaining in Jesus and communicating with God in the space of prayer.[42]

---

40. Malina, *New Testament World*, 90.

41. Malina, *New Testament World*, 97.

42. With the language of 14:12–14 in mind, the disciples do not perform works to pray but rather pray in order to perform works. All of this, of course, presupposes faith in Jesus.

Hence, the imperative to "remain" coupled with the Father's work of cleansing/pruning, amounts to a divine initiative that is centered on equipping the disciples to pray successfully. Why? Because answered prayer is prayer that brings forth fruit. Or to put it even more simply, answered prayer equates to the granting of fruit that will last. Conversely, failure to remain in Jesus results in unanswered prayers, and unanswered prayers result in fruitlessness. But as long as the disciples remain in the relational space of Jesus, the vine, they may expect an open line of communication that results in open demonstration of answered prayer. In addition to the aforementioned privileges of being a child of God, the disciples may have understood one aspect of their status in terms of the fruit they produced. By producing fruit, the disciples confirmed their status in the family and brought honor to the Father.

Neyrey and Stewart note moreover, "If honor is symbolized by family and wealth, especially land, loss of honor can be symbolized by loss of family, land, and wealth."[43] They point out that some cases of loss were due to the fault of the person, while in other cases certain people endured loss due to no fault of their own.[44] They write, "While it is no fault of a wife that her husband dies or of a farmer that drought ruins his crops, if a 'fool' loses his wealth, it is shameful."[45] In the case of the disciples, the crop of "fruit" they have been promised may be squandered if they fail to remain, since they will be "thrown away" and "thrown into the fire and burned" (15:6). Such a consequence necessarily entails the inability to pray in a manner that is supported by Jesus, the vine. Therefore, in order to avoid bringing shame on themselves and the Father, they must remain in him. As they remain, the disciples maintain their privileged status as those who, by offering prayer in Jesus' name, are promised a harvest of fruit that brings glory to the Father. In the final analysis, it may be said that disciples who bear fruit and perform "greater works" ascribe a sense of importance to God in both word and deed. To the degree that fruit is brought forth, the perception of God's worth is increased and his reputation enhanced.

Prayer, Love, and Friendship: John 15:13–15

As noted above, Jesus commands his disciples to remain in his word. But as the pericope expands, Jesus introduces the particular concept of remaining

---

43. Neyrey and Stewart, *Social World of the New Testament*, 90.

44. For a fuller discussion of honor and how it is symbolized, see Neyrey and Stewart, *Social World of the New Testament*, 90–91.

45. Neyrey and Stewart, *Social World of the New Testament*, 91.

in his love. In verses 9–10 and 12, the Evangelist provides a foundational paradigm for reciprocal love where the call to abide in Jesus' love, to keep his commandments, and to love one another is stated (which is an expanded recapitulation of 13:34–35). In verse 9 Jesus issues a statement concerning the origination and the application of the Father's love. He states, Καθὼς ἠγάπησέν με ὁ πατήρ, κἀγὼ ὑμᾶς ἠγάπησα·μείνατε ἐν τῇ ἀγάπῃ τῇ ἐμῇ. Such love originates with the Father but clearly extends to the Father/Son relationship. Then the Father's love is recapitulated through the Son to the disciples. The adverbial comparative term Καθὼς establishes the origination and genre of love that was expressed by both the Father and the Son. Accordingly, Garcia Sison says, "The imperative, 'remain in my love' echoes v. 4 where the theme of indwelling is expressed: 'Remain in me as I remain in in you.'"[46] He says further:

> On the basis of this literary link, v. 9b must therefore be seen in light of the indwelling theme. If in the immanent formula of v. 4a the word "love" is substituted for the person of Jesus, then what is meant is subjective love, namely, the love Jesus has for his disciples. "Remain in me as I remain in you" will be the equivalent of "Remain in my love as my love remains in you."[47]

But Jesus remarks in verse 10, ἐὰν τὰς ἐντολάς μου τηρήσητε, μενεῖτε ἐν τῇ ἀγάπῃ μου, καθὼς ἐγὼ τὰς ἐντολὰς τοῦ πατρός μου τετήρηκα καὶ μένω αὐτοῦ ἐν τῇ ἀγάπῃ. Thus, obedience to Jesus' commandments unites the believer to him and keeps him in his love. Such love is not earned through obedience; obedience to Jesus is the corollary of being loved by Jesus (13:1, 34). Hence, the disciples are called to remain in a relationship with Jesus and abide in his love by believing in his person and obeying his commandments. In fact, the evidence that one remains in his love is seen in commandment-keeping.

Further, the notion of friendship ethics is prevalent in ancient culture and maintains a crucial role in the Fourth Gospel. For example, there are several references to the concept and reality of "friends" (φίλων) and friendship in the Fourth Gospel (see 3:29; 11:11; 15:13–15; 19:12). Lazarus is called a friend of Jesus (11:11). John the Baptist refers to himself (figuratively) as the friend of the Bridegroom (3:29). Pilate is called a friend of Caesar (19:12). But 15:13 introduces an explicit statement concerning the nature of Jesus' love for his "friends" in particular. Jesus already issued the command to the disciples to remain in his love and to love one another as he loved them (vv. 9–12). But in verse 13 Jesus relates the highest degree of

---

46. Garcia Sison, Verb "Menéin," 49–50.
47. Garcia Sison, Verb "Menéin," 49–50.

his love to the context of friendship. He states, μείζονα ταύτης ἀγάπην οὐδεὶς ἔχει, ἵνα τις τὴν ψυχὴν αὐτοῦ θῇ ὑπὲρ τῶν φίλων αὐτοῦ. In this case, the serviceable term (for love) used by John is ἀγάπην. Carson is right to suggest, "Because John does not normally distinguish the two most common roots for 'to love' (*agapao* and *phileo*), we are probably justified in rendering this 'that one lay down his life for those he loves' (cf. 10:15)."[48] Thus, John informs the reader that Jesus' friendship with the disciples is not a matter of mere common interests, relational dependence, or neighborly dealings but is rather seen in specific, altruistic expressions of self-sacrifice.

The concept of giving one's life for a friend is scattered throughout ancient literature and is seen in various contexts. In particular, the OT does make a small qualitative contribution in certain passages that speak about friendship with God in the context of laying down one's life. For example, James (2:22–24) reflects on Abraham's obedience in his willingness to offer his son Isaac on the altar (Gen 22:1–12) and calls Abraham a "friend of God" (2:23, φίλος θεοῦ ἐκλήθη). It was God's covenant with Abraham that placed him in relational proximity (Gen 12:1–3; 15:1–6). But Abraham's faith and obedience worked together to validate and authenticate his friendship with God. In short, Abraham proved his friendship with God by being willing to lay down the life of his son, his only son. Of course, this example is the inverse of John 15:13 in that man, rather than God, is the subject who is willing to complete the action of sacrifice. Regardless, the corollary remains intact; Abraham's title, "friend of God" was gained through his own experience of obedience to God. Van der Watt says additionally:

> The bond of loyalty between David and Jonathan was beyond question (see 1 Sam 18–20). This observation makes the following conclusion possible: the embryonic dynamics and reasoning for laying down one's life for a friend that are present in the Greco-Roman thought are also present in the Jewish literature, which potentially opens up the way within a Jewish context for accepting the maxim in John 15:13.[49]

Jesus' love is already seen manifest throughout the Fourth Gospel, especially as it pertains to giving up one's life.[50] For example, in 12:24 Jesus presents the idea of a seed that falls into the earth and dies in order to bear fruit (ἀμὴν λέγω ὑμῖν, ἐὰν μὴ ὁ κόκκος τοῦ σίτου πεσὼν εἰς τὴν γῆν ἀποθάνῃ,

---

48. Carson, *Gospel According to John*, 523.
49. Van der Watt, "Some Reflections," 486.
50. Beasley-Murray remarks that "the context of mutual love and sacrifice for others, as well as the Jewish tradition relating to the friends of God, makes it needless to look for the inspiration of the saying elsewhere" (*John*, 274).

αὐτὸς μόνος μένει· ἐὰν δὲ ἀποθάνῃ, πολὺν καρπὸν φέρει.). Clearly, the key to fruitfulness is both the falling and the death of grain. On its death, fruit is brought forth. The one who hates (μισῶν) his life enough to give it up, will preserve or keep (φυλάξει) his soul for eternal life (12:25).

The concept of the good shepherd also presents the idea of the shepherd laying down his life for his sheep because he knows them and cares for them (10:11–18). Jesus was prepared to lay his life down for his sheep/friends, and he eventually did so through cross-death (19:16–30). Van der Watt notes, "Within the Christian context, with the death of Jesus as a central event, this makes even greater sense. It does not take much imagination to see how the death of Jesus on a cross could have been interwoven with the Greco-Roman conception of 'laying down your life for others/friends.'"[51] But who are the sheep/friends that benefit from such self-sacrificial love? According to John, the answer lies in verse 14, namely, ὑμεῖς φίλοι μού ἐστε ἐὰν ποιῆτε ἃ ἐγὼ ἐντέλλομαι ὑμῖν. By laying down his life, Jesus proves his love and friendship toward the disciples. But as indicated by Jesus, his friends are those who are obedient to his commandments.

The Consequence of Friendship

The concept and practice of Johannine friendship, then, has several consequences for prayer. First, by laying down his life, Jesus demonstrated that he is loyal in nature and personally invested in his friends, even to death. But Jesus' loyalty extends beyond his earthly life to include answering prayers that are made in his name. But the disciples are not merely left with Jesus' name, but with his example, which provides further credibility to his name. In this model, Jesus' example provides further substance to the promise that Jesus will answer prayer that is offered in his name. One can have assurance that prayer will be answered because Jesus' name stands for his love and loyalty for his friends.

Further, the model provided by Jesus stands in contrast to Greek aspects of religion in which the gods accepted sacrificial gifts but did not offer themselves in sacrifice for others. Greek worshippers sought the gods' favor through ritual, but the gods did not seek the worshippers' heart through altruistic deeds. The Greek gods had to be persuaded through sacrifice. The Johannine God persuades his disciples through love. The Greek gods may answer prayer, but there are no guarantees even if one prays in the correct name and performs the prescribed ritual. Burkert remarks, "The sense in which men need the gods is quite different from the sense in which the gods

---

51. Van der Watt, "Some Reflections," 486.

need men. Men live by the hope of reciprocal favor, *charis*. 'It is good to give fitting gifts to the immortals'—they will show their gratitude. But it is never possible to count on this with certainty."[52] Put simply, there is no guarantee that the gods will respond favorably to the worshipper.

However, Jesus' willingness to lay his life down plausibly points to his (and the Father's) willingness to do precisely what he promises and to go the "extra mile" for his friends. If he lay down his life, he will plausibly open his ears to prayers offered in his name. Or to state things another way, Jesus does not merely provide a theoretical space for prayer; for those who believe in him, Jesus offers his name and his example as indications of his willingness to do what he promises, namely, answer prayer. Moreover, if "hate" equates to rejection and disloyalty, then the disciples may be assured that the world will not listen to them (15:18–25). Conversely, if "love" equates to loyalty and trustworthiness, then the disciples, by virtue of Jesus' example, may have full assurance that he will listen to them.

Second, by virtue of their friendship with Jesus, the disciples are granted a new relational status that grants them the privilege of receiving inside knowledge/revelation that shapes the contours of their prayers. In 15:15 the Evangelist addresses the intimate nature of friendship, albeit in notably different terms. Here a notable shift in emphasis occurs in Jesus' statement, οὐκέτι λέγω ὑμᾶς δούλους, ὅτι ὁ δοῦλος οὐκ οἶδεν τί ποιεῖ αὐτοῦ ὁ κύριος· ὑμᾶς δὲ εἴρηκα φίλους, ὅτι πάντα ἃ ἤκουσα παρὰ τοῦ πατρός μου ἐγνώρισα ὑμῖν. According to Jesus, part and parcel of true friendship is the transmission of knowledge/revelation that is otherwise hidden or secret. Neyrey writes:

> Jesus elevates the status of the disciples from "servant" to "friend"; that is, they share the most precious benefaction of Jesus' patron, in this case "*everything* that I have heard from my Father" (15:15). With his departure, he acknowledges them as his preferred clients. Ideally, this kind of discourse will confirm them in their relationship to him and thus to God.[53]

Thus, verse 15 presents the notable contrast between δούλους and φίλους and the qualifying statement, ὅτι πάντα ἃ ἤκουσα παρὰ τοῦ πατρός μου ἐγνώρισα ὑμῖν. However, it is important to note that the concept of servanthood and/or the status of being a "slave" (as in NASB) must be distinguished from their various forms, both ancient and modern. In cases, a servant/slave is thought of as someone who serves a master in an impersonal, uninformed, and unquestioned manner; he simply works and labors without questioning or demanding knowledge. As noted by Morris, "The slave is

---

52. Burkert, *Greek Religion*, 189.
53. Neyrey, *Gospel of John*, 260.

no more than an instrument. It is not for him to enter intelligently into the purpose of his owner."⁵⁴ Thus, in the context of 15:15, it may be tempting to assert that the disciples (as servants) were those who served Jesus in the same manner. However, another understanding best serves both the context of the NT in general,⁵⁵ but also the Evangelist's usage in particular. Outside of 15:15 and 15:20, the closest that Jesus comes to referring to his disciples as servants/slaves is seen in 13:16 (ἀμὴν ἀμὴν λέγω ὑμῖν, οὐκ ἔστιν δοῦλος μείζων τοῦ κυρίου αὐτοῦ οὐδὲ ἀπόστολος μείζων τοῦ πέμψαντος αὐτόν.). But here the emphasis is not placed on impersonal and uninformed service to Jesus but rather on the call for the disciples to follow their master's example by serving and loving each other. And this example was set forth clearly before their very eyes (13:3–10). Notwithstanding, Jesus indicates that, in addition to being subordinate servants who follow their master's example, they also receive a new status that includes epistemic privileges.⁵⁶

Accordingly, by virtue of the true Son (Christ), slaves may enjoy the status of son-ship (ἐὰν οὖν ὁ υἱὸς ὑμᾶς ἐλευθερώσῃ, ὄντως ἐλεύθεροι ἔσεσθε.). Therefore, the son is granted special access to the father and to privileges that would naturally include knowledge of the father's affairs. Neyrey says that Jesus mediates several benefactions to his clients, but perhaps the most relevant one is "secret knowledge" or revelation.⁵⁷ Brown remarks, "In NT thought the Christian remains a *doulos* from the viewpoint of service that he should render, but from the viewpoint of intimacy with God he is more than a *doulos*. So also ... from the viewpoint of revelation given to him the Christian is no mere servant."⁵⁸ Finally, Turner notes Jesus' imagery of friendship derives from courtly circles rather than from the context of equality. He says:

> The king has many servants, but those who serve him with love and loyalty he may come to call his "friends." These are marked out from the rest who remain mere "servants" (and note the contrast in vv. 14–15) not by a freedom to disobey, but by the fact that the monarch shares with them his innermost counsels and trusts them. He does this *because* they love him and obey him.

---

54. Morris, *Gospel According to John*, 675.

55. For example, in Luke 17:10, the disciples are instructed to say, λέγετε ὅτι δοῦλοι ἀχρεῖοί ἐσμεν, ὃ ὠφείλομεν ποιῆσαι πεποιήκαμεν. Paul begins his letter to the Romans (1:1) with the statement, Παῦλος δοῦλος Χριστοῦ Ἰησοῦ. Brown points out that "in John xiii13 the disciples were commended for addressing Jesus as 'Lord,' an address that has the implication that they are his servants" (*Gospel According to John [XIII–XXI]*, 683).

56. See Neyrey, *Gospel of John*, 262.

57. Neyrey, *Gospel of John*, 260.

58. Brown, *Gospel According to John (XIII–XXI)*, 683.

And it is these people whose petitions are liable to be answered; for they ask out of a knowledge of the king's counsel, and out of a will to serve his interests. Such is the friendship Jesus offers the disciples: if they loyally obey him, he does not treat them as servants (who merely blindly follow orders), but as privileged "friends" to whom he has revealed what he has learned from the Father.[59]

Thus, the concept of friendship has practical implications for the topic of prayer. Much like what was indicated in the previous chapter of this analysis, the transcendental narrative (from above) is communicated through the Son to those who are below. The onus, then, is on the disciples to commit themselves to this narrative and to actualize it through their obedience to Jesus. It is within the unified relational space of the vine, gardener, and branches that friendship occurs and is fleshed out. It is those who share and remain in Jesus' interests, aims, and outlook who are granted the privilege of asking whatever they wish in prayer. And those who remain in this friendship will be granted the very things they wish for (15:7). Furthermore, verse 14 expands the theme of "remaining in" Jesus as is explicated in 15:4–5, 7. Remaining in Jesus, at a very basic level, involves remaining in agreement with Jesus in every respect. Hence, the one who remains in, agrees with, and is obedient to Jesus will inevitably make requests that are in alignment with who Jesus is and what he requires.

Hence, Jesus viewed his disciples as those who were not deficient of their Father's business; but by virtue of their friendship with Jesus, the disciples were recipients of knowledge/revelation that was otherwise hidden or secret. By virtue of their connection to the vine, the disciples had the privilege of abiding with Jesus and receiving his words and commandments. As the disciples kept Jesus' commandments, they not only confirmed their status as Jesus' friends but also demonstrated that they were knowledgeable of the very will of the Father to whom they prayed. Thus, as true sons who abide in Jesus, the disciples were prepared to pray according to the words of Jesus, they were positioned to bear much fruit for Jesus, and they were privileged in the task of bringing glory to the Father.

Friendship as Frankness and Boldness

By virtue of their friendship with Jesus, the disciples are granted the privilege of speaking plainly and boldly to God in prayer. The theme of friendship as boldness of speech and action is seen in Hellenistic literature, especially as

---

59. Turner, "Prayer in the Gospels and Acts," 82 (emphasis added).

it relates to the term παρρησία. This term occurs nine times in the Gospel of John, more often than in any other NT book (7:4, 13, 26; 10:24; 11:14, 54; 16:25, 29; 18:20). In most cases, the term is employed in both public (or political) and private spheres. For example, in 7:3–4 the term is used in the context of Jesus' brothers, who urge him to perform his works openly for the disciples and the world. Verse 13 portrays the people as those who did not want to speak openly about him (οὐδεὶς μέντοι παρρησίᾳ ἐλάλει περὶ αὐτοῦ διὰ τὸν φόβον τῶν Ἰουδαίων.). During the middle of the feast, Jesus is seen teaching in the temple. The people responded by saying (vv. 25–26), λεγον οὖν τινες ἐκ τῶν Ἱεροσολυμιτῶν· οὐχ οὗτός ἐστιν ὃν ζητοῦσιν ἀποκτεῖναι; καὶ ἴδε παρρησίᾳ λαλεῖ καὶ οὐδὲν αὐτῷ λέγουσιν. μήποτε ἀληθῶς ἔγνωσαν οἱ ἄρχοντες ὅτι οὗτός ἐστιν ὁ χριστός. Here the emphasis is placed on the visible nature of Jesus' ministry in light of the authoritative nature of his speaking, which according to verses 16–17, is derived from his father.

In 10:24 the Jews demand that Jesus speak plainly concerning his identity as the Christ (εἰπὲ ἡμῖν παρρησίᾳ). After speaking somewhat ambiguously in 11:11 (Λάζαρος ὁ φίλος ἡμῶν κεκοίμηται), Jesus seeks to clear up any subsequent confusion in 11:14 by speaking plainly concerning Lazarus (Λάζαρος ἀπέθανεν). Similarly, in 16:25 and 16:29 Jesus states that an hour is coming when he will no longer speak in figures of speech (ἐν παροιμίαις λελάληκα) but plainly (παρρησίᾳ). Finally, in 18:20 Jesus addresses the high priest and notes that his speech has been in open before the world, not in secret. These passages demonstrate that as far as the Johannine witness is concerned, the meaning of παρρησία centers on working and speaking openly, publicly, and plainly.

The concept of παρρησία is present in certain OT prayers, most notably in Habakkuk's prayer in 1:2–4 and 12–17. In the context of Habakkuk's plea, the author speaks freely to God by offering a lament concerning the injustice in Judah. The question is posed in 1:3, "Why do you make me see iniquity, and why do you idly look at wrong?" Also, in 1:13 the author asks, "Why do you idly look at traitors and remain silent when the wicked swallows up the man more righteous than he?" The language of these passages assumes a degree of boldness/confidence as one approaches the space of prayer. In particular, the above questions presuppose that one may pray in a sentiment of disappointment or lament and still be heard. The LORD's reply indicates not only that he hears but also that he will respond (2:2–4).

Further, in the context of Nehemiah 1:4–11, a prayer is offered that also assumes a degree of confidence in approaching God. In this case, Nehemiah boldly reminds God of his promise to restore his people after they have sinned if they return to him and keep his commandments (1:9). As such, Nehemiah's prayer assumes confidence in God's covenant-keeping nature. Even in the face of sin and rebellion, Nehemiah boldly approaches God with an appeal for restoration and personal success. Interestingly, Nehemiah (1:8–9) reminds God concerning the words he spoke to Moses, namely, "If you are unfaithful, I will scatter you among the peoples, but if you return to me and keep my commandments and do them, though your outcasts are in the uttermost parts of heaven, from there I will gather them and bring them to the place that I have chosen, to make my name dwell there." In the final analysis, Nehemiah's boldness toward God stems from his certitude concerning God's covenant faithfulness toward his people.

Concerning the Fourth Gospel, although the concept of παρρησία is not explicitly used in connection with prayer between believers and Jesus, it fits well within the general framework of prayer as it is prescribed in 14:13–14 and 15:7, 16. In Nehemiah's prayer, an appeal is boldly made within the context of covenant. However, in John 15 in particular, the emphasis centers on union with Jesus, the vine. It is within this relational context that prayers may be offered from the new place where God's name dwells, namely the believer. Thus, παρρησία occurs in light of patron-broker-client relationship where access to God is granted on the basis of Jesus, the Son. Thus, union with Jesus and the possession of his name provides boldness in one's prayer requests. As such, the phrases, "whatever you ask" (14:13; 15:16) and "whatever you wish" (15:7) both imply frankness and freedom of speech. As noted in the previous chapter, in 13a the phrase ὅ τι ἄν, best translated as "whatever," "anyhow," is followed by the verb αἰτήσητε. Thus, the literal translation is as follows: "whatever, anyhow you ask." In this case, the action of the verb is determined by the contents of the request itself, which is not stated but rather open-ended and undetermined. However, the request itself had to be congruent with the phrase ἐν τῷ ὀνόματί μου. The same is true in 15:16, where prayer is directed to the Father in Jesus' name. In the case of 15:7, the condition to having one's prayer answered involves abiding in Jesus and allowing his word to abide within. If the conditions are met, believers may ask whatever they wish (ἐὰν θέλητε) and thus have confidence that their prayers will be heard and responded to.

Moreover, asking in Jesus' name and according to Jesus' indwelling word does not involve the usage of flattery, but rather involves the utilization of one's friendship with Jesus. Because Jesus has disclosed the nature, purpose, and mission of his father to the disciples (14:8–11), they may in turn pray with these concerns in mind, and do so boldly. As such, the believer who abides in Jesus' word has the privilege of speaking directly and forthrightly to God without fear of losing his status as Jesus' friend.

Finally, the concept and practice of παρρησία is congruent with statements in chapters 14 and 15 that elevate the disciples' expectations concerning the works they perform and the fruit they bring forth. The Evangelist says in 14:12 that those who believe in Jesus will perform "greater works," and in 15:5, 8 it is said that those who remain in Jesus will bear "much fruit." Thus, the Evangelist provides both the *where* of prayer (in Jesus, the vine) and the *how* of prayer (in Jesus' name), but he also indicates *what* one may expect in prayer, namely, greater works and much fruit. Therefore, in light of these promises, the disciples may pray plainly and boldly to God, knowing that *no request is too great* if it is consonant with Jesus' name and if it is issued out of loyalty to Jesus, the vine, and the Father, the gardener. Perhaps one could say that the bolder the request, the greater the fruit that will be brought forth. And the greater the harvest of fruit that is brought forth, the greater the glory that will be brought to God.

Prayer and Persecution: John 15:18–16:4a

In John 15:18 Jesus begins his discourse on the topic of hatred with the clause, Εἰ ὁ κόσμος ὑμᾶς μισεῖ. This protasis describes a present reality, not a mere possibility.[60] The world hates both Jesus and the disciples. While the theme of hatred is portrayed in 15:18–25, in 16:2 the Evangelist notes that "they" will put the disciples out of the synagogue, which stands as further elucidation of Jewish persecution of the disciples. The nature of this persecution is not likely mere temporary excommunication from the synagogue with its aim of corrective punishment but permanent exclusion. Some scholars see this persecution stemming from a Jewish-Christian schism. Martyn sees the phrase, "They will put you out of the synagogue," as reflective of the *Birkat Haminim*, the twelfth benediction of the Jews[61] near the end of the first century to banish Jewish-Christians from the synagogue.[62] Additionally, the statement, ταῦτα εἶπαν οἱ γονεῖς αὐτοῦ ὅτι ἐφοβοῦντο τοὺς Ἰουδαίους· ἤδη γὰρ συνετέθειντο οἱ Ἰουδαῖοι ἵνα ἐάν τις αὐτὸν ὁμολογήσῃ χριστόν, ἀποσυνάγωγος γένηται (9:22), has led some, including Barrett and Martyn, to insist that one should envisage a late first-century *Sitz im Leben* for such expulsion. Yet this conclusion is unnecessary in light of the

---

60. For a discussion on the "Jews" and the "world," see Haenchen, *Commentary on the Gospel of John Chapters 7–21*, 136–37.

61. The benediction reads, "For the apostates let there be no hope, and let the arrogant government [Rome] be speedily uprooted in our days. Let the Nazarenes and the Minim [heretics] be destroyed in a moment and let them be blotted out of the Book of Life and not be inscribed with the righteous. Blessed art thou, O Lord, who humblest the arrogant."

62. For a fuller discussion, see Martyn, *History and Theology*.

generous evidence for Christian/Jewish conflict earlier in the first century. Alexander explains:

> It is abundantly clear from the New Testament itself that Christianity before 70 not only attracted support but also encountered strong and widespread opposition within the Jewish community. That opposition ranged from central authorities in Jerusalem (the High Priest and the Sanhédrin) to the leaders of the local synagogues. It extended from Palestine (both Galilee and Jerusalem) to the Diaspora (e.g., Asia Minor and Achaea). It began in the time of Jesus himself and continued unabated in the period after the crucifixion.[63]

Further, the statement in 16:2, ἀλλ' ἔρχεται ὥρα ἵνα πᾶς ὁ ἀποκτείνας ὑμᾶς δόξῃ λατρείαν προσφέρειν τῷ θεῷ, introduces a new challenge into the discussion. To which particular hour is Jesus referring? The Evangelist speaks of Jesus' hour in 2:4; 4:23; 7:30; 8:20-21; 12:23, 27. Schnackenburg sees the Evangelist's use of "hour" in 4:23 as referring to the eschatological presence of Jesus, but he notes that 16:2 is more closely connected with the prophetic and apocalyptic expression, "the days are coming" (Isa 39:6; Jer 7:32; 16:14; Zech 14:1 [LXX]; 2 Ezek 5:1; 13:29; etc.).[64] However, John does not connect 16:2 with these OT passages but places the concept of "hour" in a very similar semantic trajectory as seen throughout his Gospel. But context must decide the decisive meaning in each instance. Carson has pointed out that the employment of "'hour' (hora) when unqualified always points in John's Gospel to the hour of Jesus' cross, resurrection, and exaltation, or to events related to Jesus' passion and exaltation (as in 16:23)."[65] The language of 16:2, coupled with John's usage of "hour" throughout his Gospel, indicates that the disciples' hour is closely associated with his own.

Notwithstanding, the language of 15:18-25 implies that persecution came from certain Jews in general or those who are categorized as being "of the world" in particular. For example, Jesus states in 7:7, οὐ δύναται ὁ κόσμος μισεῖν ὑμᾶς, ἐμὲ δὲ μισεῖ, ὅτι ἐγὼ μαρτυρῶ περὶ αὐτοῦ ὅτι τὰ ἔργα αὐτοῦ πονηρά ἐστιν. In 8:23 Jesus states in response to those who opposed him, ὑμεῖς ἐκ τῶν κάτω ἐστέ, ἐγὼ ἐκ τῶν ἄνω εἰμί· ὑμεῖς ἐκ τούτου τοῦ κόσμου ἐστέ, ἐγὼ οὐκ εἰμὶ ἐκ τοῦ κόσμου τούτου. Here Jesus posits two distinct categories of reality in two different manners of speaking: (1) "below" and "above" and (2) "of the world" and "not of this world." The ones who are from below will accept those from below. The ones from above will accept those from above.

---

63. Alexander, *Parting of the Ways*, 19.
64. Schnackenburg, *Gospel According to St. John*, 121.
65. Carson, *Gospel According to John*, 223.

The ones from below will hate those from above. But Jesus notes that both he (8:23) and his disciples (15:19) are not of this world. They have been chosen out of the world (15:19). In keeping with the language and theme of chapter 15, the disciples have been called out of the world and have been called into the vine to bear fruit for God. Therefore, Jesus reminded them that their position with him and in him would naturally draw hatred and opposition. Those who identify with Jesus and remain with him can expect to be recipients of the same hostile sentiment that he received since οὐκ ἔστιν δοῦλος μείζων τοῦ κυρίου αὐτοῦ (15:20).

What follows is the natural corollary, εἰ ἐμὲ ἐδίωξαν, καὶ ὑμᾶς διώξουσιν· εἰ τὸν λόγον μου ἐτήρησαν, καὶ τὸν ὑμέτερον τηρήσουσιν. Once again, whatever happens to Jesus will inevitably happen to those who follow him. In verse 21 Jesus states the cause of hatred and persecution in more precise terms, namely, διὰ τὸ ὄνομά μου. As indicated by the clause ὅτι οὐκ οἴδασιν τὸν πέμψαντά με, negative responses toward Jesus are rooted in a lack of true knowledge of God. And to reject and/or fail to recognize God's representative was to reject and/or fail to recognize God himself. In light of Jesus' words and works (vv. 22–24), the world had a plethora of evidence concerning Jesus and the Father. Therefore, since the Evangelist presents Jesus as the revelation of God in flesh (e.g., 1:1, 14, 18), Jesus is essentially stating that the world hates him because of his name, that is, what his name represents.

Furthermore, Schnackenburg remarks that the phrase διὰ τὸ ὄνομά μου is from a Synoptic tradition (Mark 13:9, 13; Luke 21:12) since it is not included elsewhere in the Fourth Gospel.[66] This may be the case, but previous statements concerning prayer in Jesus' name (14:13–14; 15:16) do indicate a unique Johannine emphasis. Here the Evangelist's purpose is not merely to highlight the persecution drawn on account of Jesus' name, but also to remind his audience of the power and efficacy of prayer in his name during times of persecution. In the face of Jesus' departure, the disciples had access to Jesus' name, which, in effect, would grant them the privilege of praying effectual prayers that would further their mission in the world, in spite of the world's hostility. Thus, the phrase in 16:1, Ταῦτα λελάληκα ὑμῖν ἵνα μὴ σκανδαλισθῆτε, along with the warnings that follow (16:2–3), was issued for the purpose of encouraging the disciples to resist the temptation to apostatize in the face of persecution. As the disciples remained faithful to Jesus, they had access to his name and all the privileges afforded by his name. Conversely, failure to remain in Jesus would nullify this privilege and would result in being severed from Jesus, the vine. And being severed

---

66. Schnackenburg, *Gospel According to St. John*, 115–16.

from the vine precludes the possibility of answered prayer. And unanswered prayer results in fruitlessness. Therefore, the condition for bearing fruit does not center on remaining in peaceful circumstances but on remaining in relationship with Jesus. When this condition is met, the disciples may ask for anything they wish and it will be done for them. Therefore, the thrust of chapter 15 encourages offering prayer that aims at actualizing the story from "above" on the earth "below" in spite of hatred and opposition.

The Paraclete and Persecution

The previous chapter of this analysis provides a foundational examination of the role of the Helper, the Spirit-Paraclete. The Paraclete is the Spirit of Truth, who teaches the disciples and reminds them of everything Jesus spoke to them (John 14:17, 26). In short, the Paraclete is God's presence in Jesus' physical absence. He mediates the presence of Jesus to the disciples who will soon be without their earthly rabbi. However, the role of the Paraclete is expanded further in 15:26, where it is said concerning his role in relation to Jesus: ἐκεῖνος μαρτυρήσει περὶ ἐμοῦ. Some see the third Paraclete saying as a later addition from another source. Notwithstanding, it is better to view this verse as complementary to the theme at hand and providing further insight into the nature of how Jesus' witness will be perpetuated in days to come, particularly in the "hour" of the disciples' persecution (16:2). As noted, the preceding verses (18–25) state that the world's hatred of the disciples stems forth from its hatred of Jesus. Carson asks, "But if Jesus is going away—a theme already developed in ch. 14—how will this confrontation continue?"[67] Carson answers this question by stating that "the Holy Spirit joins with the disciples in testifying about Jesus to the world."[68] In spite of the threat of persecution, the Paraclete will proceed from the Father to "bear witness about" (ESV) or "testify about" (NIV) Jesus. The agency of the Paraclete's testimony is described in 15:27, καὶ ὑμεῖς δὲ μαρτυρεῖτε, ὅτι ἀπ' ἀρχῆς μετ' ἐμοῦ ἐστε. Thus, many scholars see this statement as a reference to the Paraclete's witness through the disciples for the purpose of conversion in general.[69]

In this writer's analysis, the Evangelist likely intends to convey both the (direct) inner and (indirect) outer work of the Paraclete on Jesus' behalf as the disciples face a hostile world. Bennema is correct to say, "The disciples'

---

67. Carson, *Gospel According to John*, 528.
68. Carson, *Gospel According to John*, 528.
69. Some commentators view the Spirit's ministry in this manner: Beasley-Murray, *John*, 276–77; Brown, *Gospel According to John (XIII–XXI)*, 690.

and Paraclete's witness . . . are not two distinct activities but essentially one: the Paraclete's witness is directed to the world but mediated through the witness of the disciples, because (1) the Paraclete is sent to the disciples (15:26), and (2) the world cannot receive the Paraclete (14:17)."[70] This emphasis includes the necessity of inner edification that leads to outward proclamation. Therefore, while the focus of verse 26 is the role of the Paraclete in witnessing about Jesus to the disciples, the focus of verse 27 is the role of the disciples utilizing the Paraclete's witness about Jesus in their own witness.

In this model, the Paraclete draws from the example provided by the earthly Jesus and provides access to the witness of the heavenly Jesus. Thus, the Paraclete provides a profile of Jesus that the disciples may benefit from as they stand before the word's prosecution and judgment. As such, the theme of "bearing witness" about Jesus (15:26–27) fits congruently with and provides supplementation to many of the subthemes threaded through chapter 15 including: the privilege of being a disciple-branch, the necessity of remaining in Jesus and Jesus' words remaining in the disciple, friendship with Jesus, and prayer in Jesus' name. As such, true disciples bear witness about their master, and friends speak boldly *to* and *about* one another. But such witness and friendship is viable only if one remains loyal. Hence, as one remains loyal to Jesus, he is afforded the privilege of offering prayer in Jesus' name, which in turn enables him to perform works and bear fruit that bear witness about Jesus. To state it another way, in his witness, the Paraclete provides a dynamic profile of Jesus' words and works that the disciples may mimic or imitate in their witness about Jesus (14:12, ὁ πιστεύων εἰς ἐμὲ τὰ ἔργα ἃ ἐγὼ ποιῶ κἀκεῖνος ποιήσει). But this occurs as the disciples remain in the space of prayer where they, as "subordinate" senders, make their petitions to the "superior" receiver who then grants their request by performing his works through them (14:13–14).[71] It is within this space that the Paraclete opens a channel of communication that informs and empowers the disciples to offer prayer in accordance with the living and dynamic testimony of Jesus, the new and final locus of God's revelation.

Finally, the consequences of failing to remain in Jesus become even clearer as chapter 15 draws to a close. In the previous chapter of this analysis, it is said that the Paraclete is sent from the patron-Father to the client-disciples to educate them in Jesus' physical absence and to mediate his presence. As such, the disciples become the dwelling place of God. In chapter 15 the Paraclete proceeds from the Father to the disciple-branches who remain in Jesus. However, if the branches fail to remain in the vine,

---

70. Bennema, *Power of Saving Wisdom*, 235–36.
71. Neyrey, *Give God the Glory*, 9.

then the Paraclete cannot proceed to the disciples and be functionally present and active with/in them. If this is the case, then the disciples not only are "removed" from the vine but also are "cut off" from access to the Spirit-Paraclete, who mediates the presence of the Father and Son to them. Further, the disciples will then fail to receive the ongoing education and reminder of Jesus' words that occurs via the Paraclete. But most pertinent to the present analysis, if the disciples are cut off from the Paraclete then the Paraclete cannot bear witness about Jesus. If this occurs, then the disciples are left without a functional model to imitate. In the end, a disciple who fails to remain in the vine is limited in his ability to offer effectual prayers. The final consequence is that one's prayers may fall on deaf ears.

CHAPTER 7

Plain and Persistent Prayer

Analysis of John 16

BUILDING UPON THE PROFILE of Jewish, Greco-Roman, and Christian prayer in general, the preceding analysis sought to determine how chapters 14–15 of the Farewell Discourse uniquely contribute to the profile of Johannine prayer. Within these chapters the topic of prayer is seen embedded in and surrounded by dominant themes such as: Jesus' departure, the necessity of faith in Jesus, the indwelling of the Father and Son, the ability to perform greater works, the necessity of abiding in Jesus, the ability to bear fruit, the role of the Paraclete, etc. As indicated, prayer functions as the means of communication that occurs between "subordinate" senders and the "superior" receiver;[1] it occurs in the relational space shared by the earthly disciples and the glorified Jesus; and it serves as the means by which God's mission continues in the earth and specific "results" are achieved.

With the above themes in mind, a careful review of the Farewell Discourse reveals that certain materials/themes appear in spiral fashion. For example, the topic of prayer initially appears in 14:13–14. However, the text moves on to address other topics but then returns to the topic of prayer in 15:7, thus providing a repetition.[2] In this fashion, the topic of prayer is seen intertwined in a matrix of other topics/themes that are gradually discussed and explicated as the text unfolds. In this textual arrangement, themes such as faith, friendship with Jesus, and the Paraclete serve to draw out the function of prayer and elucidate its unique Johannine distinction(s). In addition to summarizing and synthesizing the materials of the previous two chapters

1. Neyrey, *Give God the Glory*, 9.
2. As noted in Zumstein, *Kreative Erinnerung*.

of this analysis, the chart that follows illuminates certain problems that arise (or will arise) in light of Jesus' departure. As will become evident below, the text moves forward to provide a solution, only later to restate the problem and offer the solution in more detail, thereby demonstrating the spiraling nature of the text. For example:

Problems	Solutions
The disciples' troubled hearts/sorrow (14:1; 14:27; 16:5)	Jesus gives his peace to the disciples (14:27).
	Jesus speaks "these things" so their joy may be full (15:11).
	Jesus appears for their joy (16:16–22).
	The disciples may ask and receive so their joy may be full (16:24).
Separation from Jesus (13:36–14:1, 25; 16:7, 16–17)	Jesus will come again to the disciples, the Paraclete will mediate the presence of the Father and Jesus, and the Spirit will provide help to the disciples (14:2–3, 23, 26; 15:26; 16:7–15, 22).
	Jesus will abide/remain in his disciples, and the disciples will abide/remain in him (15:4–7).
The persecution and hatred of the world (15:18–25; 16:1–4a)	The Paraclete will "bear witness" about Jesus (15:26).
	The disciples will "bear witness" about Jesus in the face of persecution (15:27).
Potential inability to continue the mission and work of Jesus.	By faith in Jesus the disciples are promised the ability to do "greater works" (14:12), and those who "remain" will bear "much fruit" (15:5, 8).
	Jesus promises that he will "do" whatever the disciples request (14:13–14). Whatever they ask will be "done" for them (15:7).
(Implied) Potential deficit of knowledge/education	The Paraclete will teach the disciples, bring to their remembrance all that Jesus said to them, bear witness about Jesus, guide them into all truth, speak and declare all that is to come, etc. (14:26; 15:26; 16:13–14).

Problems	Solutions
	As Jesus' friends, the disciples are granted inside knowledge/revelation (15:14–15).
(Implied) Potential inability to communicate with Jesus.	Jesus says that the disciples may ask for anything in his name (14:13–14; 15:16; 16:23), which implies that dialogue with the Father/Jesus will continue in his physical absence.

Although the spiral is imprecise[3] and somewhat unpredictable, it is evident that the Evangelist sought to provide a gradual but illuminating presentation of how the disciples are to function in Jesus' physical absence through the repetition of key topics.[4] The Father and Jesus will make their home with the disciples, their education will continue, they will be "in" Jesus and he will be "in" them, and they will continue to do the works of Jesus and bear fruit in order to bring glory to the Father. It is within the spiral that the Evangelist indicates how prayer not only serves as the means by which communication with God continues to take place, but also serves as the means by which certain actual/potential problems will be solved (or "results" are achieved).[5] In short, the disciples will retain their ability to communicate with Jesus by the implementation of his name, and Jesus will retain his ability to communicate with the disciples by the mediatorial work of the Paraclete. As this loop of communication is formed, the disciples will not only receive knowledge/truth from the Paraclete but will also be able to pray in a manner that results in "greater works" being performed and "much fruit" being produced. But asking/praying in Jesus' name and in accordance with Jesus' word is the means by which these realities occur. In the final analysis, faith in Jesus, that is, believing and trusting in him, grants one

---

3. The repetition of topics and themes does not always occur in the same language but rather conceptually and categorically. Schnackenburg is correct to note that the vocabulary of sadness is absent from chapter 14 but present in chapter 16. However, the "troubled hearts" of the disciples in 14:1 gives way to and is congruent with the concept of sorrow in 16:6, 20, etc. Even more, the antonym "joy" (vv. 20–22, 24) stands in contrast to both the condition of a troubled heart in general and sorrow in particular. Thus, the spiral of various themes yields thematic nuance(s) as the text builds and progresses. See Schnackenburg, *Gospel According to St. John*, 125.

4. This approach allows each chapter to offer a unique but complementary contribution to each topic as it unfolds. Chapter 14 emphasizes faith, while chapter 15 emphasizes the need to abide, and chapter 16 centers on the joy that ensues irrespective of Jesus' physical absence and the world's persecution and hatred.

5. Neyrey, *Give God the Glory*, 9.

access to the relational space of prayer and provides the existential motivation for offering prayer to God.

While the chart above provides an overview of the topics that spiral through chapters 14–16, there is more data to be examined, particularly in chapter 16. Thus, in order to obtain a more complete profile of prayer, one must follow the thematic spiral through the material located in this chapter.

Prayer and the Mission of the Spirit-Paraclete: John 16:4b–15

This section begins with a statement that reveals the purposeful nature of the preparatory speech that Jesus issues before his departure. Jesus declares in John 16:4b, Ταῦτα δὲ ὑμῖν ἐξ ἀρχῆς οὐκ εἶπον, ὅτι μεθ' ὑμῶν ἤμην. Jesus did not expound "these things" earlier in his ministry because he was present, but now he speaks of addressing "these things" in light of the coming persecution[6] and his imminent departure.[7] While Jesus does not want the disciples to be troubled (14:1) or sorrowful (16:6), he does want them to be prepared as hard times approach. In particular, Jesus prepares his disciples by informing them of what is to come, so that when the "hour" approaches they will be reminded of what he spoke to them (16:4a). As indicated, a further aspect of such preparation involves ensuring that the lines of communication/knowledge will remain open when the disciples undergo pressure from the world. Jesus freely addressed his disciples before his departure, and the same will be true subsequent to his departure by the help of the Paraclete, who will continue to educate and impart truth (14:26; 15:26; 16:13). On the other hand, the disciples will be able to speak freely back to God in prayer, provided that they remain in a relationship with Jesus and offer prayer in Jesus' name. As will be seen below, the disciples' sorrow and anguish will give way to the fullness of joy that is the direct corollary of asking and receiving through prayer (16:24). Thus, even in the midst of a threatening/hostile *Sitz im Leben*, the disciples will have direct access to God and freedom to enter the space of prayer.

Verse 5 yields a statement (νῦν δὲ ὑπάγω πρὸς τὸν πέμψαντά με, καὶ οὐδεὶς ἐξ ὑμῶν ἐρωτᾷ με· ποῦ ὑπάγεις;) that seems contradictory to previous questions concerning where Jesus was going (13:36; cf. 14:4–5). Numerous solutions have been proposed, none of which are completely satisfactory. Notwithstanding, the overriding concern of the Evangelist is to move his readers to the promises that follow. Jesus states in 16:7, ἀλλ' ἐγὼ τὴν

---

6. See Newman and Nida, *Handbook on the Gospel of John*, 501–2.
7. See Witherington, *John's Wisdom*, 264.

ἀλήθειαν[8] λέγω ὑμῖν, συμφέρει ὑμῖν ἵνα ἐγὼ ἀπέλθω. ἐὰν γὰρ μὴ ἀπέλθω, ὁ παράκλητος οὐκ ἐλεύσεται πρὸς ὑμᾶς· ἐὰν δὲ πορευθῶ, πέμψω αὐτὸν πρὸς ὑμᾶς. At this point the topic of the Paraclete spirals back into the discussion. Jesus will soon depart, but the disciples' hearts should not be troubled or sorrowful because they will not be left without assistance. Help is on the way. The verses that follow (vv. 8–11) serve to complement the roles of the Paraclete that have already been elucidated in 14:16–17, 26 and 15:26. While there is some textual distance between 15:26 and 16:8–11, it is best to interpret the latter in light of the former. Given the context of Jesus' departure and the world's hatred, the Paraclete's function in 16:8–11 is best understood through his witness to the world, generally, and through the disciples, particularly. These verses (8–11) may be arranged in the following manner for exegetical clarity.

και ἐλθὼν ἐκεῖνος
ἐλέγξει τὸν κόσμον περὶ ἁμαρτίας καὶ περὶ δικαιοσύνης καὶ περὶ κρίσεως
περὶ ἁμαρτίας μέν, ὅτι οὐ πιστεύουσιν εἰς ἐμέ.
περὶ δικαιοσύνης δέ, ὅτι πρὸς τὸν πατέρα ὑπάγω καὶ οὐκέτι θεωρεῖτέ με.
περὶ δὲ κρίσεως, ὅτι ὁ ἄρχων τοῦ κόσμου τούτου κέκριται.

At first glance, these verses seems to have little, if anything, to do with the topic of prayer. In fact, to my knowledge there has not been any significant scholarly attention given to how the Paraclete and prayer work together in God's mission in the world. But the following analysis will demonstrate that the Paraclete works in conjunction with prayers that are issued in Jesus' name to bring forth "fruit" and "works" that bring glory to the Father. First, it is said that the Paraclete will "convict" the "world" in certain regards. In certain cases, such as John 3:20, ἐλεγχθῇ carries the idea of the light exposing the deeds of the one who does evil. However, perhaps most closely related to 16:8 is the construction found in 8:46 (ἐλέγχει με περὶ ἁμαρτίας;), which is embedded in Jesus' question concerning his sin. The emphasis here rests on exposing and/or making his sin known, if possible. Given the lexical data, the likely meaning the Evangelist seeks to convey is that the Paraclete will come to "expose" the world in regard to its guilt. Such exposure is not generic in nature but is specifically aimed at shedding light on actions that incur guilt and blame before God. As pointed out by Aloisi, "The emphasis in John 16:8 seems to center on showing people their sin

---

8. Schnackenburg notes, "The addition, 'I tell you the truth,' is certainly not merely a way of strengthening the statement—it also provides the words and their revelatory character (see 8:40, 45)" (*Gospel According to St. John*, 127).

and convincing them that they stand guilty before God. This convicting or convincing work involves the Spirit bringing the world to a self-conscious 'conviction' of its sin and guiltiness."[9] Accordingly, the aim of the Paraclete is not merely to "expose," but to do so judiciously with the aim of forensic conviction.[10] This concept fits squarely within the context of chapter 16 (which is, in part, forensic in nature) where the activity of the Spirit centers on legal concepts such as sin, righteousness, and judgment. Thus, some scholars see the Paraclete as a prosecutor. In fact, Barrett sees the Paraclete's activity of exposing as involving both judging and prosecuting counsel in one.[11] Thus, it seems best to translate ἐλέγχω by "'to expose (the guilt of)' or 'convince (of guilt),' and it comes very close to 'convict' (cf. 3:20; 8:46)."[12]

Accordingly, from one perspective, the activity of the Paraclete is directed toward the world for soteriological outcomes. In another view, the Paraclete's activity is not directed toward the world but is "an exclusively interior activity directed to (the consciences of) the disciples."[13] Brown argues extensively for the latter perspective and sees the former view at odds with the Evangelist's view of the world as well as the Paraclete's relationship to the world (14:17). In her estimation, "the Paraclete's mission is not directed to the world; he is not sent to the world in order to 'persuade' them of their guilt. Rather, he comes to the disciples in order to continue Jesus' work and to make Jesus' presence perpetually available to them."[14] Brown goes on to say, "The Paraclete will prove *to the disciples* the guilt of the world just as Jesus, during his ministry, exposed the wrongness of the world 'so that those who do not see may see' (9:39)."[15] This view does not seem tenable given that the disciples themselves were already aware of the world's sinful condition and needed no further elucidation of this reality through the help of the Spirit. Further, Bennema disagrees with Brown's interpretation for several reasons. But perhaps most helpful is the question concerning the nature of Jesus' ministry. Was the aim condemnation or conversion? To this question he correctly responds with the latter option:

> Jesus confronted people with his revelatory wisdom teaching, and salvation or judgment is the consequence of one's response

9. Aloisi, "Paraclete's Ministry of Conviction," 60.
10. For a brief survey of divine prosecution in the OT, see Keener, *Gospel of John*, 1032–33.
11. Barrett, *Gospel According to St. John*, 90.
12. Bennema, *Power of Saving Wisdom*, 237.
13. Bennema, *Power of Saving Wisdom*, 237.
14. Brown, *Spirit in the Writings of John*, 222.
15. Brown, *Spirit in the Writings of John*, 223.

to Jesus. Jesus came to bring salvation (cf. 3:17), and judgment was the (indirect) consequence of rejecting Jesus and the life that he offered. Jesus did not come to judge but to expose the sinful reality of the world and to redeem the world. Consequently, we would expect that the Paraclete's ἐλέγχειν also has a soteriological dimension, and that judgment would be the consequence of rejecting the Paraclete's ἐλέγχειν.[16]

The thrust of Bennema's argument is that the Paraclete shows the world its sin so that it may believe, repent, and be saved (3:16). He further points out that the content of 14:17 does not preclude the Paraclete's activity in this regard. He notes, "The soteriological aspect of the Paraclete's ἐλέγχειν does not contradict what is said in 14:17; the world as 'world' cannot accept the Paraclete and his ἐλέγχειν because it loves darkness (3:19; cf. 1:10–11), but a convinced person can."[17] While the world in general will be hostile toward the disciples, there is an untold number from the world that is called out of the world to follow Jesus in a salvific relationship (15:19; 17:6). Hence, some will be saved and some will continue in unbelief. Notwithstanding, it is through the Paraclete bearing witness to the disciples and their bearing witness to the world that convincing takes place. This interpretation accords with the mission of Jesus that will take place through his disciples upon his glorification and subsequent departure. As will be discussed below, it also accords with prayers that are offered in Jesus' name for the purpose of doing greater works and bearing much fruit. Such works and fruit are part and parcel of the missionary endeavors of the disciples who carried forth Jesus' mission to the world.

Further, the three περὶ clauses (περὶ ἁμαρτίας καὶ περὶ δικαιοσύνης καὶ περὶ κρίσεως) thus relate to the Paraclete's conviction of the world. Some scholars assert that each of the three ὅτι clauses that follow should be interpreted in an explanatory sense (that is, as a mere description or defining the nature of sin, righteousness, and judgment). This reading would indicate that the Paraclete will convict the world of sin, the nature of which is unbelief. Others understand the clauses as causal (explaining why). On the causal reading the implication is that the Paraclete will convict the world because it does not believe. The approach favored in this analysis involves viewing each clause as causal rather than explanatory in nature. As such, each of these clauses serves to form the grounds of the world's conviction.

The first clause (v. 9) relates to the Paraclete convicting the world concerning ἁμαρτίας. Brown is correct to note that this term is employed

---

16. Bennema, *Power of Saving Wisdom*, 238.
17. Bennema, *Power of Saving Wisdom*, 238.

in John 16 without the article and refers to "the basic idea rather than to individual instances."[18] But how does this basic idea play out in the Fourth Gospel? Newman and Nida remark, "Here, as elsewhere in the Gospel of John, the cardinal sin of the world is the refusal to believe in Jesus."[19] Burge notes accordingly, "That this is a primary sin is clear (1:11; 3:19; 15:22). It does not refer to ignorance, as if at issue is a problem of intellect; it is a problem of will and so implies rejection (cf. 5:43–47; 9:39–41)."[20] Such unbelief places the individual under condemnation (3:18) and the wrath of God (3:36). However, the outcome of the Spirit's work is to lead individuals away from sin and to turn them to belief in Jesus. Thus, while the sin of unbelief leads to condemnation, the Paraclete's role involves bringing conviction that leads to eternal life.[21]

The second clause (v. 10) relates to the Paraclete convicting the world concerning "righteousness." Many scholars see the Evangelist as referring either to Jesus' righteousness, to a certain righteous standard, or to righteousness generally. Carson is of the opinion that the righteousness spoken of here is not Jesus' righteousness but rather a pseudo-righteousness. He notes that when the Paraclete comes, "he will convict the world of . . . its righteousness (that is, what the world takes to be righteousness but which is woefully inadequate or tainted)."[22] Moloney explains further, "Jesus' opponents have consistently failed to accept that Jesus is from the Father and that he is returning to the Father and will no longer be seen among his disciples (v. 11). Yet they have laid claim to righteousness as children of Abraham (see 8:39–59), disciples of Moses (see 6:30–31; 9:28–29), and subject to the Torah (see 5:16–18, 39–40, 45–47; 7:12, 18, 20–24, 48–49; 8:58–59; 9:16, 24; 10:24–38; 11:48–50; 16:2). . . . In their *horizontally* determined understanding of a righteousness worked out within human history (Abraham, Moses, and Torah), they have rejected the *vertical* inbreak of the Son of God (the word become flesh, Jesus Christ)."[23]

Aloisi takes into account the false-righteousness paradigm but provides a view that is more theological than locative. He sees the ὅτι-clause as indicating that the Paraclete will convict the world of its false righteousness "because Jesus' resurrection and ascension prove that he is righteous and has been accepted by his Father. Christ's ascension to heaven demonstrates that

---

18. Brown, *Gospel According to John (XIII–XXI)*, 705.
19. Newman and Nida, *Handbook on the Gospel of John*, 505.
20. Burge, *John*, 405.
21. Carson, *Gospel According to John*, 537.
22. Carson, *Gospel According to John*, 565.
23. Moloney, *Glory Not Dishonor*, 85.

the 'righteousness' of the religious leaders who rejected him is worthless."[24] Therefore, he views Christ's ascension as the basis for the Spirit's conviction of the world's false "righteousness." Keener notes that "Christ's δικαιοσύνη—justification, righteousness, or vindication—is established by the Father's witness in enthroning him."[25] Moreover, in light of these views, the most appropriate interpretation of verse 10 is as follows: Upon Christ's glorification the Paraclete will convict the world of its false righteousness, which is objectively elucidated by Christ's righteousness—a righteousness demonstrated in his life, a corollary confirmed in his unjust death, and a necessary vindication approved by the Father upon his resurrection and ascension.

The third clause (v. 11) relates to the "judgment" wrought by the Paraclete because the ruler of this world stands condemned. The statement ὅτι ὁ ἄρχων τοῦ κόσμου τούτου κέκριται is reminiscent of 12:31 where Jesus remarks, νῦν κρίσις ἐστὶν τοῦ κόσμου τούτου, νῦν ὁ ἄρχων τοῦ κόσμου τούτου ἐκβληθήσεται ἔξω. In effect, the judgment of the κόσμου and the ejection of ὁ ἄρχων τοῦ κόσμου occurs now (νῦν). Yet the term νῦν may be viewed eschatologically in terms of (in sequence) Jesus' cross-death, his resurrection, his departure to the Father, and the coming of the Paraclete. But the Paraclete does not bring conviction because men falsely judged Jesus to be condemned on the cross.[26] Rather, the Paraclete brings conviction to the world based on the judgment passed on the "ruler of this world." Satan's defeat was ensured by Jesus' death and Satan's defeat/judgment provides justification for the Paraclete's conviction of the world regarding its false judgments.[27] Hence, while there are only two outcomes, judged or acquitted, the final verdict for someone in the world is based on his response to the witness of the disciple/Paraclete. In the end, the aim of such conviction/convincing centers on elucidating the fate of the ruler of this world in order to evoke faith in Jesus and an allegiance to him that culminates in a salvific relationship.

Verses 13–15 contain the final Paraclete saying, which further expands earlier statements concerning his work on the disciples' behalf (14:26; 15:26). The text reads in the following manner:

13 ὅταν δὲ ἔλθῃ ἐκεῖνος,

τὸ πνεῦμα τῆς ἀληθείας,

ὁδηγήσει ὑμᾶς ἐν τῇ ἀληθείᾳ πάσῃ·

---

24. Aloisi, "Paraclete's Ministry of Conviction," 63.
25. Keener, *Gospel of John*, 1035.
26. Carson, "Function of the Paraclete," 562.
27. Barrett, *Gospel According to St. John*, 488.

> οὐ γὰρ λαλήσει ἀφ' ἑαυτοῦ,
> ἀλλ' ὅσα ἀκούσει λαλήσει
> καὶ τὰ ἐρχόμενα ἀναγγελεῖ ὑμῖν.
> 14 ἐκεῖνος ἐμὲ δοξάσει,
>   ὅτι ἐκ τοῦ ἐμοῦ λήμψεται
>   καὶ ἀναγγελεῖ ὑμῖν.
> 15 πάντα ὅσα ἔχει ὁ πατὴρ ἐμά ἐστιν·
> διὰ τοῦτο εἶπον ὅτι
>   ἐκ τοῦ ἐμοῦ λαμβάνει
>   καὶ ἀναγγελεῖ ὑμῖν.

As such, these verses imply that future questions, tensions, and problems will not be left open-ended but will be addressed by the Paraclete's activity. In 16:13 the Evangelist repeats an earlier statement concerning the Paraclete (14:17, 26), namely, that he is the τὸ πνεῦμα τῆς ἀληθείας. But in verse 13 the Evangelist qualifies the Spirit-Paraclete's role by saying, ὁδηγήσει ὑμᾶς ἐν τῇ ἀληθείᾳ πάσῃ. Newman and Nida say, "The verb translated *lead* appears frequently in the Greek translation of the Psalms (for example, 5:8; 27:11; 106:9; 119:35). In Revelation 7:17 it is used of the Lamb, who will guide God's people to the springs of life-giving water."[28] Keener says that "Greco-Roman philosophers and moralists could speak of God or reason as a guide.... In Wisdom of Solomon, Wisdom could lead the righteous; God as the 'way of wisdom' leads the wise to wisdom."[29] He also sees the possibility that the Evangelist may be hinting at a background concerning the theme of a new exodus. Notwithstanding, the work of the Paraclete centers on functioning as a divine guide who assumes his authority from God himself. Thus, in light of Jesus' departure, the disciples will not be left without a guide; rather they will receive ongoing guidance through the Spirit.

Implications for Prayer

As noted, the topic of prayer spirals through the Farewell Discourse and is linked to other themes that explicate how Jesus' mission will continue after his departure. As will be discussed below, the means by which prayers are answered is elucidated by the role of the Spirit-Paraclete, who is sent in Jesus' absence. It has been shown above that prayer offered in Jesus' name is prayer that accords with God's revealed will through Jesus. Curiously,

---

28. Newman and Nida, *Handbook on the Gospel of John*, 506.
29. Keener, *Gospel of John*, 1036.

the Evangelist notes that the Spirit-Paraclete is sent in Jesus' name (14:26), which likely means that he is sent on Jesus' behalf and for the cause of Jesus' mission. Thus, it may be said that the link between prayer in Jesus' name and the fulfillment of the disciples' request is the Spirit-Paraclete, who is sent in Jesus absence. However, according to 16:13 the ministry of the Paraclete is not defined by what the disciples pray but rather is based on what he hears from the Father/Son. But as one has faith in Jesus and prays in Jesus' name, the disciple places himself under God's authority, in alignment with God's will, and in possession of the Spirit, who equips him to bear witness in the face of the world's hatred and persecution. Thus, both the Spirit and the disciples are unified around and subservient to Jesus' purposes in the earth.

It may be argued that prayer in the Farewell Discourse involves praying according to what God has decreed through the Jesus-Spirit-disciple paradigm, namely, bring glory to himself through works that are performed and by salvation that is achieved. This genre of prayer accords with Millar's analysis of prayer that involves "calling on the name of the Lord." Millar remarks that the "primary biblical trajectory of prayer is not praise, or lament, or intercession, or meditation on the word of Yahweh. Prayer begins in the Bible as a cry for God to do what he has promised—to deal with the reality of sin by delivering on his covenant promises."[30] He sees Genesis 4:26 ("At that time people began to call upon the name of the Lord") as containing the first prayer of the Bible. He cites evidence from numerous OT passages that refer to those who "called upon the name of the Lord" and then says accordingly, "When this phrase is used in the Old Testament, it is asking God to intervene specifically to do one thing—to come through on his promises."[31] In the context of the Farewell Discourse, the concept of "calling on the name of the Lord" is theologically congruent with offering prayer in Jesus' name, which (in part) may summon God to keep his promise of offering eternal life to anyone who believes (3:16). Thus, the impulse of Johannine prayer involves petitioning God for the specific "result" of salvation and the accomplishment of his mission in the earth.

Returning to the role of the Paraclete: his roles may be summarized in the following manner:

1. He mediates the presence of the Father/Son to the disciples (14:16–17, 23).

2. He educates the disciples, teaches them, and guides them into all truth (14:26; 16:13).

---

30. Millar, *Calling on the Name of the Lord*, 27.
31. Millar, *Calling on the Name of the Lord*, 22.

3. He communicates, that is, he bears witness about Jesus, speaks whatever he hears from the Father/Son, and declares the things that are to come (15:26; 16:13).

4. He convicts the world in regard to sin, righteousness, and judgment, and does so in order to lead people to repentance and faith/belief in Jesus.

It is partially based on the roles of the Spirit-Paraclete that the disciples' prayers will prove effectual. As noted, the conviction of the world wrought by the Paraclete is justified in light of Jesus' life, death, and ascension to the Father. Jesus confronted the world's unbelief, exposed its false righteousness, and solidified the judgment passed on the ruler of this world. Each component of conviction is forensic in nature, Christo-centric in focus, and pneumatological in application. On his departure, Jesus' work was complete, but the Paraclete's work was just beginning.[32] In other words, the finality achieved at Jesus' departure to the Father gave way to the convicting work of the Paraclete, who works concurrently within God's people so they may bear witness for God. While the Paraclete is the agency of conviction in Jesus' absence, he does not act alone but synergistically through those in whom he dwells.

> Therefore, it may be said that the disciple who prays does so in accordance with what he has received via Jesus' word(s) and the Paraclete's witness. As such, the Spirit's witness about Jesus may close the gap that exists between one's wishing and God's willing. Prayer becomes the means by which one's wishes are offered and God's promise is actualized.

The collective evidence of the Paraclete passages that spiral through the Farewell Discourse seems to indicate that asking God to do what he promised to do naturally involves the work of the Spirit in and through the disciples. As a result of his coming, the Paraclete uniquely equips the disciples for the mission that lies ahead. And it is within this context that the disciples become part and parcel of the means by which God fulfills his saving mission/purpose in the earth. In the language of 14:12 and 15:5, 8, the works that started in Jesus ministry will later translate into "greater works," and the disciples will bear "much fruit" as they remain in Jesus. Or, with the

---

32. This is not to say that the Holy Spirit had not been active prior to Jesus' glorification. But the newness of the Paraclete's operation in the world would be defined in light of the historical achievement of Jesus' death, resurrection, subsequent ascension to the Father, and application of these events in redemptive history. In this manner, the Paraclete's work was novel.

Paraclete passages in mind, as the disciples go forth in God's mission, they bear witness about Jesus through their words and their deeds and declare to the world all that has been declared to them by the Spirit. In particular, Carson understands that the disciples share in the responsibility of bringing conviction to the world in regard to their *righteousness* through the aid of the Paraclete. He notes:

> Already the promised Paraclete has been linked with the obedience of the disciples (14:16–27); and within the context of such themes comes the astounding promise that *the disciples themselves will do what Jesus has been doing* (14:12)—indeed, even greater things than Jesus has been doing, *because Jesus is going to the Father* (= *because the blessed Paraclete will be sent*).... The Paraclete convicts the world of its pseudo-righteousness, but he accomplishes at least part of this convicting work by so operating within the believers that they themselves establish before the world true and convicting standards of righteousness. Jesus is gone, and they see him no more, but the Paraclete so works in them that they are enabled to exercise the same convicting righteousness exhibited by Jesus in the days of his flesh.[33]

Furthermore, as the words of the Son are mediated through the presence of the Spirit-Paraclete and spoken from the lips of the disciples, conviction is wrought and God's will is accomplished. For some, conviction may lead to decisive and final judgment. For others, conviction may lead to salvation. As noted in 16:8–11, the world stands under conviction regarding sin, righteousness, and judgment. Yet the world is not exclusively or finally doomed. Jesus came to save the world (3:16), and he chose the disciples out of this world (15:16). Thus, the Paraclete's role centers on convicting and convincing the world of its sinfulness, which opens the way for repentance. This role is congruent with Jesus' character and mission as seen throughout the Fourth Gospel. Thus, prayer offered in Jesus' name and informed by Jesus' words may be congruent with what God has already willed to do through the Spirit-Paraclete, namely bring forth conviction to whomever he chooses. The promise of 14:13–14; 15:7, 16; 16:23–24 is that the one who makes requests in Jesus' name and in alignment with his will may have his prayers answered. Such answered prayer yields a precise result, namely that of salvation as Jesus does "greater works" of convicting in and through his disciples. One may say that prayer to God eventuates the service of the Paraclete, who yields the fruit of new believers (who become members of the family of God).

---

33. Carson, "Function of the Paraclete," 564–65.

From Sorrow to Joy: John 16:16–24

Beginning in John 16:16, Jesus transitions the discourse away from an explicit discussion of the Paraclete to an implicit discussion of his departure, which has been previously discussed (7:33; 14:19; 16:5). In doing so, Jesus re-presents a previously alluded to problem (in different language) and then brings clarity to the problem by providing a solution in more explicit terms. As will be seen below, the topic of the Paraclete implicitly spirals back into the discussion as Jesus seeks to bring further comfort to the disciples in the midst of impending sorrow. Finally, the topic of prayer explicitly reappears for the first time since 15:16 and becomes part and parcel of the solution to the problem that awaits the troubled disciples. Thus, the spiraling of topics is seen once again as the Farewell Discourse unfolds.

Particularly, in verse 16 Jesus speaks of the μικρὸν[34] to convey the temporal duration of his appearance and disappearance, which creates confusion for the disciples.[35]

Jesus says in verse 16:

Μικρὸν καὶ οὐκέτι θεωρεῖτέ με,

καὶ πάλιν μικρὸν καὶ ὄψεσθέ με.

In verse 17 the disciples respond not to Jesus but to one another by restating in similar terms the question Jesus asked them:

μικρὸν καὶ οὐ θεωρεῖτέ με, καὶ πάλιν μικρὸν καὶ ὄψεσθέ με;

καί· ὅτι ὑπάγω πρὸς τὸν πατέρα;

In 16:16 Jesus says that his disciples will not "see" (θεωρεῖτέ) him, but then they will "see" (ὄψεσθέ) him. Some commentators view these verbs as essentially meaning the same thing. While this may be true on grammatical and lexical grounds, the Evangelist may have intended to convey the action of "seeing" as relating to both the physical and spiritual realm. Notwithstanding, to what is Jesus actually referring? Carson asks, "Does the first 'little while' mark the time until Jesus' death, or until his ascension? Does 'you will see me' after the second 'little while' refer to Jesus' resurrection, the descent of the Spirit (cf. 14:23), or the parousia (14:1–4)?"[36] Keener sees the

---

34. This term is used eight times in verses 16–19. Keener notes that this term "sometimes appears in eschatological settings (Heb 10:37; Rev 6:11) probably rooted in the vernacular of Israelite prophecy about impending judgment (Hos 1:4 [LXX]; Isa 10:25; Jer 28:33 [51:22])" (*Gospel of John*, 1043).

35. Haenchen says that "the disciples are depicted as completely dense" (*Commentary on the Gospel of John Chapters 7–21*, 144).

36. Carson, *Gospel According to John*, 542–43.

first "little while" statement as referring to the hours before the cross-event (7:33; 12:35) and the second "little while" statement as pointing to the interval between the crucifixion and resurrection.[37] Based on the last phrase in verse 17, ὅτι ὑπάγω πρὸς τὸν πατέρα, it seems that the disciples at least had a referential framework of Jesus' departure in mind. Thus, Schnackenburg does not believe the additional statement at the end of verse 17 is an arbitrary addition but rather as reflecting the author's intention to reveal that the disciples did in fact understand that Jesus was referring to his departure.[38] Bruce also connects the disciples' words seen in the last clause of verse 17 as harking back to verse 10, where Jesus mentions his departure to the Father. Yet the disciples' anguish did not merely center on the timing of Jesus' departure but, perhaps more importantly, on the fact of his departure.[39] While it is difficult to know for certain the extent of the disciples' confusion, Etienne is right in saying:

> The insight Jesus requires of them certainly exceeds their present ability to understand his words. Right at the heart of the unfolding discourse, therefore, the evangelist sets the image of "giving birth" in order to provide an existential presentiment of the time of affliction in which the disciples find themselves, to show them how they are to interpret this time of affliction and live through it. This time of affliction is likened to the "hour" of a woman in labour.[40]

Assuming their need to have an answer for their question, Jesus responds with a question (v. 19). In verse 20, Jesus once again employs the phrase ἀμὴν ἀμὴν to offer forthright assurance that, while the world rejoices (κόσμος χαρήσεται), the disciples will experience sorrow. They will weep and lament. The term θρηνήσετε ("to lament") appears only here (v. 20), while the verb κλαύσετε ("to weep") appears in John 11:31, 33; 20:11, 13, 15 as an action carried out by Mary in the context of death.[41] The Evangelist then offers the disciples an image that is analogous to the situation they are facing (v. 21):

---

37. Keener, *Gospel of John*, 1043.
38. Schnackenburg, *Gospel According to St. John*, 157.
39. Bruce, *Gospel and Epistles of John*, 322.
40. Etienne, "Birth," 233.
41. This is also seen in the LXX. Jeremiah 22:10 states, Μὴ κλαίετε τὸν τεθνηκότα μηδὲ θρηνεῖτε αὐτόν, κλαύσατε κλαυθμῷ τὸν ἐκπορευόμενον, ὅτι οὐκ ἐπιστρέψει ἔτι καὶ οὐ μὴ ἴδῃ τὴν γῆν πατρίδος αὐτοῦ.

ἡ γυνὴ ὅταν τίκτῃ λύπην ἔχει, ὅτι ἦλθεν ἡ ὥρα αὐτῆς· ὅταν δὲ γεννήσῃ τὸ παιδίον, οὐκέτι μνημονεύει τῆς θλίψεως διὰ τὴν χαρὰν ὅτι ἐγεννήθη ἄνθρωπος εἰς τὸν κόσμον.

Culpepper remarks, "The image, drawn from the prophets, is that of a woman in labor, whose travail soon turns to joy. Israel's exile was but a temporary travail that would turn to joy, but it requires faith to see that the suffering is temporary or purposeful."[42] Accordingly, in the midst of temporary travail and darkness, psalms of lament look forward in faith to God for a favorable outcome. While there are numerous examples one can cite, Psalm 12 (LXX) sufficiently indicates the nature of lament:

2 Ἕως πότε, Κύριε, ἐπιλήσῃ μου εἰς τέλος;
  ἕως πότε ἀποστρέψεις τὸ πρόσωπόν σου ἀπ᾽ ἐμοῦ;
3 ἕως τίνος θήσομαι βουλὰς ἐν ψυχῇ μου,
  ὀδύνας ἐν καρδίᾳ μου ἡμέρας;
  ἕως πότε ὑψωθήσεται ὁ ἐχθρός μου ἐπ᾽ ἐμέ;
4 ἐπίβλεψον, εἰσάκουσόν μου, Κύριε ὁ θεός μου·
  φώτισον τοὺς ὀφθαλμούς, μή ποτε ὑπνώσω εἰς θάνατον,
5 μή ποτε εἴπῃ ὁ ἐχθρός μου Ἴσχυσα πρὸς αὐτόν·
  οἱ θλίβοντές με ἀγαλλιάσονται ἐὰν σαλευθῶ.
6 ἐγὼ δὲ ἐπὶ τῷ ἐλέει σου ἤλπισα·
  ἀγαλλιάσεται ἡ καρδία μου ἐν τῷ σωτηρίῳ σου·
  ᾄσω τῷ κυρίῳ τῷ εὐεργετήσαντί με,
  καὶ ψαλῶ τῷ ὀνόματι Κυρίου τοῦ ὑψίστου.

Returning to John 16, the emphasis of verse 21a centers on the sorrow (λύπην) that ensues from the mother's labor pains. A corollary of this sorrow would likely involve anxiety about the future occasion of the labor/delivery of her baby in the form of minutes and hours. The emotional state of the mother, then, would find a place of relevance and similitude in the disciples as they experienced sorrow over Jesus' disappearance and death.

Yet, even in the midst of travail, the disciples may find a sense of comfort and finality knowing that joy awaits them. As the birth of a child causes the mother to no longer remember the anguish she experienced (οὐκέτι μνημονεύει τῆς θλίψεως διὰ τὴν χαρὰν ὅτι ἐγεννήθη ἄνθρωπος εἰς τὸν κόσμον), so the disciples will rejoice when they see Jesus again (vv. 21–22). And it is said that they will rejoice at that time and their joy will not be taken from them (καὶ τὴν χαρὰν ὑμῶν οὐδεὶς αἴρει ἀφ᾽ ὑμῶν) (see 15:11; 1 John 1:4). In

---

42. Culpepper, *Gospel and Letters of John*, 218.

contrast to the short-lived joy of seeing Jesus resurrected, this coming of the Spirit would result in a joy that would remain indefinitely throughout the disciples' lives. Moreover, the emphasis here on the Spirit is textually and thematically congruent with 16:7–15, where the work of the Paraclete is explicated. Therefore, as Etienne explains, "The disciples' sufferings acquire a new significance. These sufferings are no longer just the natural sorrow felt by those who have lost a friend who made their lives radiant by his presence, but the sufferings of a human race on the verge of a profound transformation which will result in a new life."[43] But this new life comes about only through the great sorrow and anguish that the disciples would face but also, and primarily, through the sorrow and anguish that Jesus would experience (John 19:1, 18, 28).

In verse 23 Jesus continues the discussion by addressing the benefits of seeing him again:

Καὶ ἐν ἐκείνῃ τῇ ἡμέρᾳ ἐμὲ οὐκ ἐρωτήσετε οὐδέν.
ἀμὴν ἀμὴν λέγω ὑμῖν,
ἄν τι αἰτήσητε τὸν πατέρα ἐν τῷ ὀνόματί μου δώσει ὑμῖν.

Barrett remarks, "In the New Testament 'that day' or 'those days' often refers to the last days, the end of the age; so, e.g., Mark 13:11, 17, 19, 24, 32; 14:25; Acts 2:18; 2 Tim 1:12, 18; 4:8; Heb 8:10; 10:16 (= Jer 31[38]:33); Rev 9:6."[44] Keener observes that the phrase ἐν ἐκείνῃ τῇ ἡμέρᾳ "is frequently eschatological language, which would fit John's emphasis on realized eschatology: Jesus returns in the resurrection to impart eschatological life through the Spirit (cf. 14:20)."[45] In this reading, Jesus will not merely be physically present upon his resurrection, but he will also be continually present "in that day" (and in the days that follow) through the Spirit.

Concerning this particular "day," the Evangelist indicates that the disciples will no longer ask anything of Jesus, but will instead approach the Father in his name. Therefore, the disciples will not ask Jesus questions because in the days to come they will have guidance via the Spirit of Truth. Alternately, the disciples would not need to make requests to Jesus because they have direct access to the Father in order to make requests in Jesus' name. The freedom to approach the Father in Jesus' name is, of course, grounded in the finality of Jesus' mission. To state matters further, the certainty of Jesus' death and resurrection provides certainty for the disciples as they ask and receive in prayer.

43. Etienne, "Birth," 236.
44. Barrett, *Gospel According to St. John*, 494.
45. Keener, *Gospel of John*, 1046.

Verse 24 indicates that the disciples had not made any requests in Jesus' name (ἕως ἄρτι οὐκ ᾐτήσατε οὐδὲν ἐν τῷ ὀνόματί μου), which is to be expected given that this privilege was initially introduced in 14:13. The disciples' personal interaction with Jesus precluded the necessity of employing his name in their requests. But, as noted throughout the Farewell Discourse, this would soon change. As Jesus departs, he remains functionally present both through the Spirit and by the disciples praying in his name. Accordingly, in 16:23–27 the Evangelist provides the definitive solution to the problem of Jesus' physical absence (hence, the spiraling). Jesus will be absent, but God will not be distant from them. In these verses the initial cause for the disciples' troubled hearts (14:1) is fully addressed and the larger picture is elucidated. Jesus will go to the Father (14:2–3), but his preparatory work on the disciples' behalf not only involves them becoming the dwelling place of God but also involves their ability to approach the Father (in Jesus' name) without hindrance. This ability is part and parcel of the privilege afforded to believers in light of the impending hour of sorrow/trial. Further, they will have no need to ask Jesus questions or make requests exclusively to him (hence, 16:26b: καὶ οὐ λέγω ὑμῖν ὅτι ἐγὼ ἐρωτήσω τὸν πατέρα περὶ ὑμῶν). Rather, they may approach the Father in Jesus' name and he will grant their requests.

In 16:24 the Evangelist notes that the disciples may experience χαρά as they offer prayer. This term appears in 15:11 in the context of the words Jesus spoke to his disciples (Ταῦτα λελάληκα ὑμῖν ἵνα ἡ χαρὰ ἡ ἐμὴ ἐν ὑμῖν ᾖ καὶ ἡ χαρὰ ὑμῶν πληρωθῇ.). Also, in 16:20, 22 the disciples will experience χαρά when they see Jesus again, and according to Jesus, καὶ τὴν χαρὰν ὑμῶν οὐδεὶς αἴρει ἀφ' ὑμῶν. Yet in verse 24, the disciples' fullness of joy is the corollary of receiving from the Father in prayer (αἰτεῖτε καὶ λήμψεσθε, ἵνα ἡ χαρὰ ὑμῶν ᾖ πεπληρωμένη). How do these various contexts of joy relate? Carson remarks concerning these verses:

> If that joy is part of the matrix of consistent obedience (15:11), that obedience, that remaining in Jesus (15:4) and his love (15:9) and his word (8:31), is the matrix out of which fruitbearing springs, the fruitbearing that is the direct consequence of prayer (15:7, 8). Thus the connection amongst asking, receiving and complete joy in 16:24 turns out to be a compressed version of themes developed in ch. 15, but now more clearly set within the eschatological situation introduced by Jesus' death and resurrection.[46]

---

46. Carson, *Gospel According to John*, 546.

As such, the disciples who will experience temporary sorrow will, upon seeing Jesus again, offer prayers to the Father, who will in turn grant their requests. Thus, the waiting will be over once they receive what they ask for, and their joy will be full. Finally, the nature of what they receive in prayer is to be understood in the context of the "greater works" (14:12) they will perform and the "much fruit" (15:5, 8) they will produce. Such actions recapitulate Jesus' presence in the world as his mission is advanced and his family is expanded.

The Timing of Answered Prayer

As seen above, the Evangelist integrates the topic of joy into the analogy of the woman in labor. Just as a woman rejoices over new life that has been brought into the world, so the disciples may rejoice when they see Jesus once again. But in the present case of John 16:24, the Evangelist links the fullness of joy to asking in prayer and receiving. These episodes should be read in light of each other both in content and consequence. The analogy of birth elucidates and even contrasts the conflicting emotions that are involved in bringing forth a human life. But there may be a sense in which some may feel anguish/sorrow as they await an answer to prayer. Although the Farewell Discourse states that the Father/Jesus will answer prayer, there is no explicit statement concerning how long one must wait for that answer to be granted. Jesus simply informs the disciples that if they pray in his name (14:13–14; 15:16), remain in him, and allow his words to remain in them (15:3–7), then he will do whatever is requested. Yet there is no direct mention of the length of the temporal duration that exists between one's initial asking and subsequent receiving in prayer.

While the Farewell Discourse provides no direct link to OT or other NT episodes of prayer, it is possible that the Evangelist's audience may have been familiar with specific examples where the answer to prayer was delayed. While examples may be multiple, a few select examples will suffice. The book of Habakkuk opens with the author's cry to God, namely (1:2 [LXX]), Ἕως τίνος, κύριε, κεκράξομαι καὶ οὐ μὴ εἰσακούσῃς; βοήσομαι πρὸς σὲ ἀδικούμενος καὶ οὐ σώσεις; In this instance, the petitioner suffers anguish as he waits on God's response. The reality of his waiting demonstrates that God's response to prayer cannot be precisely timed from human calculations. As indicated in Habakkuk 2:1–4, one must wait patiently and faithfully for God to act in his timing. The nature of such optimistic waiting is also highlighted in Psalm 26:14 (LXX) where the psalmist states, ὑπόμεινον τὸν κύριον· ἀνδρίζου, καὶ κραταιούσθω ἡ καρδία σου, καὶ ὑπόμεινον τὸν κύριον.

Additionally, the Gospel of Luke records the Parable of the Persistent Widow wherein a widow cried out for justice against her adversary. The context of the parable reveals that she was not answered in a timely fashion (18:2–5). As such, the parable likens this widow to the disciples, who must be persistent in their prayers to God. As the unjust judge answered the persistent widow, so God will hear and respond to those who pray and do not give up. Hence, Jesus' statement in 18:7–8, ὁ δὲ θεὸς οὐ μὴ ποιήσῃ τὴν ἐκδίκησιν τῶν ἐκλεκτῶν αὐτοῦ τῶν βοώντων αὐτῷ ἡμέρας καὶ νυκτός, καὶ μακροθυμεῖ ἐπ᾽ αὐτοῖς; λέγω ὑμῖν ὅτι ποιήσει τὴν ἐκδίκησιν αὐτῶν ἐν τάχει. πλὴν ὁ υἱὸς τοῦ ἀνθρώπου ἐλθὼν ἆρα εὑρήσει τὴν πίστιν ἐπὶ τῆς γῆς; Interestingly, the necessity of faith is highlighted in each of the examples above. As noted throughout the previous chapters of this analysis, faith in God/Jesus is the prerequisite to Johannine prayer.[47] Such faith not only involves believing that God is able to answer prayer but also involves trusting in God for the timing of God's response to prayer. Thus, although the topic of faith is not explicitly mentioned in 16:23–24, it is the basic requirement of prayer to God in general and waiting for an answer to prayer in particular. Hence, the call to "remain" in the vine, Jesus (15:4–7), becomes relevant again in the context of prayer, which will be discussed in the section below entitled "Implications for Prayer."

With the topic of faith in mind, it is necessary to briefly analyze the nature of time in the Fourth Gospel. Accordingly, Neyrey says that "'time' in this Gospel is not celebrated by clock or calendar."[48] Concerning the *past*, Neyrey points out that certain OT characters (Abraham, Jacob, etc.) are mentioned in the Fourth Gospel but only for points of comparison to Jesus, who is greater than all. Also, for the Evangelist the *present* refers to the day, days, or even months "once a process has begun." He writes, "'Present' describes what it means to 'have' eternal life in the here and now (3:15–16; 5:24; 6:40, 47, 54) or to 'abide' in the vine. We are told of an hour so imminent that it is 'now here' (4:23; 5:25; 12:23; 16:32). 'Now the Son of Man has been glorified' (13:31), but the present quality of this declaration will extend to the 'lifting up' of Jesus and his full return to the Father."[49]

In 16:32 the Evangelist makes a distinction between an hour that was coming and one that had already come (ἰδοὺ ἔρχεται ὥρα καὶ ἐλήλυθεν). This distinction brings the issue of narrative time[50] to the forefront of the

47. Faith is mentioned explicitly in 14:1, 12, and implicitly in 15:4–7. It may be argued that the requirement of faith is assumed in 14:13–14; 15:7, 16; 16:23–24.

48. Neyrey, *Gospel of John*, 272.

49. Neyrey, *Gospel of John*, 272.

50. Culpepper distinguishes between story time and narrative time in the following manner. He writes, "Story time is the passage of time during the ministry of Jesus as

discussion. O'Day summarizes the nature of the issue well. She writes, "At times Jesus speaks as if the crucifixion/resurrection/ascension were a past event (e.g., 16:33; 17:11), at times he speaks as if his departure from the world is imminent (e.g., 13:33; 14:3), and at still other times he speaks as if he were in the process of departing at that very moment (e.g., 13:31; 16:15, 28; 17:13)."[51] She draws attention to the work of Culpepper, who through critical categories developed by Genette "investigates temporal sequence, frequency, and duration as the constitutive elements of narrative time."[52] O'Day says, "Genette identifies two broad modes of temporal ordering in narrative: 'retrospection' or 'temporal analepsis,' in which the narrated sequence of events moves backward in time from the temporal locus of the main narrative line; and 'anticipation' or 'temporal prolepsis,' in which the narrated sequence of events jumps forward."[53] She also observes Culpepper's usage and application of Genette's temporal figures and cites a few examples he provides:

Analepsis

Internal: They came to John and said to him, "Rabbi, the one who was with you across the Jordan, to whom you testified, here he is baptizing and all are going to him" (3:26).

External: Isaiah said this because he saw his glory and spoke about him (12:41).

Prolepsis

Internal: Just as the Father knows me and I know the Father. And I lay down my life for the sheep (10:15).

External: They will put you out of the synagogues. Indeed an hour is coming when those who kill you will think that by doing so they are offering worship to God (16:2).[54]

Along with Culpepper, O'Day finds the above categories inadequate in light of mixed categories that appear in the Gospel.[55] Such inadequacy

---

John records it. . . . Narrative time, on the other hand, is determined by the order, duration, and frequency of events in the narrative" (*Anatomy of the Fourth Gospel*, 53–54).

51. O'Day, "I Have Overcome the World," 153.
52. Culpepper, *Anatomy of the Fourth Gospel*.
53. O'Day, "I Have Overcome the World," 154.
54. O'Day, "I Have Overcome the World," 154.
55. For example, Culpepper sees mixed prolepses as "progressive," in the sense that

is especially evident in light of the presence of what she calls "figures of anticipation." O'Day sees within the Fourth Gospel certain narrative shifts that move the reader from the present to a time of anticipation.[56] For example:

> 13:19, I tell you this now, before it occurs, so that when it does occur, you may believe that I am.
>
> 14:29, And now I have told you this before it occurs, so that when it does occur, you may believe.
>
> 15:11, I have said these things to you so that my joy be in you, and that your joy may be complete.
>
> 16:1, 4, I have said these things to you to keep you from stumbling (v. l). . . . But I have said these things to you so that when their hour comes you may remember that I told you about them (v. 4).
>
> 16:33, I have said this to you, so that in me you may have peace.[57]

O'Day notes further that "chapters 13–17 can be understood as the fourth evangelist's attempt to freeze the time of the hour in order to explain what the hour will mean before the events of the hour play themselves out in full. Once the events of the hour are put in motion, there will be no time for explanation."[58] Relevant to the present analysis is 16:32 where what is still future in terms of the narration of events in the Gospel is the present reality of the narrative. In this case the emphasis shifts from what is coming to what is a present reality. Indeed the hour is coming, but it is here. Similarly, the statement in 16:33 ("In the world you will have tribulation. But take heart; I have overcome the world") establishes a temporal trajectory that climaxes in victory. The anticipation builds with the future in mind, but the future has present implications. Thus the best approach is "not bringing the narrative present into the future, but bringing the future into the narrative present."[59] In other words, Jesus is saying that the present is the moment of victory. As such, the disciples will experience tribulation (present/future), but victory is certain (present/future). Therefore, as noted by O'Day this vantage point

"the conditions for their fulfillment are established by the end of the narrative, but their fruition lies beyond it" (e.g., John 14:16, 17, 18, 19, 20, 21) (*Anatomy of the Fourth Gospel*, 63).

56. O'Day, "I Have Overcome the World," 156.

57. Neyrey notes the presence of numerous predictions in chapter 16 (vv. 1–4, 5–6, 7–11, 12–15, 16, 20–21, 22, 25, 32), which, in his view, "provide the realistic background for the exhortation about 'abide,' 'love,' and 'hate' (*Gospel of John*, 265).

58. O'Day, "I Have Overcome the World," 159.

59. O'Day, "I Have Overcome the World," 162.

is not that of the pre-crucified/resurrected savior but the one of the risen Jesus. In fact, this is the voice heard throughout the farewell discourse. She points out accordingly, "It is only the Jesus who has made it through to the end of the story who can speak with certainty about the outcome. The fourth evangelist has not constructed his narrative according to the logic of story time, however. Before the story arrives at its conclusion, Jesus already speaks with confidence of its outcome."[60]

Moreover, the clause ἐν ἐμοὶ εἰρήνην ἔχητε stands in contrast to ἐν τῷ κόσμῳ θλῖψιν ἔχετε (16:33) and is conceptually reminiscent of chapter 15, where the call to abide in Jesus is emphasized. Taken together, chapters 15 and 16 elucidate how the disciples may experience peace in times of sorrow and tribulation. Undoubtedly, to be "in the world" meant tribulation for the disciples. Yet they could rest assured (in the present) that by virtue of his cross-death, resurrection, and ascension to the Father (Future), Jesus stands victorious over the world. In turn, they too stand victorious as they remain "in him" and bear fruit for him. Thus, the certainty of these future events offered assurance in the narrative present. Additionally, the disciples' victory is contingent upon the judgment that has been passed on to the ruler of this world (16:11) and the promise of the Spirit/Paraclete who will be "with" and "in" (14:17) them. In days to come they would not have Jesus' physical presence, but they would enjoy the abiding presence of the Paraclete who would guide them. They would no longer ask Jesus questions because the Spirit of Truth would lead the disciples in all truth.

Implications for Prayer

Thus, for Jesus' immediate disciples before his glorification, the present must be viewed in light of future promises. Or to state it another way, their present problems may be solved/viewed on the basis of guaranteed future outcomes that are existentially embraced by faith. In this reading, before the future occurs, Jesus speaks with confidence of its outcome for those who offer prayer in his name. In the midst of their sorrow and troubled hearts, the disciples' sentiment may be positively altered as they (presently) contemplate the privilege of asking the Father "in that day" (the future, John 16:23, 26). This model of time may be applied theoretically to the "little while" that the disciples had to wait, as well as to the interval that exists between their asking God and receiving from him in prayer. Although asking God and receiving from him are logically distinct activities that may be separated by minutes, days, etc., the promise of answered prayer provides a sense of

---

60. O'Day, "I Have Overcome the World," 162.

existential immediacy for the disciple who anticipates praying according to the Johannine model. Thus, the answer to prayer may be delayed in its temporal application, but such waiting may be perceived as "a little while" to the one who has faith in Jesus/the Father. Thus, one's joy is not diminished if prayer is not answered instantaneously per se since, for the Evangelist, future outcomes serve to encourage the disciples' present situation/problems. Hence, the outcome of prayer is guaranteed as long as requests are made in Jesus' name and in accordance with Jesus' words.

Yet for the disciples, the future became the present, and as time passed, the future became the actual past. Therefore, after Jesus' departure the disciples no longer needed to import the future promises into their present situation. Rather, they anticipated the present in light of what Jesus accomplished in the past. Thus, the Johannine community naturally read the Fourth Gospel as containing events that had already taken place. Jesus lived, died, and was resurrected. He had gone to prepare a place (14:2–3) and had appeared to his disciples so they could see him again (16:22). Further, the Spirit had been given since Jesus was glorified (7:39), and access to the Father was granted in Jesus' name (16:23–24). Therefore, the Johannine community contemplated the accomplished mission of Jesus as the basis for receiving whatever they requested in prayer. Once again, a delay may exist between the time of their asking God and receiving from God, but by praying according to the Evangelist's model and on the basis of Jesus' accomplishments, a believer was assured that he would eventually receive what he requested. Thus, as noted, a temporary delay in the outcome of prayer does equate to divine denial of one's request. Rather, as seen in both the OT and NT examples above, God responds to prayer in the timing he chooses. The believer's responsibility involves maintaining faith in Jesus and remaining in him as he awaits a divine response. On receiving, he will experience the fullness of joy spoken of in 16:24.

Plain Speech and Prayer: John 16:25–33

As the discourse progresses, the necessity of plain speech is brought into the center of the discussion. In contrast to John chapter 16, verse 25, where it is said that Jesus spoke about "these things" (Ταῦτα ἐν) in parables or "figures of speech" (ἐν παροιμίαις λελάληκα ὑμῖν), a time is coming when Jesus will speak plainly (ἀλλὰ παρρησίᾳ περὶ τοῦ πατρὸς ἀπαγγελῶ ὑμῖν.). In this verse, the term παρρησία is employed again, this time in reference to Jesus' statement concerning the hour (ὥρα) when he will no longer use "illustrative devices." But through what means will Jesus speak plainly about the Father?

While there is no direct mention to the Paraclete in verse 25, Bennema sees the Evangelist as "probably" referring to "the Paraclete's revelatory teaching function as described in 16:12–15." He says:

> Saving wisdom/truth is locked up in Jesus' revelatory teaching/words, and it will then be the task of the Paraclete to unlock, reveal and mediate this saving wisdom/truth to people. Thus, there seem to be two modes of mediation of revelation: (1) Jesus brings God's revelation, though veiled, in the form of παροιμία; (2) the Paraclete will, as Teacher/Revealer, uncover the meaning and significance of Jesus' revelatory teaching, i.e., the Paraclete will open up Jesus' teaching and mediate its saving truth/wisdom to people.[61]

Thus, once again, the Paraclete's work spirals (implicitly) into the discussion and serves as an aspect of the solution to Jesus' departure and the disciples' sorrowful predicament. At the Paraclete's coming, he will educate the disciples, lead/guide them in all truth, and mediate the presence of God. As these actions occur, the disciples are equipped to pray plainly according to the will of God. Hence, plain speech through the Paraclete begets plain (and bold/confident) speech in praying.

In John 16:26 the Evangelist reminds his audience that prayer must be offered not only on the basis of divine revelation but also through the medium of Jesus' name. Jesus says (v. 26), ἐν ἐκείνῃ τῇ ἡμέρᾳ ἐν τῷ ὀνόματί μου αἰτήσεσθε, καὶ οὐ λέγω ὑμῖν ὅτι ἐγὼ ἐρωτήσω τὸν πατέρα περὶ ὑμῶν. However, at face value it seems that while prayer in his name remains effectual, Jesus' role as intercessor is preluded. However, Brown notes, "Perhaps the real import of 16:26 is not to exclude intercession but to explain that in interceding Jesus will not be a *tertium quid* between the Father and His children. Rather, Jesus' necessary role in bringing men to the Father and the Father to men (14:6–11) will set up so intimate a relationship of love *in and through Jesus* that Jesus cannot be considered as intervening."[62] Accordingly, verse 26 echoes 14:6 where Jesus says, ἐγώ εἰμι ἡ ὁδὸς καὶ ἡ ἀλήθεια καὶ ἡ ζωή· οὐδεὶς ἔρχεται πρὸς τὸν πατέρα εἰ μὴ δι' ἐμοῦ. As the disciples believed in Jesus, he revealed the Father to them in their travels with him. Further, as the disciples abide in Jesus' love, they are, in turn, also brought into the Father's love (15:9–10). It is, therefore, on the basis of this relational model that Jesus says (16:27), αὐτὸς γὰρ ὁ πατὴρ φιλεῖ ὑμᾶς, ὅτι ὑμεῖς ἐμὲ πεφιλήκατε καὶ πεπιστεύκατε ὅτι ἐγὼ παρὰ [τοῦ] θεοῦ ἐξῆλθον. Finally, Jesus

---

61. Bennema, *Power of Saving Wisdom*, 230–31.
62. Brown, *Gospel According to John (XIII–XXI)*, 735.

will depart, but by virtue of their union with him the disciples will have access to the Father, who will in turn listen to their prayers.

In summary, Jesus spoke about the future in a manner that would inform, inspire, and encourage their prayer lives by bringing the future into the present. As such, the disciples' present outlook should be dramatically altered. While they would not have direct access to Jesus' physical presence, they would enjoy the privilege of approaching the Father in Jesus' name and making requests that would be granted. By offering prayer in Jesus' name, they were making requests in the name of a person who would not fail in his mission. And because Jesus succeeded, the disciples could have confidence that they would also succeed. Because Jesus overcame the world, the disciples would be fruitful in the world as they progressed into hostile circumstances. Finally, the corollary of this privilege and the hearing of the things spoken by Jesus would involve peace and assurance for the disciples as they encountered tribulation (hence, 16:33, ἐν τῷ κόσμῳ θλῖψιν ἔχετε· ἀλλὰ θαρσεῖτε, ἐγὼ νενίκηκα τὸν κόσμον).

CHAPTER 8

The Prayers of Jesus

Analysis of John 6:11; 11:41b–42;
12:27–28; 17; 19:28, 30

THE PREVIOUS CHAPTERS PROVIDED an exegetical analysis of John 14–16, with a special emphasis on the topic of prayer. In chapters 14–16, the topic of prayer spirals in and out of Jesus' farewell address to his disciples as he prepares them for his departure. Consequently, certain materials in these chapters focus on how the disciples are to address God in prayer in light of Jesus' absence. Yet a cursory reading of the Fourth Gospel reveals that Jesus also prayed to the Father on notable occasions.[1] As will be argued below, the Fourth Gospel contains five instances in which Jesus addresses the Father in prayer, namely, a thanksgiving prayer at the episode of the feeding of the five thousand in 6:11 (a prayer report in the narrative), a prayer of thanksgiving that precedes the raising of Lazarus in 11:41b–42, a prayer of boldness toward his own death in 12:27–28 (prayers attributed to Jesus), a prayer-report of completion in chapter 17, and finally, prayers from the cross just before his death in 19:28, 30. The aim of this chapter involves detecting how Jesus' communication with God in these passages further enhances one's understanding of prayer in the Fourth Gospel.

---

1. Of course, Jesus did not merely pray on special occasions, but rather he maintained a lifestyle of prayer and communion with the Father. But this chapter will focus on specific episodes of prayer and the corresponding contexts in which they occurred. These prayer events are notable not only because of the nature of what occurred but also because of what the Evangelist sought to convey by documenting each episode.

The Uniqueness of Jesus' Prayers in the Fourth Gospel

As indicated in chapter 2 of the present analysis, the Synoptic accounts provide a profile of Jesus' prayer life that demonstrates that he was the ideal man of prayer. As one examines the Synoptic accounts, the reader is left with the impression that Jesus maintained an extraordinary prayer life. For example: he prayed early in the morning (Mark 1:35), in desolate places (Luke 5:16), at night before appointing the twelve apostles (Luke 6:12), before giving thanks to God for sustenance (Mark 6:41; 8:6-7), and at Gethsemane to "Abba, Father," with full confidence in his Father (Mark 14:36). Thus, as a son, Jesus provided an extraordinary example of what prayer to the Father entails. However, the Fourth Gospel, while sharing some of the Synoptic assumptions and portrayals of Jesus, offers a unique perspective concerning Jesus and his life of prayer. Although there are only several accounts in the Fourth Gospel of Jesus praying, perhaps the most striking feature is the Evangelist's emphasis concerning Jesus' relationship with the Father. Lincoln points out:

> The Greek verb "to pray" (*proseuchomai*), which is used eleven times in Mark, fifteen times in Matthew, and nineteen times in Luke, does not occur at all in John. More significantly, however, what sets John's Gospel apart is that its portrayals of Jesus' prayer life are extensively affected by its understanding of Jesus' unique relationship as Son to the divine Father—and its teaching about prayer in the lives of Jesus' followers are also heavily colored by this relationship.[2]

This is not to say that Jesus' relationship with the Father is downplayed or precluded in the Synoptic accounts, but as will be seen below, the prayer episodes in the Fourth Gospel, collectively, paint a complementary but unique picture of how Jesus' relationship with the Father is fleshed out.[3] As such, the longest prayer, and perhaps the one that most exhaustively elucidates Jesus' relationship with the Father, is recorded in John 17 and will be examined in this chapter.

---

2. Lincoln, "God's Name, Jesus' Name," 155.

3. Turner says, "John's witness adds fresh perspective and new depth to themes already raised in Matthew, Mark, and Luke. We have observed that in the Synoptic accounts, Jesus' prayer brings to expression his filial obedience (focused in his addressing God as 'Abba' and in his willingness even to drink the terrible cup, if it be the Father's will), and through prayer 'all things' have been revealed *to* the Son who in turn reveals the Father (Luke 10:22)—especially the dawn of his End-time rule. John extends the horizons of our vision on each of these points" ("Prayer in the Gospels and Acts," 75).

A Prayer of Thanksgiving: John 6:11

The Setting

The episode reported in John 6:1-15 provides the context for Jesus' fourth sign, the feeding of the five thousand. As will be demonstrated below, Jesus' offering of thanksgiving to God prior to the feeding may be rightly viewed as a prayer to God that is issued before the miracle itself. Before examining the nature of Jesus' so-called prayer, it is necessary to offer some brief remarks about the setting and context of the episode reported in 6:1-15.

In the case of the feeding of the five thousand, the opening four verses provide the geographical context for the events that follow. In particular, Jesus traveled to a place on a mountain (v. 3, ἀνῆλθεν δὲ εἰς τὸ ὄρος Ἰησοῦς) on the other side of the Sea of Galilee, that is, on the east side of the Sea of Tiberias (v. 1). The reason for Jesus' movement is stated in verse 2, namely, ἠκολούθει δὲ αὐτῷ ὄχλος πολύς, ὅτι ἐθεώρουν τὰ σημεῖα ἃ ἐποίει ἐπὶ τῶν ἀσθενούντων. At the place on the mountain/hill (v. 3, ἀνῆλθεν δὲ εἰς τὸ ὄρος Ἰησοῦς) the reader is told that Jesus sat down with his disciples at the time of the Passover (v. 4). In verses 5-6 Jesus made an observation about the apparent crisis that had arisen in light of the quantity of people (v. 5, πολὺς ὄχλος) who were coming toward him and subsequently put Philip to the test by asking him, πόθεν ἀγοράσωμεν ἄρτους ἵνα φάγωσιν οὗτοι. Philip's response (v. 7, ἀπεκρίθη αὐτῷ [ὁ] Φίλιππος· διακοσίων δηναρίων ἄρτοι οὐκ ἀρκοῦσιν αὐτοῖς ἵνα ἕκαστος βραχύ [τι] λάβῃ.) indicates that not even eight months' of wages (NIV) could meet the need in the present crisis of feeding five thousand people (v. 10). Notwithstanding, Andrew identified a boy who possessed five barley loaves and two fish. Malina and Rohrbaugh say concerning the loaves, "Barley was used for making bread among lower-status people because it was much cheaper than wheat (and less nutritious)."[4] Thus, the Evangelist is highlighting the severity of the situation not only from a numerical perspective but also from a socio-economic standard. In short, in light of the large crowd of five thousand men, the only apparent solution was a cheaper form of nutritional substance, albeit in limited supply. As such, the concern would naturally center on the hunger of those gathered. Van der Watt remarks concerning hunger in the ancient world:

> In the writings of the Greek philosophers hunger is mainly described as something unpleasant. It is linked to pain, discomfort and even sickness, as Socrates remarks in Plato's *Philebus*: "Hunger, for example, is a dissolution and a pain" (par. 349)

---

4. Malina and Rohrbaugh, *Social-Science Commentary*, 126.

and "Thirst again is a destruction and a pain" (par. 351). In Plato's *Rep.* III.101 we read: "The saddest of fates is to die and meet destiny from hunger?" Hunger is indeed a "killer," both of animals and of people and is obviously something which was feared. Epictetus maintains that a person who is not suffering from thirst and hunger is indeed fortunate. Even in the Old Testament hunger and thirst are reckoned as serious forms of lack and in the New Testament they count among the terrors of the end time.[5]

Most familiar to a Jewish audience is the episode reported in Exodus 16 where it is implied that the Israelites grumbled due to their hunger, generally, but even more, against the leadership of Aaron and Moses in particular. For example:

καὶ εἶπαν πρὸς αὐτοὺς οἱ υἱοὶ Ἰσραήλ Ὄφελον ἀπεθάνομεν πληγέντες ὑπὸ Κυρίου ἐν γῇ Αἰγύπτῳ, ὅταν ἐκαθίσαμεν ἐπὶ τῶν λεβήτων τῶν κρεῶν καὶ ἠσθίομεν ἄρτους εἰς πλησμονήν· ὅτι ἐξηγάγετε ἡμᾶς εἰς τὴν ἔρημον ταύτην, ἀποκτεῖναι πᾶσαν τὴν συναγωγὴν ταύτην ἐν λιμῷ. (16:3 [LXX])

Accordingly, John 6:31 indicates that the Jews issued (implicit) credit to God (via Moses) for meeting the needs of their forefathers.[6] Notwithstanding, in the present case of John 6:11–12, Jesus rises to the occasion in order to meet the needs of his disciples and the crowd who came to him. By doing so, Jesus fulfilled the role of their provider and savior,[7] thereby providing qualification for his statement in 6:32–35.

Jesus' Prayer

In John chapter 6, verse 10 the Evangelist notes that Jesus had the men sit down in an area with much grass (χόρτος πολὺς ἐν τῷ τόπῳ). Köstenberger writes, "The feeding of the multitude ... conveys the image of presiding as a host over an abundant meal, a theme found already in the prophets (e.g., Isa

---

5. Van der Watt, *Family of the King*, 171–72.

6. See Exod 16:11–36; Ps 78:23–24; 105:40. Newman and Nida remark, "The Scripture quotation, 'He gave them bread from heaven to eat' is interpreted by the crowd to mean that Moses gave them bread, and therefore the people desire a miracle greater than the one Moses performed" (*Handbook on the Gospel of John*, 196).

7. Smith sees the Bread of Life Discourse as being "imbued with meal symbolism, primarily from the messianic banquet tradition" (*From Symposium to Eucharist*, 274). For an overview of the messianic banquet, see Smith, *From Symposium to Eucharist*, 167–71.

25:6)."[8] Keener notes, "That the multitude must 'recline' (6:10) may suggest an allusion to the Passover (6:4). For normal meals people sat on chairs, but they reclined at banquets and festivals in accordance with the Greek custom probably adopted during the Hellenistic period."[9] As such, Jesus' leadership is consistent with the role of a host at a Greco-Roman banquet. Smith remarks, "The host would generally be the same one in charge of the guest list, the menu, and the provision of the place of the banquet. In addition, the host would designate the positions that the guests would occupy at the table."[10] In this setting, then, Jesus, as a good host, offers thanksgiving for the food. The episode reports in 6:11:

ἔλαβεν οὖν τοὺς ἄρτους ὁ Ἰησοῦς καὶ εὐχαριστήσας διέδωκεν τοῖς ἀνακειμένοις ὁμοίως καὶ ἐκ τῶν ὀψαρίων ὅσον ἤθελον.[11]

Louw and Nida state concerning this term:

> Thanks is often expressed in highly idiomatic ways. For example, in some languages one says thank you by saying "may God pay you." Such a phrase may be so standardized as to even be used in expressing thankfulness to God himself. In other instances, thankfulness may be expressed as "you have made my heart warm."[12]

Neyrey is right to point out that "we must be extra sensitive to the meanings of 'thanksgiving' in Greek, for they differ considerably from our modern understandings of this word. Better to think of this as 'showing appreciation for' or 'praising' or 'telling of God's wondrous deeds.'"[13] In the case of John 6:11, the term εὐχαριστήσας is issued in the context of communication to God that verbally expresses gratitude for God's provision in the immediate crisis, namely, the multiplication[14] of the loaves and fish. The nature of Jesus' address elucidates his dependence on God and his willingness to give him credit for the wondrous deed that was performed. Bruce notes, "The verb rendered 'gave thanks' in verse 11 is *eucharisteō*, from which we derive the term Eucharist ('thanksgiving'), commonly used of the Holy Communion. But this in itself would not require a eucharistic significance

---

8. Köstenberger, *Encountering John*, 100.
9. Keener, *Gospel of John*, 666.
10. Smith, *From Symposium to Eucharist*, 33.
11. Emphasis added.
12. Louw and Nida, *Greek-English Lexicon*, 428.
13. Neyrey, *Give God the Glory*, 26.
14. This is implied, not asserted (Bruce, *Gospel and Epistles of John*, 145).

for the feeding; the verb is perfectly common and untechnical in Greek."[15] Carson says also, "If John were trying to project Eucharistic symbolism, he missed many good opportunities; he does not mention the breaking of bread, or the distribution of the pieces (unlike Mark). What John stresses, instead, is the lavishness of the supply."[16]

If the significance of the events of 6:11 is not seen in the context of the Eucharist, then where is it seen? Some have suggested that in order to appreciate the significance of Jesus' thanksgiving, one must look to the Jewish background of his prayer. When this background is considered, it would not be surprising to learn that Jesus prayed much like other Jews of his day, most particularly, as they prayed before meals. Carson points out, "If Jesus used the common form of Jewish thanksgiving, he said something like this: 'Blessed art thou, O Lord our God, King of the Universe, who bringest forth bread from the earth.'"[17] In this prayer, God is simply acknowledged as the one responsible for granting sustenance to his people.

As might be expected, there is some disagreement concerning the nature of the content that Jesus may have prayed when he gave thanks. Hendriksen says, "It is often said that Jesus must have used a customary table-prayer. This is barely possible. . . . It must be borne in mind in this connection that our Lord's address delivered to the multitudes were always characterized by freshness and originality—he never spoke like the scribes, merely copying the words of former rabbis. Is it probable, then that when he addressed his Father in heaven he borrowed a formula prayer?"[18] Hunter outlines the assertions of Barrett and Lenski, who believe that Jesus did nothing unusual or out of the ordinary from the Jewish meal. On the other hand, he notes the conclusions of some scholars who assert that Jesus employed a free approximation (of the Lord's Prayer) of the benedictions (Beyer) or gave Berakot 6.1, a form of its own (Jeremias).[19] Of course, it is impossible to be certain, but Hunter is probably right to conclude, "The view that he [Jesus] offered a more or less 'traditional' Jewish blessing seems less likely than the idea that Jesus probably offered a characteristically unique form of thanksgiving which may have taken account of his special relationship to the Father and the special circumstances which attached to the situation of the feeding miracle." With these conclusions in mind, the summary below

---

15. Bruce, *Gospel and Epistles of John*, 145.
16. Carson, *Gospel According to John*, 270.
17. Carson, *Gospel According to John*, 270.
18. Hendriksen, *Exposition of the Gospel According to John*, 222.
19. Hunter, "Prayers of Jesus," 100.

will seek to draw out and bring together the important implications for the topic of prayer in the Fourth Gospel in general and 6:11 in particular.

If Jesus is the good host of a banquet-like gathering based on the amount of food that was produced/distributed (John 6:12–13), and if Jesus' thanksgiving is directed to the Father, and if the Father responds to Jesus by performing his works through Jesus, then it is possible that the Evangelist sought to present the feeding of the multitude as a banquet-like gathering to honor the Father-Son relationship. In this relational model, Jesus is the one through whom thanksgiving is offered, and is the one through whom the miracle is performed. Thus, as indicated by Jesus, the works he performs are the works of the Father (5:19, 36; 14:10–11). Therefore, Jesus' offering of thanksgiving to the Father for the miracle is, in other words, an offering of thanksgiving to the Father who hears him and performs works/signs through him. Further, upon belief in Jesus, disciples enter into this union, pray in light of this union, and thereby become the vehicles through which the works of God are performed. Thus, it is possible that the Evangelist presents Jesus as one who, by honoring the Father in thanksgiving to him, provides a model of prayer that is formed and issued on the basis of his union with the Father. Therefore, as indicated in previous chapters of this analysis and as seen above, in light of Jesus' coming, prayer is no longer offered to the Father without consideration of the Son. Rather, the Son is the one through whom prayers are offered and is the one who does whatever is requested (thus anticipating, 14:13–14; 15:7, 16; 16:23–24).

Moreover, one may ask, "Why did Jesus pray?" Whether Jesus chose to offer a short, traditional Jewish prayer or a modified benedictory prayer, the fact remains that the Evangelist (or redactor) chose to provide limited textual data. Thus, it is likely the Evangelist intends for his audience to discover the significance of Jesus' prayer primarily, but not exclusively, within the immediate context of the Fourth Gospel. As indicated, by issuing a prayer of thanksgiving, Jesus revealed the intimate/dependent nature of his relationship with the Father.[20] Viewed within the family dynamic, prayer in the form of thanksgiving, then, is simply the outworking of a heart of gratitude for what God is willing and able to do. And his message to the Father is in the form of thanksgiving that presupposes a "subordinate/superior" relationship (14:28). Although the Father and Son are one (10:30), Jesus submits himself to the Father's will (6:38) and acts for the Father's glory (17:4). In short, by thanking God, Jesus honors his Father. In return, the Father honors the Son by performing the miracle through his hands.

---

20. Michaels notes, "'Giving thanks' shows Jesus' dependence on the Father, and consequently, the five thousand were fed" (*Gospel of John*, 349).

Finally, one might ask: Could the miracle have occurred without the prayer? Based on the testimony of the Fourth Gospel, there is nothing to suggest that prayers of thanksgiving are necessary for a miracle/sign to occur. In fact, aside from 6:11 and 11:41–42, no other miracle/sign reported in the Fourth Gospel is preceded or followed by prayer. Accordingly, there is nothing from 6:1–15 to suggest that the Evangelist intends for his audience to expect miracles to occur when they give thanks to God. Rather, for Jesus and the believer, the prayer of thanksgiving is a sign of his dependence on God as the source of every form of provision. As the believer issues prayers in Jesus' name and asks according to Jesus' words, he may have confidence before God. And confidence before God is the impetus for issuing thanksgiving to God, since the one praying is assured of his relational status and that his requests will be granted.

A Prayer for Lazarus: John 11:41b–42

The Setting

The events surrounding and leading up to Jesus' seventh sign began with Mary and Martha reporting to Jesus that their brother Lazarus, the one Jesus loved (κύριε, ἴδε ὃν φιλεῖς ἀσθενεῖ), was ill (John 11:3). Whether he was ill or dead at the time Jesus received the message is debated. One reconstruction of this report views Lazarus as dying after his sisters sent the message.[21] But Carson is right to argue that Lazarus was still alive when Jesus heard the news of his illness.[22] In short, following Carson, there seems to be congruence between what the sisters reported (e.g., Lazarus was ill and not dead) and the way Jesus perceived the situation (e.g., Lazarus was ill and not dead). Ironically, it is said that on hearing the news about Lazarus, Jesus remained where he was for two more days (v. 5). Lazarus's sure death set the context for prayer and the subsequent miracle of resurrection.

As δόξα relates to prayer, it is said in John 14:13–14 that Jesus will do whatever is asked in his name. In particular, verse 13 says, καὶ ὅ τι ἂν αἰτήσητε ἐν τῷ ὀνόματί μου τοῦτο ποιήσω, ἵνα δοξασθῇ ὁ πατὴρ ἐν τῷ υἱῷ. This statement is congruent with 11:4, where the sickness itself will eventuate a revelation of God's glory. The sisters' statement to Jesus in verse 3 is not prayer in the formal sense of the term. Nor do they address Jesus by name. But they do verbally communicate with Jesus believing that he is the one who has the ability to (at the very least) sympathize with them in

---

21. Keener, *Gospel of John*, 839; Brown, *Gospel According to John (I–XII)*, 431.
22. Carson, *Gospel According to John*, 407.

their distress over Lazarus. And Martha's statements in 11:22 indicate they believed that Jesus could do even more. Keener says:

> When Martha indicates that she trusts that whatever he asks of God, God will give him (11:22), she is probably making an implied, oblique request as in 11:3 (cf. 2:3, 5). Her expression of confidence in Jesus—that God would grant whatever he asked (11:22; cf. 3:35; 13:3)—thus would illustrate the sort of prayer God might hear in Jesus' name (16:24). While this could be a request for comfort, it is more likely a request that Jesus raise her brother.[23]

Yet Jesus' immediate response to the sisters' initial statement of distress (v. 3) was not likely what they had in mind. As noted, Jesus remained behind for two days and then traveled to Lazarus's tomb. While it may be argued that God's self-revelation could have been manifested through the healing of a sickness/illness, this episode indicates that Jesus chose to reveal himself in the dire situation of death. Thus, he did not respond to the crisis in the sisters' timing or in earthly terms, but at the time and by the manner he chose to display God's glory. Therefore, this episode may be viewed as a retrospective paradigm of Jesus' initiative to hear requests and his intention to grant whatever is requested, albeit with certain conditions in mind. As such, Jesus' statement concerning prayer in 14:13–14 may be read and understood through the events that occurred in chapter 11. Jesus does not grant every request made in his name in the manner humans always expect; rather he responds to prayer in the manner and timing he chooses. Moreover, the unfolding of this narrative reveals that the sisters' request encouraged Jesus' gradual movement toward Lazarus. As such, both the sisters' requests and Jesus' prayer for Lazarus were part and parcel of the mission of God that culminated in Jesus' cross-death.

Thus, requests made for Lazarus were informative and indicative of a perspective that viewed Jesus in terms of his true identity and nature (particularly in light of Martha's statement in verses 22 and 27). Culpepper says concerning Martha's statement in verse 21 (κύριε, εἰ ἦς ὧδε οὐκ ἂν ἀπέθανεν ὁ ἀδελφός μου), "Martha opens the conversation, not with a greeting, but with words that express both faith and implied criticism."[24] In her distress, Martha insists that Lazarus would not have died if Jesus had been present. Mary issues the same response in verse 32. Yet Martha states in verse 22, [ἀλλὰ] καὶ νῦν οἶδα ὅτι ὅσα ἂν αἰτήσῃ τὸν θεὸν δώσει σοι ὁ θεός. This statement indicates that Martha's confidence in Jesus is based on his relationship

---

23. Keener, *Gospel of John*, 844.
24. Culpepper, *Gospel and Letters of John*, 187.

with God (9:31, for God does not listen to sinners). The implication of her statement indicates a degree of intimacy and oneness between Jesus and the Father. The Father grants authority to the Son because the Son is submitted to the Father.

According to Jesus, Lazarus will rise again (v. 23). Yet Martha's response in verse 24 (οἶδα ὅτι ἀναστήσεται ἐν τῇ ἀναστάσει ἐν τῇ ἐσχάτῃ ἡμέρᾳ) indicates that she did not seem to understand the immediate efficacy of Jesus' ability. Jesus did not disagree with her assertion but instead issued a statement that would be applied in the events that followed, namely, ἐγώ εἰμι ἡ ἀνάστασις καὶ ἡ ζωή· ὁ πιστεύων εἰς ἐμὲ κἂν ἀποθάνῃ ζήσεται, καὶ πᾶς ὁ ζῶν καὶ πιστεύων εἰς ἐμὲ οὐ μὴ ἀποθάνῃ εἰς τὸν αἰῶνα (vv. 25–26). This statement was followed by the question, πιστεύεις τοῦτο (v. 26). Martha responded in the affirmative. Hence Martha's statement in 11:27, ναὶ κύριε, ἐγὼ πεπίστευκα ὅτι σὺ εἶ ὁ χριστὸς ὁ υἱὸς τοῦ θεοῦ ὁ εἰς τὸν κόσμον ἐρχόμενος. Though her confession was firm and genuine,[25] it is too much to insist that Martha understood the full implications of the immediate ability of the Christ in whom she professed faith (so the phrase, ἀναστήσεται ὁ ἀδελφός σου). Nonetheless, in the event that followed, Jesus demonstrated his commitment to fulfill the mission of God, and in doing so revealed to Martha (and the onlookers) both his nature and ability as the one who is the resurrection and the life.

While a discussion concerning divine passibility and impassibility is beyond the scope of this book, it is important to note Jesus' emotional response in 11:33 and 35. Jesus states in verse 11, Λάζαρος ὁ φίλος ἡμῶν κεκοίμηται· ἀλλὰ πορεύομαι ἵνα ἐξυπνίσω αὐτόν. Although the disciples interpreted Jesus' words to mean that Lazarus had fallen asleep for temporary rest (vv. 11–12), Jesus confirmed that Lazarus had indeed died (v. 14). And by the time Jesus arrived, the Evangelist notes that Lazarus had been in the tomb four days (v. 39). At this point, there was no doubt that Lazarus was dead indeed. On hearing the weeping of Mary and the Jews (v. 33), the Evangelist notes that Jesus "was deeply moved in his spirit and greatly troubled" (ESV). Accordingly, in 11:35 Jesus demonstrates his character as one who suffered *with* humanity (at Lazarus's tomb) before he suffered *for* humanity (on the cross). Moreover, Jesus' display of emotional sentiment toward the situation is followed directly by his movement toward the tomb and his prayer to the Father. As such, Jesus was not satisfied to merely show emotion toward the situation, but his desire was to respond with a prayer that would drastically change the situation.

---

25. Bruce says, "The perfect tense (*pepisteuka*) differs but little in force from the present (*pisteuo*): 'I have come to believe,' she means, 'and now, as a settled attitude of soul, I believe'" (*Gospel and Epistles of John*, 245).

Jesus' Prayer

Jesus' display of emotion gave way to a brief dialogue with Martha concerning the removal of the stone at the mouth of the cave (John 11:38–40) and the prayer of thanksgiving offered to the Father. Martha's concern about the odor from the cave notwithstanding, Jesus asked the question, οὐκ εἶπόν σοι ὅτι ἐὰν πιστεύσῃς ὄψῃ τὴν δόξαν τοῦ θεοῦ; After removing the stone, Jesus lifted up his eyes and said (vv. 41b–42):

πάτερ, εὐχαριστῶ σοι ὅτι ἤκουσάς μου.
ἐγὼ δὲ ᾔδειν ὅτι πάντοτέ μου ἀκούεις,
    ἀλλὰ διὰ τὸν ὄχλον τὸν περιεστῶτα εἶπον,
ἵνα πιστεύσωσιν ὅτι σύ με ἀπέστειλας.

Most notable is Jesus' upward gaze (likely toward heaven, 17:1) as he addressed the Father in a prayer of thanksgiving (εὐχαριστῶ). What is the significance of this posture? An analysis of Jewish/Hebrew tradition reveals the practice of a similar posture when praying. Kneeling and standing are common postures of OT prayer that also involve the lifting of one's hands toward heaven (2 Chr 6:12). The Tefillah was recited while facing toward the land of Israel, or more specifically, toward the temple. The implication is that God, who resides in heaven, will hear the prayers of his people on the earth and respond accordingly. Further, Greco-Roman prayer was often issued in a standing posture with arms extended toward the deity being addressed. Burkert says, "Kneeling down to pray is unusual. The gesture of entreaty is outstretched arms. To invoke the heavenly gods, both hands are raised to the sky with upturned palms; to call on the gods of the sea, the arms are extended to the sea."[26]

With these background examples in mind, the Evangelist's inclusion of Jesus' gaze toward heaven (and his prayer that follows) serves to highlight his union with the Father, his dependence on the Father, and his thanksgiving (εὐχαριστῶ) concerning the corollary of his union with the Father in the form of the miracle that would follow his command in verse 43 (Λάζαρε, δεῦρο ἔξω). In this reading, the implication involves the narrative of heaven (above) being applied on earth (below) in the miracle that transpires. Bryant remarks accordingly:

> Based on the evidence found in the Gospels (Matt 14:19; Mark 6:41; Luke 9:16; John 17:1a) it seems to have been a typical gesture performed by Jesus prior to prayer. Nevertheless, it most likely simply indicates an attempt to focus one's attention upon

---

26. Burkert, *Greek Religion*, 75.

God where he resides. Support for this understanding of the action may be found in the Jewish practice of praying toward Jerusalem (e.g., 1 Kgs 8:44; Dan 6:10). In other words, in the same way that Jews who sought God in prayer directed their attention toward the place traditionally associated with his presence (Jerusalem), so does Jesus in 11:41a look upward that he might direct his attention to another place traditionally associated with God's presence (heaven).[27]

Jesus' posture of confidence centers on being united to the Father and thus heard by the Father in heaven. The verb ἀκούεις (hear) is used approximately fifty-eight times in the Fourth Gospel. It is employed in the context of those who fail to hear (9:31; 12:29), but it is also seen in the context of the Father/Son relationship. In John 5:30 it is said that Jesus does nothing on his own but judges as he hears; in 8:40, which speaks of Jesus hearing truth from the Father; and 15:15, where it is said that Jesus has made known all that he has heard from the Father. Each of these examples demonstrates Jesus' unity with and dependence on the Father. In this relationship, knowledge is exchanged and God's will is elucidated and executed. With the Father/Son union in mind, prayer is not a mere formality but rather a top priority in order for Jesus to maintain a life of revelation and power.

The culmination of Jesus' prayer occurs when Jesus cried out in a loud voice, Λάζαρε, δεῦρο ἔξω (v. 43). Kok says concerning Jesus' statement, "John makes it abundantly clear that the words of Jesus create life (cf. John 6:68, ῥήματα ζωῆς αἰωνίου ἔχεις; cf. 8:51), but that the words of Jesus are actually and in effect, the words of the Father (cf. 14:10). In the background, one hears the echo of Jesus' words in John 5:19–21:

> Ἀπεκρίνατο οὖν ὁ Ἰησοῦς καὶ ἔλεγεν αὐτοῖς· ἀμὴν λέγω ὑμῖν, οὐ δύναται ὁ υἱὸς ποιεῖν ἀφ' ἑαυτοῦ οὐδὲν ἐὰν μή τι βλέπῃ τὸν πατέρα ποιοῦντα· ἃ γὰρ ἂν ἐκεῖνος ποιῇ, ταῦτα καὶ ὁ υἱὸς ὁμοίως ποιεῖ. ὁ γὰρ πατὴρ φιλεῖ τὸν υἱὸν καὶ πάντα δείκνυσιν αὐτῷ ἃ αὐτὸς ποιεῖ, καὶ μείζονα τούτων δείξει αὐτῷ ἔργα, ἵνα ὑμεῖς θαυμάζητε. ὥσπερ γὰρ ὁ πατὴρ ἐγείρει τοὺς νεκροὺς καὶ ζῳοποιεῖ, οὕτως καὶ ὁ υἱὸς οὓς θέλει ζῳοποιεῖ."[28]

With this passage in mind, it is plausible to suggest that Jesus' words in 11:43 are indicative of the authority he shared with the Father and elucidate the efficacy of speaking/praying in a manner that is consistent with his Father's will. In this model, Jesus vocalizes the Father's will, yet speaks as God's agent who possesses the authority to grant life to whomever he chooses.

27. Bryant, "Examination of Prayer," 25.
28. Kok, *New Perspectives on Healing*, 238.

> ### Excursus: Healing through Prayer?
>
> A question that thematically relates to the raising of Lazarus was issued in the second chapter of this analysis, namely, "The Amidah contains prayers that center on reviving the dead, healing the sick, and freeing the captives. How does this genre of prayer relate to prayer in the Fourth Gospel? According to the Fourth Gospel, what specific "result(s)" may one seek to obtain through prayer?" The second prayer of the Amidah (the *Gevurot*) states:
>
>> *You sustain the living* with loving kindness,
>>
>> *Revive the dead* in great compassion,
>>
>> *Support* the falling,
>>
>> *Heal* the sick,
>>
>> *Free* the captives,
>>
>> And keep faith with those who sleep in the dust.
>>
>> Who is like You,
>>
>> *Master* of mighty deeds,
>>
>> And who resembles you, King,
>>
>> *You who kill and bring back to life.*
>>
>> And make salvation flourish?[29]
>
> In John 11:41–44, one sees a partial fulfillment of the Amidah as Lazarus is healed, revived, freed from the tomb, and brought back to life by the agency of the voice of the Son of God. As such, this episode clearly indicates that Jesus is ἡ ἀνάστασις καὶ ἡ ζωή (11:25) who, by a word, can reverse the effects of death. Kok says:
>
>> The restoration of Lazarus serves as the great undisputable sign in the Gospel that Jesus can give life, especially against the background that Lazarus had already been dead for more than three days and had started to decay.... The question then arises whether Jesus would be able to create life if and when he lost his own. When Jesus dies and ultimately raises from the dead, the eschatological era of the Spirit arrives and new existential possibilities are created (cf. 7:37–39). The resurrection is the culminating sign in John, which proves that Jesus truly is the sent Son of God and that he has the ability to grant life.[30]

---

29. Emphasis added.
30. Kok, *New Perspectives on Healing*, 344.

> Accordingly, one may view Jesus' death and resurrection as the events that not only ushered forth the era of the Spirit but also eventuated the era in which the disciples were granted the privilege of praying in Jesus' name and performing "greater works" for the Father's glory (14:2, 12–14). As noted in chapter 5 of this analysis, prayer that is issued in Jesus' name involves offering requests and petitions that center on the advancement of God's mission in the earth. Following Kok, part and parcel of this mission involves the salvation of the world (3:16) through healing of spiritual death and blindness (5:24; 9:41; 12:40).[31] In this paradigm the healing of the sick[32] and the raising of the dead are signs that point to the fullness of eschatological life that is promised to all who believe in Jesus.
>
> Finally, while the Fourth Gospel does not provide explicit license for the disciples to pray for the sick to be healed or for the dead to be raised, the nature of the document does not preclude the possibility since such signs/miracles may consequently provoke others to faith in Jesus (11:42, 45; 20:30–31). If physical healing points to the restoration of spiritual life in the Fourth Gospel, why should it cease having that quality in the lives of praying disciples in the first-century community and beyond? In this model, prayer for the restoration of the sick fits well within the paradigm of the Johannine concept of "greater works" (14:12) as long as one maintains that physical restoration is an eschatological preview of spiritual healing and eternal life. Therefore, based on a careful reading of John 11 and 14, it seems plausible to suggest that believers may offer prayer to the Father in Jesus' name that aims at the reversal of biological diseases and (ultimately) at the spiritual restoration of the world. Yet, one must remember that while the disciples maintain the privilege of praying, the Son reserves the prerogative to give life (both physical and spiritual) to whomever he chooses (5:21).

On hearing the prayer and seeing the miracle, there was no question concerning "the source of the power."[33] The dynamic of Jesus' prayer, the Father's response, and the belief of the audience is illustrated/summarized below.

31. Kok, *New Perspectives on Healing*, 268–69.

32. For a discussion on prayers of forgiveness and healing, see Koenig, *Rediscovering New Testament Prayer*, 95–113.

33. Brown, *Gospel According to John (XIII–XXI)*, 437.

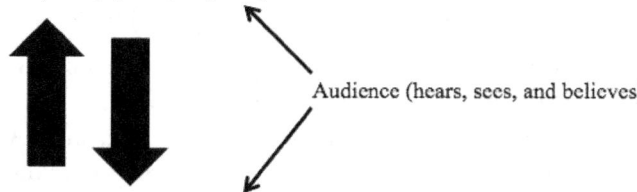

Jesus promised in 11:4, αὕτη ἡ ἀσθένεια οὐκ ἔστιν πρὸς θάνατον ἀλλ' ὑπὲρ τῆς δόξης τοῦ θεοῦ, ἵνα δοξασθῇ ὁ υἱὸς τοῦ θεοῦ δι' αὐτῆς. In 11:43-44 Jesus' words were fulfilled. By seeing Lazarus rise from death, the onlookers saw the τὴν δόξαν τοῦ θεοῦ (v. 40). If δόξα is that which conveys a sense of importance to God, if it involves the splendor and/or the weightiness of his revelation, then τὴν δόξαν τοῦ θεοῦ is to be understood as that which flows forth freely from the Father through the Son in the resurrection of Lazarus. In other words, the glory of God is seen in the Son thanking the Father, the Father hearing the Son, and Lazarus responding to the voice of Jesus. This sign not only displayed the glory of God but also provoked believers to a deeper level of faith. As indicated in 11:45, many Jews who had not previously believed came to faith in Jesus (see also 12:11, 18). In retrospect, such individuals would naturally interpret Jesus' thanksgiving to the Father, his command to Lazarus, and the corresponding "result" as τὴν δόξαν τοῦ θεοῦ. As with each sign that Jesus performed, the raising of Lazarus at Jesus' command added a sense of splendor, weightiness, and/or importance to Jesus and the Father, whom he acknowledged.

As indicated above, Jesus' prayer to the Father not only was indicative of the type of relationship he maintained with the Father but also was instructive/didactic, that is, it was designed to teach his audience a valuable lesson concerning how this relationship can be mirrored in their own prayerful experience. Crump writes:

> These earlier statements [both in John 11:41-42 and Martha's statement, "Lord ... I know that even now God will give you whatever you ask" (11:21-22 [NIV])] establish the proper context for Jesus's later promise concerning prayer. The Farewell Discourse elaborates how the impregnable efficacy of Jesus' prayer life will eventually be transferred to his followers. The Father will receive our prayers in the same fashion as he received

the Son's, promising to advance his mission through those who learn to live as Jesus lived and to pray as Jesus prayed.[34]

With this in mind, the following points may be offered: First, Jesus' response to the crisis of Lazarus's death demonstrates his own humanity and his corresponding emotional relatability with humanity. As Nehemiah wept over the state of Jerusalem (1:4), so Jesus wept over the state of his friend Lazarus, who died. Yet, the narrative (of John chapter 11) moves the reader from Jesus' weeping toward his upward gaze as he gives thanks to the Father for hearing him. A juxtaposition of these events demonstrates the inevitability of sorrow in the face of death on one hand, and the necessity of offering prayer of thanksgiving to the God who hears on the other. Such thanksgiving is indicative of a relationship defined by friendship and faithfulness (John 15:4-7, 9-15) as well as open communication and divine accessibility (14:13-14; 15:7, 16; 16:23-24). Moreover, Jesus' display of emotional sentiment toward the situation is followed directly by his movement toward the tomb and his prayer to the Father. Thus, Jesus was not satisfied to merely show emotion about the situation, but his desire was to respond to it with a prayer that would drastically change the situation. Such sentiment and action may also be present in believers who seek to imitate Jesus (*mimesis*) and do the works that he did (14:12; 15:7-8).

Second, as Jesus looked upward and prayed, the believer may also pray to God by directing his gaze toward the place where God dwells. One's upward gaze toward heaven symbolically demonstrates his dependence on God, his longing to be heard in prayer, and his desire for the transcendental narrative of heaven to become actualized on the earth. By thanking God, Jesus gave honor to God, thereby publicly affirming his union with and dependence on God. The same occurs when believers, who offer prayer in Jesus' name, offer thanksgiving to God. As such, disciples may offer thanksgiving to God in the name of Jesus, that is, in the name that yields greater works that bring honor/glory to God.

But it must be noted that, in light of Jesus' coming, one's actual posture in prayer is less important than maintaining relational proximity by faith (14:1, 12; 15:4-7) in Jesus. As one comes to faith, the disciple becomes the dwelling place (temple) of the Spirit, who mediates the presence of the Father and Son (14:17, 23). And since God is near, the disciple may be assured that he will indeed hear his prayers. As the Father hears Jesus, so the Father will also hear those who pray to him in Jesus' name. Therefore, the disciples' prayer should be issued with the same sense of expectation and confidence,

---

34. Crump, *Knocking on Heaven's Door*, 161-62.

provided they walk in communion with and obedience[35] to God. Van der Watt says:

> In God's family, communication *inter alia* takes place in the form of prayer, based on the open communication within which believers have confidence to approach their Father. Because *Jesus* is sure that the Father always hears his prayers (11:22, 41–42), he communicates freely with his Father (11:41–42; 14:16; 16:26; 17:1–26). Like Jesus the *disciples* should also pray with confidence (14:13–14; 15:7, 16; 16:23–26; 1 John 3:21–22; 5:14) in the name of, and in obedience to Jesus (14:13–14; 15:16; 16:23–27; 1 John 3:22). Through prayer believers may ask for whatever they need in order to fulfil their duty and remain true to the wishes of their Father (15:16–17; 1 John 5:14–15).[36]

And finally, the "result" of the glory of God is displayed in Jesus' thanksgiving to the Father, in the Father hearing Jesus' prayer(s), and in Lazarus's resurrection. As believers remain in union with the Father and the Son (15:4–7), they may confidently offer prayers in the name of Jesus (14:13–14; 15:16; 16:23–24) and have their prayers answered. As this occurs, they too will also see the glory of God. In this model, prayer to God and God's response to prayer ensure that the Father is glorified in the Son (14:13). In the final analysis, whatever one asks God (14:13) does not merely refer to anything without qualification but to anything in association with the revealed mission of God. As Jesus acted, so the disciples will act. As Jesus brought glory to the Father, so the disciples may also bring glory to him as they pray.

A Prayer for the Father's Glory: John 12:27–28

The Setting

The event of Jesus' prayer in John 12:27–28 is directly preceded by the wish of certain Greeks who desired to see Jesus (vv. 20–22). In verse 23 Jesus speaks of the impending hour of his glorification in agricultural terms. As such, he implicitly describes his death in light of a grain of wheat that falls

---

35. Keener notes the importance of Jesus stating that the Father heard him. He says that in doing this "Jesus iterates his dependence on the Father, a frequent Johannine theme; the Father 'always' heard him because of his perfect obedience (8:29), a model for John's audience (14:12–15; 15:7)" (*Gospel of John*, 849). As believers walk in obedience to the Father, they too may expect to be heard and have their prayers answered.

36. Van der Watt, *Introduction*, 58.

into the earth and dies but subsequently bears much fruit (v. 24). He then remarks concerning the corollary of someone loving and/or hating his life (v. 25) saying that one must be willing to follow him (presumably) even to death (v. 26). Such a commitment not only grants one eternal life but also confers the honor of the Father. Just as the Father honors Jesus in his death, so the Father will honor the disciples who follow Jesus in life and death.[37] With this context in mind, Jesus offers the following prayer.

Jesus' Prayer

John 12:27–28 reads as follows:

> Νῦν ἡ ψυχή μου τετάρακται, καὶ τί εἴπω;
> πάτερ, σῶσόν με ἐκ τῆς ὥρας ταύτης;
> ἀλλὰ διὰ τοῦτο ἦλθον εἰς τὴν ὥραν ταύτην.
> πάτερ, δόξασόν σου τὸ ὄνομα.

With the theme of Jesus' glorification at the forefront, Jesus addresses the Father with words that elucidate his emotional disposition. As such, 12:27a indicates Jesus is "troubled" (τετάρακται, or "disturbed"). Carson is right in pointing out that the source of Jesus' troubled soul did not center on his concern for the disciples but rather centered on the approaching "hour" of his death.[38] This "hour" involves both the physical and psychological pain that Jesus would soon endure. Much like the Synoptic accounts at Gethsemane, this account reveals the humanity of Jesus. Further, the language of verse 27a is thematically congruent with Psalm 6, in which the psalmist faces the fear of death. The psalmist prays in 6:2–6 (LXX):

> 2 Κύριε, μὴ τῷ θυμῷ σου ἐλέγξῃς με,
>   μηδὲ τῇ ὀργῇ σου παιδεύσῃς με.
> 3 ἐλέησόν με, Κύριε, ὅτι ἀσθενής εἰμι·
>   ἴασαί με, ὅτι ἐταράχθη τὰ ὀστᾶ μου.
> 4 καὶ ἡ ψυχή μου ἐταράχθη σφόδρα·
>   καὶ σύ, Κύριε, ἕως πότε;
> 5 ἐπίστρεψον, Κύριε, ῥῦσαι τὴν ψυχήν μου,
>   σῶσόν με ἕνεκεν τοῦ ἐλέους σου.
> 6 ὅτι οὐκ ἔστιν ἐν τῷ θανάτῳ ὁ μνημονεύων σου·

---

37. Neyrey, *Gospel of John*, 215.
38. Carson, *Gospel According to John*, 439.

ἐν δὲ τῷ ᾅδῃ τίς ἐξομολογήσεταί σοι.[39]

As indicated in this passage, the cry of the psalmist is for salvation and deliverance from physical calamity and death. When applied in the life of Jesus, deliverance would bring him emotional and physical relief, but such deliverance would nullify the mission for which he was sent.

Notwithstanding, the concept of παρρησία, or frankness of speech, appears in verse 27. Of all that Jesus could have prayed, he elucidates the inward condition of his soul in a manner that his disciples would relate to in their own hour of suffering (16:2). Jesus experienced a troubled soul; they too would experience a troubled heart (14:1; 16:1–4, 6; etc.). The implications are clear: If Jesus spoke to God in a frank, revealing, and honest manner about his troubled soul, the disciples could do likewise. Jesus prayed for his approaching hour, so the disciples will need to pray for their approaching hour (16:2) with frankness and honesty.

Accordingly, scholars are divided on whether the phrase καὶ τί εἴπω; πάτερ, σῶσόν με ἐκ τῆς ὥρας ταύτης; forms a question raised by Jesus followed by an actual prayer, or a question raised by Jesus followed by a hypothetical prayer.[40] Is Jesus issuing an actual prayer for deliverance or simply posing a hypothetical scenario in the face of death and suffering ("Father, save me from this hour!" or "Father, save me from this hour?")? As indicated by Bryant, those who regard Jesus' words as an actual prayer for deliverance find congruence with the Synoptic portrayal of Jesus' suffering in the garden prior to his crucifixion (Matt 26:39; Mark 14:36; Luke 22:42).[41] Yet he is right in saying that Jesus' emotional distress (in 12:27) does not require insisting that he actually petitioned the Father to escape the cross. Following Morris, Bryant suggests that the second option above (that Jesus is offering a hypothetical prayer) is most plausible due to the following reasons: "First, the second interpretation avoids the awkward proposal that Jesus makes a request of the Father and then immediately rejects his petition. Second, the latter view takes seriously the deliberative subjunctive εἴπω ('shall I say') in verse 27. Finally, the 'strong adversative' (ἀλλά) that follows also seems to favor this view as it points to a firm resolve on the part of Jesus."[42] It is difficult to say which view is correct. The tentative conclusion of this writer is that Bryant's position is the most plausible.

As in 11:41; 17:1, 5, 21, 24, here Jesus addresses God as "Father," which highlights intimacy, oneness, and submission. As such, in his brief prayer,

39. Emphasis added.
40. Bryant, "Examination of Prayer," 36–37.
41. Bryant, "Examination of Prayer," 37.
42. Bryant, "Examination of Prayer," 38.

Jesus manifests loyalty to his Father (information) but also makes the request (petition) that the Father would bring glory to his name. The Son's request for the Father's name to be honored and respected is consistent with the Jewish prayers such as those seen in the Amidah (*Kedusha*), which states:

> *We will sanctify your name in the world*
> Even as they sanctify it *in the highest heavens.*[43]

Concern for the name of God is also echoed in Psalms 8:1, 9 (ESV):

> O LORD, our LORD, how majestic is *your name* in all the earth!

The psalmist says in 115:1 (ESV):

> Not to us, O LORD, not to us, *but to your name give glory.*

Jesus' request in 12:28 also accords with the sentiment of the Lord's Prayer[44] in Matt 6:9 (ESV):

> Our Father in heaven, *hallowed be your name.*

In each instance above, concern for God's name is central: his name is to be revered, esteemed, and set apart. Jesus' request in 12:28 encapsulates and assumes each of these components with the central aim of the Father's name being honored and praised. In essence, Jesus' prayer inevitably places the Father's reputation and honor above his own life and comfort and anticipates Jesus' statement (in prayer) in John 17:4, ἐγώ σε ἐδόξασα ἐπὶ τῆς γῆς τὸ ἔργον τελειώσας ὃ δέδωκάς μοι ἵνα ποιήσω. Furthermore, concern for the Father's name is congruent with prayer offered in Jesus' name (14:13–14; 15:16; 16:23–24). In short, to honor one is to honor the other. To live and/or die for the glory of one is to live and/or die for the glory of the other. As noted in chapter 5 of this analysis, Jesus' name stands for who Jesus is and all that Jesus' mission represents. Since Jesus came to do the Father's will (6:38), to finish his work (17:4), and to glorify his name, prayer in Jesus' name results in works that are congruent with God's will and works/fruit bring glory to the Father (14:13; 15:8). Hence, although the names are distinct, they are congruent in their implication and evoke equal honor.

Finally, immediately following Jesus' prayer (v. 28) a voice from heaven stated, καὶ ἐδόξασα καὶ πάλιν δοξάσω. The Father's response serves as

---

43. Emphasis added in this and the following three passages.

44. Schnackenburg notes, "The short prayer [12:28] can be regarded as a Christological rephrasing of the petition in the Our Father, 'Hallowed be thy name' (Mattt 6:9 = Luke 11:2)" (*Gospel According to St. John*, 387).

reaffirmation that his name has been glorified (past) and the confirmation that his name will be glorified again (future); Jesus' prayer has been heard and will be answered. He brought glory to the Father in the past through the signs he performed, and he will bring glory to him again through the suffering/death he will endure. Although the Father spoke audibly, the crowd mistook his voice for thunder or an angel (v. 29). Jesus' explanation for the verbal response to his prayer is seen in the phrase, οὐ δι' ἐμὲ ἡ φωνὴ αὕτη γέγονεν ἀλλὰ δι' ὑμᾶς (12:30). Although Jesus' prayer did not require an audible response—and although Jesus did not require divine comfort, it is possible that the Father's response may have served to console Jesus. But Carson notes the more likely implication by pointing out that after Jesus' death, the disciples will find themselves in "urgent need of making sense of it all."[45] As such, there were some statements they could not grasp in the moment. To this Carson says, "But eventually they would remember what Jesus had told them the voice had uttered, and it would be for them a divine confirmation that the shameful cross, and all that flowed from it, was not a defeat but a victory, not final destruction, but ultimate glorification."

As the hour of his glorification approached, Jesus' contemplation of the cross caused emotional distress. As noted above, Jesus was fully aware of the consequences of his obedience to the Father. To the extent that he was obedient, Jesus would experience pain, suffering, and death. Conversely, to the extent that he was disobedient, Jesus would experience temporary comfort and life. Yet the Johannine Jesus knew of only one option, namely, that the Father's name would be glorified through his life and in the hour of his death. In short, Jesus' prayer in John 12:27-28 demonstrates the emotional tension that accompanies suffering, on the one hand, but it ultimately demonstrates the triumph of Jesus' obedience to the Father, on the other. Prayer, then, is the space in which this tension is communicated but ultimately resolved. With this basic summary in mind, the following points may be offered:

This episode demonstrates that Jesus spoke frankly and openly with the Father about the condition of his soul. As such, this episode provides a Johannine model concerning how the disciples, who are children of God (1:12–13), may approach the Father in prayer in their hour of distress without fear of rejection. A troubled soul in prayer shares Jesus' sentiment in prayer. As the Father heard Jesus, he will also hear those who pray in Jesus' name. Yet the aim of prayer is not merely the pouring out of one's soul, but it also involves conformity to the will of God. The episode above, then, demonstrates that Johannine discipleship is not a one-time profession of faith in

---

45. Carson, *Gospel According to John*, 442.

Jesus but rather involves a lifestyle of continual faith and obedience to the Father. In particular, faithfulness to the Father is expressed as one subordinates his desires to the wishes of God, even at the expense of his own life.

Second, as indicated in 6:11; 11:41-42; 12:27-28, prayer to the Father is followed by public ramifications in the form of signs performed before people's eyes or an audible voice. Such encounters are designed to display the unity and oneness that exists between the Father and the Son. But such encounters might naturally remind one of the unity that exists between the Father/Son and those who pray in Jesus' name. As such, the corollary of such unity involves the privilege of offering prayer that results in works/fruit that increase honor and respect for the Father. As the Father performs his works through the Son, so the Son performs his works through the believers who remain in relationship with him. Hence, both the Father and Son receive glory when prayer is issued with the Father-Son mission and reputation in mind. Again, to honor one is to honor the other since they are unified in mission.

In the final analysis, prayer is the medium through which Jesus' humanity is expressed, but it also serves as the means by which he submits to the will of God and the name of God is honored. Therefore, Jesus' prayer in 12:27-28 provides the conceptual foundation for what Jesus later communicates through didactic discourse in 14:13-14; 15:7, 16; 16:23-24. Disciples may experience emotional distress as they contemplate their hour of trial in prayer. But true disciples who exercise faith in Jesus are those who submit and subordinate their wishes to the Father for the sake of his honor/reputation.

Jesus' Prayer of Completion: John 17

In John 17 the Evangelist provides the longest prayer recorded in the Gospel accounts. Since much scholarly attention has been given to this chapter, I will not repeat or analyze in detail what has been stated elsewhere.[46] Rather,

---

46. See Moule, *High Priestly Prayer*; Dodd, *Interpretation of the Fourth Gospel*, 417-23; Thüsing, *Herrlichkeit und Einheit*; Käsemann, *Testament of Jesus*; Brown, *Gospel According to John (XIII-XXI)*, 737-82; Barrett, *Gospel According to St. John*, 499-515; Hunter, "Prayers of Jesus," 189-360; Carson, *Farewell Discourse and Final Prayer*, 173-207; Newman and Nida, *Handbook on the Gospel of John*, 523-48; Brodie, *Gospel According to John*, 505-518; Haenchen, *Commentary on the Gospel of John Chapters 7-21*, 150-59; Turner, "Prayer in the Gospels and Acts," 77-80; Becker, *Das Evangelium nach Johannes*, 608-31; Witherington, *John's Wisdom*, 266-71; Cullmann, *Das Gebet im Neuen Testament*, 140-45; Countryman, "Jesus' 'High Priestly Prayer,'" 222-27; Rosenblatt, "Voice of the One Who Prays," 131-44; Beasley-Murray, *John*, 291-307; Culpepper, *Gospel and Letters of John*, 219-21; Moloney, *Glory Not Dishonor*, 102-126;

what follows is an overview of the formal aspects of Jesus' prayer, a discussion of its didactic nature and value, and a discussion concerning how this prayer is best understood in terms of a final report that Jesus uttered before his hour of suffering and cross-death. This so-called "report" not only involves an account of Jesus' completed work, but also involves his request(s) for the mission that lies ahead. The aim is to discover how Jesus' prayer enhances our understanding of the relationship between prayer and the unfinished task of advancing God's mission in the world.

The Setting

Jesus' prayer is issued subsequent to his farewell address but prior to his departure with his disciples across the Kidron Valley to the garden where he is arrested (John 18:1-12). Jesus is the Logos (1:1, 14), who came from God and is about to return to God after his glorification on the cross. Thus, the theological implications of this prayer center on what has been and what is yet to be accomplished through Jesus' mission. Its practical outcome centers on the continuation of Jesus' ministry via disciples/believers for whom he offers prayer.

The Structure and Genre

While numerous suggestions have been put forth concerning the structure of chapter 17,[47] Carson following Beasley-Murray and Schnackenburg offers one of the more straightforward examples:

1. Jesus prays for his glorification (17:1-5)
2. Jesus prays for his disciples (17:6-19)
   a. Jesus' grounds for this prayer (17:6-11a)
   b. Jesus prays that his disciples may be protected (17:11b-16)
   c. Jesus prays that his disciples will be sanctified (17:17-19)

Schenke, *Johannes Commentar*, 320-28; Karris, *Prayer and the New Testament*, 103-7; Lincoln, "God's Name, Jesus' Name," 160-72; Wengst, *Das Johannesevangelium*, 188-209; Keener, *Gospel of John*, 1050-64; Sadananda, *Johannine Exegesis of God*, 133-49; Neyrey, *Gospel of John*, 284-88; Michaels, *Gospel of John*, 856-82; Von Wahlde, *Gospel and Letters of John*, 714-43; Beutler, *Das Johannesevangelium*, 450-60; Thyen, *Das Johannesevangelium*, 675-96; Millar, *Calling on the Name of the Lord*, 180-83; Schnelle, *Das Evangelium nach Johannes 4*, 333-39.

47. For a helpful and thorough overview, see Diehl, "Puzzle of the Prayer," 137-51. See also Newman and Nida, *Handbook on the Gospel of John*, 523-24; Karris, *Prayer and the New Testament*, 105-6; Moloney, *Glory Not Dishonor*, 104-6.

3. Jesus prays for all who believe (17:20–23)
4. Jesus prays that all believers may be perfected so as to see Jesus' glory (17:24–26)[48]

Scholars are right to point out that chapter 17 recapitulates themes that appear in previous chapters and then reframes them as they spiral through the prayer itself. For example, Jesus prays that the disciples will be kept in the Father's name and that they will be one (v. 11); he prays that the disciples will be kept from the evil one (v. 15); he asks that the Father sanctify them in truth (v. 17); he prays that all believers will experience oneness (vv. 20–21), and he prays that believers will be with him and that they will see his glory (v. 24). Each petition is congruent with key theological themes that appear within the Farewell Discourse.[49] As such, the concept of oneness assumes faith in Jesus (14:1, 12), the necessity of remaining in Jesus (15:1–7), and friendship with Jesus (15:14–15). Also, being kept from the evil one is compatible with the theme of "the ruler of this world" (14:30). Since the evil one has no hold on Jesus, it is natural for Jesus to pray that his disciples will be free of his hold. Further, being sanctified in truth is conceptually/practically congruent with knowing the truth (14:6), being indwelt by the Spirit of truth (14:17, 26), bearing witness to the truth (15:26–27), and being guided in(to) all truth (16:13–14).

Further, chapter 17 is framed in a manner that repeats and expands our understanding of the Father-Son relationship. Therefore, we see the following theological themes/actions in Jesus' prayer, namely: his dependence on the Father (v. 1), his obedience to the Father (vv. 4, 6, 12), the revelation of the Father through the Son (vv. 8, 14, 22, 26), and his completion of the Father's work/mission (v. 4). These elements are theological recapitulations of Jesus' ministry in general and his earlier prayers to the Father in particular (6:11; 11:41–42; 12:27–28). As such, Jesus' prayer in chapter 17 provides the theological content and the emotional sentiment that his disciples and future believers may utilize and express as they offer prayer to the Father in Jesus' name (14:13–14; 15:16; 16:23–24). Therefore, this prayer has premiere didactic value for the onlookers (and eavesdroppers).

---

48. Carson, *Gospel According to John*, 553.

49. Further points of theological congruency are seen in the following examples: The disciples "know" the Son and the Father (John 17:3; cf. 14:5–11). The disciples, like Jesus, are to "glorify" the Father (John 17:10; 13:31–32; cf. 14:13; 15:8). The disciples are to keep the Father's "word" and manifest God's "name" (John 17:6, 8; cf. 14:13–14; 15:4–7, 10, 16; 16:23–24, 26). The disciples will have "joy" (John 17:13; cf. 15:11; 16:22, 24). The disciples will experience the "love" of the Father (John 17:26; cf. 14:21; 15:8–10; 16:27).

As Jesus looked to heaven in dependence on the Father, so the disciples must depend on God in prayer. As Jesus could do nothing on his own, so the disciples could do nothing on their own. As Jesus brought glory to the Father, so the disciples must seek to pray and live in a manner that brings glory to God. As Jesus performed the works of the Father and communicated the words of the Father, so the disciples must seek to make God known in their works and words. As Jesus remained in the Father, so the disciples must remain in him. In the final analysis, Jesus' prayer for the disciples is one of the primary means through which these ends are accomplished. As such, a juxtaposition of John chapters 14–17 demonstrates that Jesus did not merely instruct his disciples concerning how to pray in his absence but also sealed his instruction with prayer to the Father on their behalf. Since the Father always hears Jesus (the "subordinate" sender), the disciples/believers for whom Jesus prays may rest assured that such prayers will be answered.

As the appropriate conclusion to the Farewell Discourse, chapter 17 has often been labeled Jesus' "High Priestly Prayer" (since the sixteenth century by David Chyträus), largely because it presents Jesus as offering intercession in a manner similar to a priest in the OT. However, in my view the textual evidence to justify this label is lacking. Several suggestions have been offered concerning the background of this chapter. Keener points out that chapter 17 "reflects the standard Jewish motifs, such as the unity of God's people, their love for God, God's glory, obedience to God's message, and the importance of obeying God's agent (Moses in the Jewish tradition)."[50] Moloney notes further, "Closer parallels have been urged between John and the Hermetic writings (see *Poimandres* 1:31–32; *Corpus Hermeticum* 13:21–22)—in which God is praised and there are certain verbal similarities—and the Mandean writings (see *Book of John* 236–39); Mandean Liturgy [Qolasta 58:9–2])—in which 'the Great Life' is asked to raise up and give the splendor of light to disciples and children who are locked in the darkness of the lower world."[51] Notwithstanding, there is little if any evidence that the Fourth Gospel depended on any of the aforementioned traditions. In my view, Jesus' prayer is best viewed as a "report of completion" to the Father. Van der Watt points out that, in ancient times, an agent would report back to his sender in order to provide a report of the mission. Additionally, the agent would seek to discover what further action would be needed in order to complete the mission (if anything). He notes concerning Jesus:

> He reports back to his Father in the prayer of John 17. He has completed his mission with success (17:1–5). As a result of his

---

50. Keener, *Gospel of John*, 1050.
51. Moloney, *Glory Not Dishonor*, 103.

mission, the family of God was established in this world (17:6–8). However, what will happen to them now that he returns to the Father? Jesus asks the Father to protect and equip them for their sake in the world (17:19). Jesus also prays for those who will still become believers in the future through the missionary work of the original believers (17:20–23).[52]

The analysis that follows directly below will unpack the particulars concerning the nature of Jesus' report to the Father and the nature of his requests for the completion of his earthly mission.

Analysis of Jesus' Prayer Report and Requests

As one reads the language of chapter 17 it becomes evident that the Evangelist's desire centers on highlighting the work completed by the Son. As such, the Fourth Gospel portrays Jesus as the obedient Son of the Father par excellence. For example, Jesus reports:

ἐγώ σε ἐδόξασα ἐπὶ τῆς γῆς τὸ ἔργον τελειώσας ὃ δέδωκάς μοι ἵνα ποιήσω (17:4).

Ἐφανέρωσά σου τὸ ὄνομα τοῖς ἀνθρώποις οὓς ἔδωκάς μοι ἐκ τοῦ κόσμου (17:6).

ὅτι τὰ ῥήματα ἃ ἔδωκάς μοι δέδωκα αὐτοῖς, καὶ αὐτοὶ ἔλαβον καὶ ἔγνωσαν ἀληθῶς ὅτι παρὰ σοῦ ἐξῆλθον, καὶ ἐπίστευσαν ὅτι σύ με ἀπέστειλας (17:8).

ὅτε ἤμην μετ' αὐτῶν ἐγὼ ἐτήρουν αὐτοὺς ἐν τῷ ὀνόματί σου ᾧ δέδωκάς μοι, καὶ ἐφύλαξα, καὶ οὐδεὶς ἐξ αὐτῶν ἀπώλετο εἰ μὴ ὁ υἱὸς τῆς ἀπωλείας, ἵνα ἡ γραφὴ πληρωθῇ (17:12).

καθὼς ἐμὲ ἀπέστειλας εἰς τὸν κόσμον, κἀγὼ ἀπέστειλα αὐτοὺς εἰς τὸν κόσμον (17:18).

These examples demonstrate that Jesus, the agent who came from "above," completed the mission he was assigned "below." As seen throughout the Fourth Gospel, the relationship between the Father and Son is eternal (17:5, 24) but manifests in time and space. Each of the instances outlined above demonstrates Jesus' honor/esteem for his father and the family of God. In summary, Jesus accomplished the Father's work, manifested his name, spoke his words, preserved the disciples whom the Father gave to him, and sent them into the world with esteem for God's name and

---

52. Van der Watt, *Introduction*, 43.

equipped for his mission. This latter aspect is most particularly outlined in the Farewell Discourse where Jesus highlights the necessity of faith (14:1) in God and remaining in relationship with him (15:1-7), provides instruction concerning how to perform "greater works" (14:12-14) and bear "much fruit" (15:7-8), and assures them of God's abiding presence "in" them and "with" them via the agency of the Paraclete (14:17, 26; 15:26; 16:7). By equipping the disciples in this manner, Jesus was ensuring their success in the face of hostile circumstances.

It is upon the foundation of Jesus' completed work in preparing the disciples that he makes several notable petitions to the Father. For example,

Ταῦτα ἐλάλησεν Ἰησοῦς καὶ ἐπάρας τοὺς ὀφθαλμοὺς αὐτοῦ εἰς τὸν οὐρανὸν εἶπεν· πάτερ, ἐλήλυθεν ἡ ὥρα· δόξασόν σου τὸν υἱόν, ἵνα ὁ υἱὸς δοξάσῃ σέ,

καὶ νῦν δόξασόν με σύ, πάτερ, παρὰ σεαυτῷ τῇ δόξῃ ᾗ εἶχον πρὸ τοῦ τὸν κόσμον εἶναι παρὰ σοί (17:5).

οὐκ ἐρωτῶ ἵνα ἄρῃς αὐτοὺς ἐκ τοῦ κόσμου, ἀλλ᾽ ἵνα τηρήσῃς αὐτοὺς ἐκ τοῦ πονηροῦ (17:15).

Οὐ περὶ τούτων δὲ ἐρωτῶ μόνον, ἀλλὰ καὶ περὶ τῶν πιστευόντων διὰ τοῦ λόγου αὐτῶν εἰς ἐμέ, 21 ἵνα πάντες ἓν ὦσιν, καθὼς σύ, πάτερ, ἐν ἐμοὶ κἀγὼ ἐν σοί, ἵνα καὶ αὐτοὶ ἐν ἡμῖν ὦσιν, ἵνα ὁ κόσμος πιστεύῃ ὅτι σύ με ἀπέστειλας (17:20-21).

Πάτερ, ὃ δέδωκάς μοι, θέλω ἵνα ὅπου εἰμὶ ἐγὼ κἀκεῖνοι ὦσιν μετ᾽ ἐμοῦ, ἵνα θεωρῶσιν τὴν δόξαν τὴν ἐμήν, ἣν δέδωκάς μοι ὅτι ἠγάπησάς με πρὸ καταβολῆς κόσμου (17:24).

These requests provide several insights into our understanding of the nature of the Father-Son relationship and the basis for the advancement of God's mission beyond the crucified and resurrected Jesus. First, like we saw in John 11:41, 17:1 states, Ταῦτα ἐλάλησεν Ἰησοῦς καὶ ἐπάρας τοὺς ὀφθαλμοὺς αὐτοῦ εἰς τὸν οὐρανὸν εἶπεν·πάτερ, ἐλήλυθεν ἡ ὥρα· δόξασόν σου τὸν υἱόν, ἵνα ὁ υἱὸς δοξάσῃ σέ. The lifting of Jesus' eyes toward heaven is not only consistent with his prayer in 11:41, but also with certain prayers in Judaism (4 Macc 6:6). Perhaps Jesus' upward gaze is indicative of both his dependence on the Father and his desire to complete the earthly mission the Father assigned to him so that he may return to heaven. Further, it is possible that Jesus' upward gaze anticipates his desire for the Father to glorify the Son in his presence with the glory that the Son had with him before the world existed (17:5, 24).

Nevertheless, Jesus' request (17:1) centers on the glorification of the Father through the work of the Son as his hour approaches. Moloney says, "The link between the revelation of God's glory and the glorification of the Son was made explicit in 11:4, and its relationship with Jesus' oncoming death was reinforced by the decision taken by 'the Jews,' the final negative response of this group to Jesus' words and actions (see 11:45–50, 57; 12:9–11)."[53] As I will argue in the following section (Jesus' prayer in John 19:28, 30), the answer to Jesus' prayer for the glorification of God's name through the Son is seen in Jesus' willingness to remain obedient to the point of death, thereby completing the mission he was assigned (12:23–24; 13:31–32). Although Jesus had been obedient to the Father, it was necessary for him to remain obedient. As noted in 14:12, the basis for the disciples performing "greater works" is founded upon Jesus "going" to the Father. In chapter 17, Jesus reports that he had successfully run the race marked out for him. But he also prays that he will be able to "cross" the finish line (at the cross). This truth takes on special relevance in light of Jesus' words concerning answered prayer in the Farewell Discourse since the disciples' ability to cross the finish line, which entails enduring their own hour of trial, performing greater works, and bearing much fruit, is dependent upon Jesus' obedience. In light of Jesus' person and work, the disciples are empowered to pray for whatever they want in Jesus' name so "that the Father may be glorified in the Son." If obedient, glory is achieved. If disobedient, glory is diminished.

Second, in 17:15 Jesus prays that the disciples will not be taken out of the world, but that they will be protected from the "evil one" (see Matt 6:13) as they advance God's mission. In 14:30 it is said that the "ruler of this world" (presumably Satan) had no hold on Jesus.[54] If this is the case for Jesus, then it is logical to view Jesus' request as a reference to the disciples being protected from the "hold" or influence of the evil one. With chapter 14 in mind, one might naturally think of Jesus' request in light of his disciples being the "house of God" that bears his name. In this understanding, Jesus is asking that the Father protect the place (or relational space) where his name and Spirit dwells (14:13–14, 17). But perhaps most relevant to this formal aspect of prayer is the vine-branch-gardener discussion in 15:1–8. While Jesus is the vine, the disciples are the branches, and the Father is the gardener (or vine-dresser). Here it is implied that Jesus prays that the Father-gardener will offer spiritual protection for his investment, namely that he will protect the branches from influence of the evil one. It is clear that the world "hates" those who possess the Father's word (17:14). Yet, the

---

53. Moloney, *Glory Not Dishonor*, 108.
54. See also 12:31; 16:11.

disciples will not be removed from the tumultuous and hostile climate of the world. Rather, Jesus prays that they will be protected from the evil one so they will bear "much fruit" (15:8). In short, the greater the growth, the greater glory the Father-gardener receives. Just as the Father tended to the vine (Jesus) in particular, he will also tend to the branches that are inextricably connected by virtue of unity of relationship and shared purpose. Finally, the so-called loss of the "son of destruction" elucidates the cutting away and disposal of a branch that was never truly "in him" to begin with.

Third, in 7:20-23 Jesus prays for those who "will believe" in him via the words of the original disciples. The thrust of this petition is aimed at future generations of disciples who will believe in the Father through the Son (17:20b, ἀλλὰ καὶ περὶ τῶν πιστευόντων διὰ τοῦ λόγου αὐτῶν εἰς ἐμέ). In this understanding, Jesus prays for a unity among believers that replicates the Father-Son relationship. As the Son is in the Father and the Father is in the Son, so believers are to remain in relationship with God and with one another. The unity displayed among believers replicates the unity that exists between the Father and Son. Perhaps one should read such unity in familial terms to highlight the believability of one's claim to son-ship. Unity displayed is unity proven, particularly unity based on the love of God (3:16; 17:26). As disciples of Jesus display love for one another, they display, in part, the love that exists in the Father-Son relationship. Jesus completed the task of walking in unity with the Father and displaying his glory; now the disciples must continue where Jesus left off. They must replicate and reproduce God's love in their community. Once this mission is accomplished, Jesus' final desire will be realized, namely, Πάτερ, ὃ δέδωκάς μοι, θέλω ἵνα ὅπου εἰμὶ ἐγὼ κἀκεῖνοι ὦσιν μετ' ἐμοῦ, ἵνα θεωρῶσιν τὴν δόξαν τὴν ἐμήν, ἣν δέδωκάς μοι ὅτι ἠγάπησάς με πρὸ καταβολῆς κόσμου (17:24).

Finally, as noted in the brief analysis above, Jesus approaches the Father to issue a report concerning the work he completed. Yet, more work lies ahead. Therefore, Jesus prays for the work to continue through the disciples (in every generation) who have faith in his person, pray according to his name, and advance God's assignment in the power of the Spirit. This prayer not only has didactic value concerning the nature of the Father-Son relationship, it also looks backward as well as forward to the fulfillment of God's mission through the disciples who replicate the Father-Son relationship in their lives and communities. In keeping with Neyrey's basic definition of prayer, Jesus' prayer assumes a "subordinate/superior" relationship that seeks "to have some effect on the person with whom the prayer communicates; that is, it seeks results . . . petitions for goods and services or as maintenance of relationships."⁵⁵ In the case of chapter 17, the nature of the "results" centers on the completion of God's mission and the glorification of his name.

A Prayer from the Cross? John 19:28, 30

Many scholars do not recognize John 19:28, 30 as containing prayers in the traditional sense. This is to be expected given the lack of features that clearly characterize prayers in 6:11; 11:41–42; 12:27–28. Thus, many commentaries and scholarly works highlight the potential theological implications of Jesus' final words without respect to how they might be understood as prayer to God. However, as will be demonstrated below, a careful examination of Jesus' words centers on the question concerning whom Jesus is addressing and the implications of his address in light of various psalms in general, but also in light of the overall scope of Jesus' mission (as enunciated in the Fourth Gospel) in particular. Therefore, the following analysis will seek to ascertain whether Jesus' final words may be viewed as prayer to God, and it also will explore several possibilities concerning how prayer functions in the final moments of Jesus' life. Yet before analyzing the text in detail, it is necessary to offer a brief remark concerning the setting.

The Setting

The Evangelist provides a straightforward account of the events leading up to and including Jesus' cross-death. In particular, after his arrest Jesus appeared before Annas and Caiaphas (John 18:12–14, 19–24) but was subsequently handed over to Pilate (18:29–38), who questioned him and then sentenced him to flogging (19:1) and finally death (19:16). The Evangelist indicates that Jesus carried his own cross to Golgotha, where he was crucified with two others (19:17–18). Further, the Fourth Gospel states that the soldiers took his garments and divided them into four parts. But they did not tear his tunic; instead they cast lots for it (19:23–24). Finally, at the cross Jesus' mother, his mother's sister, Mary the wife of Clopas, and Mary Magdalene were gathered. At this point Jesus assigned the role of providing care and protection of his mother to the Beloved Disciple (19:26–27). It is within this context that Jesus offers his final words.

---

55. Neyrey, *Give God the Glory*, 9.

Jesus' Final Words/Prayers

Although the following analysis will focus almost exclusively on the Johannine materials, it is necessary to outline Jesus' final words from the Synoptic accounts (and the corresponding psalms) in order to sensitize the reader to the unique nature of the Johannine account. Consider the Markan and Matthean accounts:

> ὁ Ἰησοῦς φωνῇ μεγάλῃ ελωι ελωι λεμα σαβαχθανι; ὅ ἐστιν μεθερμηνευόμενον ὁ θεός μου ὁ θεός μου, εἰς τί ἐγκατέλιπές με; (Mark 15:34)
>
> ὁ Ἰησοῦς φωνῇ μεγάλῃ λέγων ηλι ηλι λεμα σαβαχθανι; τοῦτ' ἔστιν θεέ μου θεέ μου, ἱνατί με ἐγκατέλιπες; (Matt 27:46)

Compare with Psalm 21:2 (LXX):

> Ὁ θεὸς ὁ θεός μου, πρόσχες μοι· ἵνα τί ἐγκατέλιπές με; μακρὰν ἀπὸ τῆς σωτηρίας μου οἱ λόγοι τῶν παραπτωμάτων μου.

Luke's account says:

> καὶ φωνήσας φωνῇ μεγάλῃ ὁ Ἰησοῦς εἶπεν· πάτερ, εἰς χεῖράς σου παρατίθεμαι τὸ πνεῦμά μου (Luke 23:46).

Compare with Psalm 30:6 (LXX):

> εἰς χεῖράς σου παραθήσομαι τὸ πνεῦμά μου.

The Fourth Gospel states:

> Μετὰ τοῦτο εἰδὼς ὁ Ἰησοῦς ὅτι ἤδη πάντα τετέλεσται, ἵνα τελειωθῇ ἡ γραφή, λέγει· διψῶ (19:28).

Compare with Psalm 68:22 (LXX):

> καὶ ἔδωκαν εἰς τὸ βρῶμά μου χολὴν καὶ εἰς τὴν δίψαν μου ἐπότισάν με ὄξος.

Finally:

> ὅτε οὖν ἔλαβεν τὸ ὄξος [ὁ] Ἰησοῦς εἶπεν· τετέλεσται, καὶ κλίνας τὴν κεφαλὴν παρέδωκεν τὸ πνεῦμα (John 19:30).

It is notable that each of the Synoptic passages above is a direct address to God/Father, which indicates that Jesus is likely offering prayer. In Mark and Matthew, Jesus' words are issued in the form of a question to God in the midst of his feeling of separation and suffering. In the Lukan account, Jesus' words may be viewed as a statement of finality and trust as his life draws to a close. Notwithstanding, some scholars have pointed out the unique distinction of the final words of Jesus from the Fourth Gospel, which are also issued in the form of a prayer. Karris highlights the Evangelist's rendering of the cross event and draws special attention to the associations that exists between the language of John chapter 19 and the Jewish Passover festival.[56] He points out that only in John is it implied that Jesus is crucified at the same time the lambs were being slaughtered for Passover. Accordingly, he notes that only in John is Jesus presented with a sponge of water laced with vinegar on a hyssop branch. Furthermore, he notes that only in John does the author mention that the soldiers did not break Jesus' legs, which follows the historical antecedent of the Passover lamb in Exodus 12:46 (ESV), which says, "You shall not break any of its bones."

Finally, Karris sees the hyssop branch mentioned in 19:29 against the backdrop of Exodus 12:22 (ESV), which states, "Take a bunch of hyssop and dip it in the blood that is in the basin, and touch the lintel and the two doorposts with the blood that is in the basin."[57] He joins with other scholars who view the hyssop branch as containing a deeper level of meaning. In short, the branch of 19:29 may be connected with Exodus 12:22 in reference to shedding of blood that is necessary for the taking away of sin (1:29).[58] Brown remarks further, "Plausibly the reference to hyssop in John 19:29 is meant to alert readers to an inclusion with the Gospel's opening description of Jesus by JBap ... (1:29)."[59] He says elsewhere that the Evangelist's notation of the ὁ ἀμνὸς τοῦ θεοῦ ὁ αἴρων τὴν ἁμαρτίαν τοῦ κόσμου (1:29) may be in reference Deutero-Isaiah's Suffering Servant and to the paschal lamb. Thus, with these references in mind, the Johannine account may have been penned in a manner that connects the final events of Jesus' life and death with the Passover tradition in order to highlight the concept of sacrifice for sin.[60] On the other hand, Coloe points out that the Passover lamb was not expiatory or sacrificial but apotropaic. She says, "The primary purpose of the blood of the Passover lamb is to provide a salvific sign marking the household of the Israelites."[61] Thus, Coloe views (with the Exodus motif in mind) the Johannine mode of salvation as liberation from the dominion of slavery to sin (Deut 6:12–14a; cf. John 8:34–36). She remarks:

---

56. Karris, *Prayer and the New Testament*, 109–110.
57. Karris, *Prayer and the New Testament*, 110.
58. See also Moloney, *Glory Not Dishonor*, 145–46.
59. Brown, *Death of the Messiah*, 2:1077.
60. Brown, *Gospel According to John (I–XII)*, 63.
61. Coloe, *God Dwells with Us*, 194–95.

The liberation model of salvation is very different from Israel's sacrificial system. Jesus' death, although presented as a Paschal sacrifice, is never described as a "laying down of life" **for sin**, where sin is the cause or reason for his death. All the expressions describing Jesus' death are couched in terms of the people who will benefit by this death:

> "The bread which I shall give *for the life of* the world is my flesh" (6:51).
>
> "The good shepherd lays down his life *for the sheep*" (10:11, also v. 15).
>
> "It is expedient for you that one man should die *for the people*" (11:50, cf. 51, 52; 18:14).

She says, moreover, "It is love rather than sin which is the dominant power leading to Jesus' death" (15:13–15).[62] Notwithstanding, whether one opts for the removal of sin or for the motivation of love, obedience to the Father and perseverance to the point of death was of utmost importance. In this context, then, Jesus' words in 19:28 become relevant in the discussion of prayer. The Evangelist states, Μετὰ τοῦτο εἰδὼς ὁ Ἰησοῦς ὅτι ἤδη πάντα τετέλεσται, ἵνα τελειωθῇ ἡ γραφή, λέγει· διψῶ. What does the Evangelist intend to convey by stating that Jesus knew that all was finished? Brown has no problem seeing ὅτι ἤδη πάντα τετέλεσται as referring to the previous episode "when Jesus, lifted up, began drawing to himself disciples as he had promised (12:32) and referring forward to the completion of Scripture that is about to take place."[63] He points out further that "*teleioun* has been previously used in John for Jesus' completing the work the Father gave him to do (4:34; 5:36; 17:4) and so makes clear that Jesus' finishing all things also includes his christological task." Yet the Evangelist seems to indicate that Jesus' past work and his present task of obedience to the Father in death are brought together and solidified in a statement that implies a longing for the achievement of finality, namely, διψῶ. Karris sees the words "I thirst" as a symbolic reference that transcends the natural, literal meaning. While it was undoubtedly true that Jesus was thirsty for physical water in light of his anguish, Karris sees this statement as a reference for Jesus' desire to carry forth the will of God. The most notable evidence for this assertion is seen in 18:11 where Jesus says to Peter, τὸ ποτήριον ὃ δέδωκέν μοι ὁ πατὴρ οὐ μὴ πίω αὐτό; He writes, "Jesus thirsts to do his Father's will and to finish the work the Father has given him. Just as a person needs drink to sustain life, so too

---

62. Coloe, *God Dwells with Us*, 194–95.
63. Brown, *Death of the Messiah*, 2:1071–72.

does Jesus need obedience to and communion with his Father to sustain his life and his life's work. Jesus is needy to do his Father's will."[64]

Some scholars see Jesus' longing in connection to Psalm 69:21. Yet Brown says that if one follows this reading, then the scriptural element is not in Jesus' actual words but in the response provoked, the giving of vinegar to drink.[65] Notwithstanding, Carson is right to suggest:

> If we grant that Jesus knew he was fulfilling this Scripture, presumably he knew that by verbally confessing his thirst he would precipitate the soldiers' effort to give him some wine vinegar. In that case, the fulfillment clause could be rendered, "Jesus, knowing that all things had been accomplished, in order to fulfil [the] Scripture [which says 'They ... gave me vinegar for my thirst'] said 'I thirst.'" Either way, John wants to make his readers understand that every part of Jesus' passion was not only in the Father's plan of redemption, but a consequence of the Son's direct obedience to it.[66]

Karris points out that some scholars view Psalm 69:21 fulfilled in Jesus' reception of the sponge filled with vinegar/sour wine. He says, "By alluding to this psalm text, John assimilates it into his own text and context. What may have been a real physical thirst in the situation envisioned in Psalm 69:21 is now a symbolic thirst: the thirst to do God's will to its nth degree and to drink the cup the Father has set out for him."[67] Thus, in all likelihood, Jesus' word(s) may be viewed as a prayer to finish in death what began in his life, namely, unswerving obedience to the Father. To state matters further, Jesus' perseverance to the end may be viewed as the answer to his prayer in John 17. In light of Jesus' union with the Father's will and by virtue of the Father's answer to his prayer, Jesus crossed the finish line and completed his mission.

But as indicated above, Jesus' desire for full obedience to the Father would necessarily benefit the "sheep" (10:7–11) for whom he lay down his life. Thus, the end (τέλος) that the Evangelist speaks of in 13:1 anticipates Jesus' completed work and final words in 19:30, τετέλεσται. This expression also has the sense of completeness (compare the use of τετέλεσται in 19:30). In the incarnation, the Word became flesh for the sake of the world (6:51c) and lived a life of self-giving love to the end of his life Jesus' final word(s) (τετέλεσται) is a declaration of nothing less than the fulfillment of

---

64. Karris, *Prayer and the New Testament*, 110.
65. Brown, *Death of the Messiah*, 2:1072–73.
66. Carson, *Gospel According to John*, 619–20.
67. Karris, *Prayer and the New Testament*, 110.

his earthly tasks. In this understanding, Jesus has proved victorious in his obedience to the Father and his mission to secure salvation. Although Jesus' final words were followed by his physical death, his death brought forth eternal life for those who believe (3:16).

But on completion of Jesus' obedience to the Father and his mission for the world, the Evangelist notes in 19:30, καὶ κλίνας τὴν κεφαλὴν παρέδωκεν τὸ πνεῦμα. Coloe interprets Jesus' final statement in terms of him handing down the promised gift of the Spirit. She sees Jesus' final act as the granting of the Spirit, thereby "constituting the believers into a new household of God."[68] She says, "As the soldiers destroy the 'body/temple' of Jesus, the Nazarene temple-builder is in the process of raising up a new temple/household of God, thus fulfilling Jesus' words, 'destroy this temple and in three days I will raise it up.'"[69] In this reading, the Spirit was handed down to Mary the mother of Jesus and to the small group of believers gathered at the cross. But Coloe is careful to note that the Evangelist does not present two bestowals of the Spirit but rather "two moments within one hour."[70] As such, the Spirit-Paraclete was granted to indwell those who were in [of] the new household of faith and to fulfill the roles assigned by Jesus in 14:26; 15:26; 16:13–14.

Finally, the question remains concerning whether or not the term τετέλεσται may be viewed as a prayer to the Father. For some the answer is an obvious *yes*, but others may not be convinced since Jesus' last words contain no direct form of address ("Father"). Accordingly, no petition is presented and no thanksgiving or adoration is offered. However, with the Johannine emphasis on Jesus' obedience (in life and death) to the Father in mind, Jesus' final words may be understood as prayerful communication between a "superior" receiver and a "subordinate" sender. In this reading, Jesus, the "subordinate" sender, enters into the space of prayer in order to communicate/declare the completeness and finality of his mission to the Father, the "superior" receiver. This model accords with the nature of Jesus' prayer in 12:27 where he asserts boldness and fidelity to the purpose of the hour of suffering assigned to him. Or, in other words, the "superior/subordinate" model is congruent with Jesus' petition that the Father's name be glorified (12:28a; 17:1, 5) through submission to his will/purpose, Jesus' troubled soul notwithstanding. The Johannine Jesus is presented as the one who is thirsty to do the will of God and to bring honor to his name. All that

---

68. Coloe, "Nazarene King," 847.
69. Coloe, "Nazarene King," 847.
70. Coloe, *God Dwells with Us*, 197.

Jesus does is out of submission to him. Hence, the term τετέλεσται serves as a prayer through which Jesus affirms that this purpose is now completed.

What about other possibilities? Did Jesus offer these words as a personal declaration for his own benefit? In this writer's estimation, such a suggestion is possible but not probable since the textual evidence is substantially lacking. However, this is not to say that Jesus' prayer was merely offered to the Father without benefit to those gathered at the cross. His final words may have been issued to inform believers that, in light of the completeness of his mission, they are now qualified to be dwelling places of the Spirit and carriers of his name. The finality of Jesus' words, then, might naturally evoke a sense of anticipation for the approaching "day" when their sorrow would turn to joy and they would be able to approach the Father directly in Jesus' name (16:20–23).

Moreover, the following questions were raised in chapter 2 of the present work: "Penner demonstrates that Jewish prayers were spontaneous, but oftentimes offered in conjunction with the timing of the sacrificial enterprise. Does the Fourth Gospel make this connection? How does prayer and sacrifice relate in the Fourth Gospel?" In light of Penner's research, it is possible, but not provable, that worshippers who saw a link between sacrifice/incense and prayer may have viewed Jesus' death as the means by which their prayers would become effectual. Although the Fourth Gospel does not make this connection in such precise terms, it does highlight the completion of Jesus' mission as the key to the answered prayer and the performance of "greater works" (John 14:2–3, 12–14). Although the terminology of sacrifice is not used in 19:30, the evidence above suggests that Jesus' final words on the cross were offered in the context of his completed mission (14:2–3; 17:1; etc.). Since his work is complete, effectual prayer is now possible for those who approach the Father in his name (16:16–24).

Second, the Fourth Gospel offers a unique but complementary account of the final moments of Jesus' life. By associating certain events from the cross-event with the Passover festival, the Evangelist draws attention to Jesus as the one who, on the basis of fidelity to the Father and love for his sheep, emancipates believers from slavery to sin. By virtue of Jesus' obedience, believers are afforded the privileges of becoming members/children of the new household of God and possessors of both the Spirit of God and the name of Jesus. As they pray in his name, the works of the Father/Jesus are performed through them (14:12–14) and the Father is glorified.

Accordingly, the following questions were raised in chapter 2 of the present work and are relevant in the present discussion: "In light of the destruction of the first temple and the abolition of cultic sacrifice, the synagogue participants were transformed into a praying community. What is the scope of prayer in the Fourth Gospel? Is prayer presented as a private or communal activity?" While communal prayer is not prescribed in the Fourth Gospel, it is certainly not precluded. In light of the analysis performed in previous chapters, the Synoptic accounts reveal that Jesus prayed both in public and in private. Yet the Johannine examples above, in particular, reveal the public nature of Jesus' prayer life. As indicated, Jesus did not pray/speak out loud for his sake, but for the sake of those watching and listening. Thus, once again, it is plausible to suggest that Jesus' prayer had didactic value for disciples who approached the Father in Jesus' name and on the basis of his example. In light of Jesus' final public prayer and the destruction of his body on the cross (John 2:19), a new temple/household was created. Thus, it is possible, but not provable, that believers were inspired to offer communal prayer within and in the presence of this newly formed household of faith.

Finally, the evidence above demonstrates that Jesus' final words, "I thirst" and "It is finished," are best viewed as prayers through which Jesus declares his desire for obedience to the will of the Father and proclaims the completion of his mission, respectively. Thus, it may be plausible to suggest that Jesus' words in 19:28, 30 serve as a model for the disciples who would face hardship in the approaching hour (16:2-4). As Jesus thirsted to do the will of the Father, so the disciples may thirst to do the will of the Father, both in life and in death. As Jesus, through a short prayer in 19:30, declared that his mission was complete, so the disciples and the Johannine Community, through the means of prayer and obedience to his will, could offer a similar declaration upon completing the works the Father assigned to them.

CHAPTER 9

Conclusion

THE PREVIOUS CHAPTERS OF this book have been dedicated to analyzing the topic of prayer. With consideration to the surrounding Jewish, Greco-Roman, and Christian traditions, the present work has aimed at drawing forth and establishing the unique contributions made by the Fourth Evangelist to the topic of prayer. Further, specific questions were raised in chapters 2–4 that served to sensitize the reader to the prayer materials that would be examined in subsequent chapters. Moreover, in chapters 5–7 I devoted a significant amount of attention to ascertaining the theological function of prayer in the Farewell Discourse. I have shown that the concept and practice of prayer is surrounded by numerous topics including: Jesus' departure, belief/faith in Jesus, the Father's house, greater works, Jesus' name, the Spirit-Paraclete, the world's hatred, the vine-gardener-branches, remaining in Jesus, friendship with Jesus, Jesus' love, bearing much fruit, the glory/honor of God, and the disciples' sorrow/joy. Each of these topics form the theological and historical network that prayer is situated within and serves to contextualize Johannine prayer within the larger framework of belief in Jesus and the advancement of God's mission through him.

As seen, prayer in the Farewell Discourse is located within the context of what, at first glance, appears to be an eschatological crisis: Jesus' departure is imminent, the mission of God is incomplete, and opposition from the world is certain. Thus, Johannine prayer is issued within the context of Johannine problems. Jesus' speech began in the upper room as he announced his betrayal and subsequent departure (13:36–38). Although the disciples were not definitively clear concerning the nature of Jesus' departure, their emotional sentiment (14:1) indicates that they experienced a sense of apprehension and reservation in light of Jesus' announcement. As Jews, the disciples could naturally pray to God and expect him to answer accordingly.

However, in light of the incarnation, a new situation has developed. Jesus is the Logos (1:1, 14) sent from God, who claimed to be the way, and the truth, and the life (14:6). To have seen Jesus is to have seen the Father. To have seen the works that Jesus performed was to have witnessed the Father working in the disciples' midst (14:9–10). To have conversed with Jesus was to have conversed with God. Therefore, most problematic is the question concerning how the disciples were to carry on in light of Jesus' absence. How will the disciples communicate with God? What will they communicate to God? How will discipleship continue? How will they perform Jesus' works and bear fruit for God? How will they endure their own hour of hardship and tribulation? How will the mission of God be accomplished? How will they bring glory to God?

Of course, it may be tempting to posit *prayer* as the immediate answer to the questions raised above. This present work has asserted that prayer is the means by which one may communicate with God and achieve specific results. However, when approaching the Farewell Discourse, the Evangelist does not place immediate stress on the topic of prayer, but rather locates prayer within a larger matrix of themes that make it relevant. Particularly, the dominant theme of the Farewell Discourse centers on the necessity of being in and remaining in a relationship with God, Jesus' absence notwithstanding. As such, the Evangelist indicates that Jesus will depart, but the disciples' relationship with God will not be disrupted. Instead it will rather undergo a fundamental reorientation in and around the glorified Jesus, who brokers access to God. The emphasis placed on Jesus provides a distinct point of divergence from Greco-Roman and Jewish prayer traditions. In the Johannine model, the solution to one's problems is not prayer, generally, but prayer that is offered in the context of a relationship with Jesus, particularly. Since Jesus brokers access to God, then a relationship with Jesus guarantees a response from God. In sum, the Johannine God will "do" (14:13–14) anything for the one who is "in" him (15:4–7). The synthesis below will explicate how a relationship with Jesus is maintained in light of his absence.

The New Location of Worship: Where Is Prayer Offered?

The Space of Prayer

Throughout the Fourth Gospel, the disciples' communication with Jesus involved normal aspects of human interaction, namely: speaking, seeing, and hearing (John 1:38; 6:32; 11:6; etc.). And it was within the context of relational space with Jesus where questions were raised and answers were provided (3:4–5; 13:6–20; 21:21–22). But the nature of this space was altered on Jesus' departure. They no longer had access to Jesus in the flesh. So how could their relationship with Jesus continue? The Evangelist's solution to the problem of Jesus' physical absence centers on the indwelling of God's presence through the Paraclete. As indicated in 14:2, the Father's house has many "rooms." Some scholars relegate this so-called space to heaven, but this interpretation is too restrictive. Following Coloe, "In the Hebrew Scriptures, 'my father's house' always means the group of people who make up the household [or home], such as the family and servants, or even the future descendants."[1] If this interpretation is correct, then Jesus departed to prepare the disciples who would occupy and comprise the Father's house on earth (but also inevitably in heaven). Thus, the disciples would become the dwelling place of God via the Spirit-Paraclete, who would come to be in and with the disciples (14:17). By virtue of the indwelling presence of the Spirit, believers have access to Jesus and the Father. Hence, the presence of God will be brokered/mediated through the Spirit-Paraclete, as well as the necessary provision that accompanies his presence in the form of education, conviction, and so forth (14:26; 15:26; 16:8–11, 13). In this model the Paraclete perpetuates one's relationship with Jesus and provides the space in which communication with God/Jesus may continue. And because God is always present in this space, one can have confidence that he is always listening and willing to respond to one's prayers. Therefore, the Evangelist labors to demonstrate that the disciples should not fear relational distance with Jesus or the consequences thereof. Jesus will not only be present via the Spirit, but his name will be present on the lips of every disciple who approaches God.

Furthermore, the concept of relational space with Jesus is highlighted in John 15, albeit in different terminology. As in the case of chapter 14, the primacy of physical space is precluded in the Evangelist's discussion in chapter 15. Rather, the disciples are portrayed as branches who must remain in relationship with Jesus, the vine (15:1–6). The very act of remaining in relational space with Jesus ensures that the nourishing sap of the vine permeates the disciple-branches (15:5). As believers remain in Jesus and Jesus' words remain in them, they may ask for anything they wish and they will have it (15:7). Thus, once again, remaining in the vine, not in a physical structure, is the key to effectual praying and fruit bearing. Yet the Evangelist is careful to highlight the necessity of remaining in the vine by faith. If one fails to remain, he is like a branch that has been severed from the vine and will be

---

1. Coloe, "Temple Imagery in John," 375.

burned (15:6). The consequence is that his prayers will not be answered and no fruit will be produced (15:4–6). In order to be successful in prayer, then, one must successfully remain in Jesus. This model of prayer assumes that God is not obligated to answer anyone's prayers, generally, but only prayers that are offered from faithful believers, particularly. Such prayers are forged in the relational context where Jesus' words and will form the very fabric of one's prayer requests. Thus, relational closeness, intimacy, and faithfulness are the keys to understanding prayer in the Farewell Discourse. Once again, without a relationship with Jesus, prayer is not possible. On the other hand, without prayer, a fruit-bearing relationship is not possible. Therefore, the Evangelist is careful to uphold the importance of both dynamics throughout the discourse.

Moreover, the Fourth Gospel indicates that in light of the incarnation, worship is no longer tied to a particular city (Jerusalem) or structure (the temple), but it occurs in Spirit and truth (John 4:23–24). As such, worship that the Father accepts is that which is offered on the basis of the Son who reveals God's truth to the world. And those who have faith in Jesus (14:1) become the new dwelling places of God. Although temple imagery is not explicitly present in chapters 14–16, certain elements may be present in the background.

As noted previously, the first and second temples were the metaphorical dwelling places of God and the places where sacrifice was offered. The temple that bore God's name was the structure from which prayers were channeled heavenward to God (1 Kgs 8:17–19, 20, 29). As such, an informal connection between prayer and the temple was established over the course of time. Penner has shown convincingly that certain Jews believed that prayer in connection with sacrifice in the temple increased the efficacy of their prayers. If this was the perception of Jews in the first century generally, then access to Jesus, the new temple (John 2:19–20), may have been viewed as the necessary requirement for increasing the efficacy of one's prayers. Theoretically, this may have been the perception after the fall of Jerusalem and the destruction of the temple in 70 CE. Much like the physical structure of the temple, Jesus' physical body was no longer present after his ascension. Yet one could approach the space of prayer as he stood in relationship with the risen Jesus. Therefore, prayer would be heard by virtue of Jesus' preparatory work (i.e., death as sacrifice, 19:30) and by virtue of all that Jesus' name represents. Free outpouring of the heart may be offered to God apart from the physical temple, but not apart from Jesus, the new temple. He is the conduit through which prayer is offered heavenward to the Father. Thus, disciples who remain in Jesus stand in relational proximity to God and are therefore beneficiaries of that relationship. The synthesis that follows explicates the nature and function of prayer within the context of a relationship with Jesus.

The Timing and Posture of Prayer

The following question was raised in chapter 2 of this book: "Both the Shema and Tefillah were prayed at certain times of the day. According to the Fourth Gospel, what time of day should prayer occur?" As far as the Farewell Discourse is concerned, prayer is not tied to fixed times or liturgical sequence. Rather, the Evangelist portrays prayer as an act of communication that may take place at any time. Since prayer is tied to the mission of God, it may be offered whenever one desires since the mission of God will not be finally completed until the Parousia. Since God is always working (John 5:17), the disciples should never cease praying. As they offer prayer in Jesus' name and according to the indwelling word, greater works will be performed and much fruit will be produced. Therefore, in the context of John 14–15, prayer in connection with the temple (or any physical space) is a moot point. Rather than prayer being offered in the temple, the Fourth Evangelist highlights prayer as taking place in the context of one's relationship with Jesus, the vine. One may pray at any place and at any time as long as he prays according to the mandates outlined by the Evangelist. Further, as noted previously, Jewish prayer/worship was offered in various postures and positions. For example, when praying the Tefillah/Amidah, the worshipper stood with his or her feet together and prayed toward Jerusalem/the temple. The biblical record indicates that Joshua fell on the ground before God (Josh 7:6). Moses bowed his head to the earth (Exod 34:8). Solomon stood before the altar of the Lord and spread out his hands (2 Chr 6:12). Concerning prayer in the NT, before Jesus performed a miracle he looked up toward heaven, most presumably in an attitude of prayer (Mark 7:34). In other cases he knelt down to pray (Luke 22:41). Finally, we are told Jesus fell on his face and prayed (Matt 26:39).

As such, one's posture of prayer is revealing. Bowing down conveys a sense of humility before God and dependence on God. Looking up toward heaven conveys a sense of acknowledgement of where one's help comes from. Interestingly, in the context of the Farewell Discourse, the Evangelist does not prescribe a particular posture or stance in prayer. While Jesus is portrayed as looking toward heaven in his address to the Father in John 17:1, Jesus does not prescribe this posture as mandatory for believers who offer prayer in his name. Although such a posture may be assumed out of respect, it should not be assumed out of necessity. By virtue of the indwelling presence of the Father and Son through the Spirit-Paraclete, God is particularly immanent, that is, he is present in relational space with believers. Thus, one may bow down or look up to heaven in prayer, under the condition that he acknowledges that God is not merely above him, but most specifically within him. Moreover, a worshipper need not face toward one particular city in prayer (i.e., the Tefillah/Amidah). Instead he or she may face any direction since salvation is offered to the entire world (3:16; 4:42; etc.). In brief, prayer in the Farewell Discourse is less about a physical place or posture than it is about a relational place and the theological privileges granted to believers.

Posture in prayer is largely determined by one's presuppositions concerning the one being addressed in prayer. As noted throughout the present work, Johannine prayer occurs in relational space that is occupied by subordinate (human) and superior (divine) parties. Neyrey says that "the receiver of the prayer is the person perceived as supporting, maintaining, and controlling the order of existence of the one praying, which presupposes a superior/subordinate relationship."[2] This element of Neyrey's definition of prayer draws attention to the nature and ability of the one praying, as well as the one being prayed to. Theoretically, depending on one's religious presuppositions, one may view prayer as simply a means by which dialogue occurs between equal parties. Of course, in this understanding Neyrey's definition loses its relevance. However, prayer within each of the religious traditions examined in this book is offered from the lesser party to the greater party, from the weaker member to the stronger member, from the "subordinate" sender to the "superior" receiver.[3] This is clearly the case with prayer within the Jewish and Christian traditions, but it is also seen in Greco-Roman prayer where petitions are offered to gods who are like men, but superior to

---

2. Neyrey, *Give God the Glory*, 9.

3. Neyrey's definition provides the proper context wherein one offers prayers of petition, adoration, contrition, and/or thanksgiving. Each of these genres of prayer is congruent with the superior/subordinate framework. For example, prayer of petition assumes that the receiver of prayer is superior and is therefore able to grant one's request. Adoration and thanksgiving is the proper response to answered prayer and rightly focuses on esteeming the one who granted the request. Finally, prayer of lament is the natural emotional response one may feel when unfortunate circumstances coalesce with unanswered prayer. Yet the very act of praying assumes that one is dependent on a superior receiver to hear and grant his request. Furthermore, lament is also indicative of one's emotional state that may drive him to prayer. Such is the case with Nehemiah, the psalmists, and most notably, Jesus, who wept over Lazarus's death. In brief, while words of petition, adoration, contrition, and thanksgiving may be offered among equals, they are best understood and applied in the context of relational subordination and superiority.

them in notable respects. Notwithstanding, the act of petitioning conveys a sense of vulnerability and dependency on the part of the worshipper.

As seen in the Lord's Prayer (Matt 6:9; Luke 11:2), Jesus says that one is to approach God as Father, that is, the head of the family; he is the one who provides for his children and cares for them. Further, although God is like a father, his dwelling space is in heaven and should therefore be addressed with honor and reverence. The superior nature of the Father is highlighted throughout the Gospels but is most particularly typified in the Fourth Gospel where Jesus is presented as the one who can do nothing without the Father (5:19, 30; 14:10–11). Jesus thanks the Father, petitions the Father, and looks upward to the Father in prayer. By doing so, Jesus is the obedient/dependent son par excellence.

Yet Neyrey's definition not only elucidates the nature of Jesus' prayer to the Father, but it also serves as a foundational basis for understanding the disciples' prayers to the Father. The Fourth Gospel presents Jesus as the new place of worship. In the OT, one may approach God on the basis of a relationship established by faith in Yahweh. But the Fourth Evangelist indicates that relational access to the "superior" receiver (the Father) is predicated on one's belief in the Word-made-flesh-mediator (Jesus). In this model the "subordinate" sender (disciple) may freely offer prayer to the "superior" receiver (the Father) as he remains in relationship with the Son. In the final analysis, Neyrey's definition, when applied in the context of the Fourth Gospel, serves to elucidate the demarcation of prayer: just as Jesus (the "subordinate" sender) could do nothing without his Father (the "superior" receiver), so the disciples could do nothing except through prayer as they approach the Father in their mediator's name (16:23–24). As such, a relationship with Jesus provides the relational space where prayer is offered and results are produced. The nature of such results will be discussed further below.

The Substance of Prayer: What Is the Content of Prayer?

With the above synthesis in mind, it is necessary to highlight the particular substance of prayer as indicated in John 14–16. First, the Evangelist prescribes that prayer be offered in Jesus' name (14:13–14; 15:16; 16:23). In ancient culture, an individual's name was a symbol for personal identity, status, and character. For the Jews, the name of God was a symbol for his nature, character, and glory. As such, God's name appears throughout the OT in various contexts and is associated with the terms "I am." Yet as the

Logos, Jesus' mission is relational and revelational in nature. By using the phraseology "I am,"[4] Jesus connected his person and work to Yahweh. By performing signs, Jesus revealed his power and glory. In the incarnation, Jesus revealed his identity as the only Son who has always existed with the Father (1:1, 18). By taking on the role of rabbi (1:38, 49; 3:2; 4:31; 6:25; 9:2; 11:8), Jesus revealed his intention to instruct. By laying down his life on a cross (19:16–30), Jesus revealed his role as a good shepherd (10:11, 14). Thus, Jesus came to reveal, not conceal. So when a person prays in Jesus' name, he is praying on the basis of what that name symbolizes, namely God's person, authority, and mission.

The following questions were raised in chapter 2, "In Psalm 8, the psalmist extols the Lord's name through prayer/hymn. Does the Fourth Gospel link prayer and praise together? If so, how is God's name involved?" As noted, the OT refers to prayers of thanksgiving and praise for the name of God (Ps 69:30; 148:13; etc.). The NT evidence suggests that the Father's name was to be hallowed (Matt 6:9; Luke 11:2). Jesus glorified the Father by manifesting his name to the disciples (John 17:6, 26). He further offered praise to the Father, "Lord of heaven and earth" (Luke 10:21). Yet one may wonder why the Evangelist does not prescribe prayers of praise to Jesus. While there are no direct injunctions of this genre, it is possible that prayer in his name may function as shorthand praise for his name. Thus, one may pray: "Father, in Jesus' name I ask that you will enable me to love the world as you have loved me." As such, in light of Jesus' promises to do whatever one requests in his name, this simple prayer may be viewed as a prayer of petition and praise/thanksgiving since the results are guaranteed. In other words, by offering petitions according to Jesus' will and on the basis of his name, one may be asking God and thanking him at the same time since he is convinced that his prayers cannot fail.

Accordingly, one may praise and/or thank Jesus by the usage of his name, not merely for the promised results that prayer in his name yields, but for the person that his name represents ("I am"). And the granting of such honor to the Son does not minimize or diminish one's honor for the Father since the Father is glorified in the Son (14:13). In essence, glorifying the Son's name is analogous to glorifying the Father's name since they are one (10:30).

---

4. See John 6:35, 48, 51; 8:12; 9:5; 10:7, 9, 11, 14; 11:25; 14:6; 15:1.

Prayer and Jesus' Word

In Greco-Roman prayer, exactness of speech and precision of wording were essential when addressing the gods. A pertinent question centers on whether or not the Fourth Gospel prescribes a formal approach of prayer according to certain words. In John 15:7, the Evangelist indicates that one must remain in Jesus and that Jesus' words must remain in the believer in order for prayer to be effectual. But remaining in Jesus involves more than mere profession of faith in him, but necessarily involves total commitment to him and his words (6:66–69; 8:31). When the condition of loyalty to remain/dwell is met, the words of Jesus shape the trajectory of one's entire life. Thus, the believer will not merely pray in Jesus' name, but he or she will pray in a manner that is consistent with Jesus' words and self-revelation. Jesus' words are to be absorbed into the minds and hearts of believers to such a degree that the substance of their prayers will conform in content and consequence. Much like disciples who pray in Jesus' name (14:13–14), which means praying with all that his name represents, a disciple educated by the words of Jesus will pray in a specific manner that is congruent with his education.

Therefore, the aim is for the nourishing words from the vine to transfer to the hearts and minds of the disciples. As this occurs, the disciples' word-informed prayers are offered to the Father-gardener, who hears and responds. In this model, Jesus' will becomes the disciples' will. Honor for God is established when this blending occurs and when one offers requests that are congruent with his will. By allowing Jesus' words to remain within, the disciples collectively share a group-oriented language that esteems, rather than diminishes, the wishes of their master. Thus, as one approaches God in prayer he does not merely pray for his own good but for the good of all. In short, the disciples are not commissioned to offer self-centered prayers that focus on their own interests. Rather, they are commissioned to offer prayers that contribute to the fruitfulness of the vine, which in turn bring glory to the Father-gardener. This model differs greatly from Greek models of prayer whereby the worshipper must recite the exact words in ritualistic format in order to gain the gods' attention and approval. Thus, the Fourth Evangelist knows nothing of fixed, liturgical, or ritualistic prayers. Instead the content of one's prayers is uttered in the individual's own words that have been shaped by his relationship with Jesus. Instead of the Evangelist providing a script of what to pray, he provides a prerequisite that, once fulfilled, equips the believer to pray in his own words, yet pray in a manner that is consonant with Jesus' stated will.

Further, the Evangelist does not specify how the name of Jesus is to be implemented in one's prayers. Therefore I would like to suggest that a degree of latitude should be offered as Johannine models of prayer are constructed. The following are possible suggestions concerning how prayer may be offered:

> "In Jesus' name, I approach you, Father, to make my requests known."

> "I approach you, Father, in the name of Jesus, to make my requests known."

> "Father, I ask that you grant my requests, in Jesus' name."

Alternatively, on the basis of John 15:7, it is possible that one's prayers to God may not include the phrase, "in Jesus' name," but since the prayer's content is forged on the basis of Jesus' words, it is nonetheless analogous to prayer in his name. The strength of this approach is that it stresses the primacy of being in a relationship with Jesus over against the mere recitation of a name. Although the former examples above do not prescribe a ritualistic approach to prayer, the possibility of implementing such an approach is not precluded. It is possible that one may offer prayer in Jesus' name without having his requests shaped and fashioned by his word. In such a case, the usage of Jesus' name will lose its effectual basis and force. The weakness of this approach centers on the fact that a plain reading of John 14:13-14; 15:16; 16:23 seems to allow "Jesus' name" to function as either a prefix or a suffix to one's prayers. While the evidence is not conclusive, in my view each of the examples above may be implemented insofar as one grasps why effectual prayer is predicated on Jesus' person and work.

Prayer and the Paraclete

The role of the Paraclete is discussed throughout John chapters 14–16. Unfortunately, in most cases interpreters center their attention on the work of the Paraclete apart from prayer. Yet given the immediate context of the Farewell Discourse, I have argued that the Paraclete is sent to further educate and equip the disciples for prayer in Jesus' absence. As such, the Spirit-Paraclete is the Spirit of Truth, who teaches the disciples all things, reminds them of everything Jesus said to them, mediates the presence of Jesus to them, leads them into all the truth, brings conviction to the world, and brings glory to Jesus (14:26; 15:26; 16:8, 13, 14). As the Father educated the Son, so Jesus (as their Rabbi) educated the disciples. In Jesus' absence, the

Paraclete assumes the role of an educator who carries forth the teaching(s) of Jesus and expounds it further. In short, the Paraclete keeps the words and profile of Jesus before the disciples as they advance his mission in the earth. To the degree the disciples were educated via the Paraclete, they were able to offer prayer to God that accorded with his mission and will.

Additionally, the Paraclete functions in a prophetic role, communicating the heavenly, transcendental story to the disciples on earth, who in turn offer prayer back to the Father. In this role, a circular model of communication is formed that begins with the Father, is mediated through the Son, is communicated/taught by the Spirit, is received by disciples, and is finally prayed back to God in Jesus' name. Thus, in this manner the disciples become educated with God's story in order to make his story their earthly reality through prayer. By praying in Jesus' name, the disciples are equipped to bring heaven to the earth, thus actualizing the transcendental story.

Part and parcel of this story is the salvation of the world wrought through the work accomplished by the Son and applied by the Spirit-Paraclete. In this model, salvific initiative that the Paraclete bears witness to is the same initiative that he helps the disciples to complete. Hence, the Spirit convicts the world in regard to sin, righteousness, and judgment (16:8), and does so in order to lead people to repentance and faith/belief in Jesus. Therefore, while the Paraclete is the agency of conviction in Jesus' absence, he does not act alone but synergistically through those in whom he dwells. Therefore, it may be said that the disciple who prays does so in accordance with what he has received via Jesus' word(s) and the Paraclete's witness. In brief, the Paraclete inspires the disciples to pray for the salvation of the world and works concurrently in the world to bring it to pass.

Insofar as salvation is concerned, the Spirit's witness about Jesus may close the gap that exists between one's wishing for salvation and God's willingness to accomplish it. Prayer becomes the means by which one's desires for salvation is offered and God's initiative to save is actualized. As such, prayer to the Father in Jesus' name naturally involves asking for God's heavenly story to become an earthly reality. One may say that prayer to God activates the Spirit of God, who works in the world to produce the result of new believers (who become members of the family of God). In this model, then, prayer becomes the means by which the family of God grows through disciples who continue the mission of God in Jesus' absence. In the context of John 14, such growth is set in the context of the Father's house and the occupation of many rooms. With John 15 in mind, the aim of prayer is the same, yet it is set in the context and language of viticulture wherein it functions as the means by which the vine grows quantitatively as more and more disciple-branches are produced.

Friendship with Benefits

The disciples' initiative to pray is set squarely in the context of friendship with Jesus where relational intimacy occurs and common outlooks are shared. It is worth citing Burge again who says, "Where true friendship exists, true disclosure (or revelation) accompanies it (John 15:15b). Disciples possess the word of Jesus (thanks to the Spirit, 14:25–26), and they will receive ongoing revelations of Jesus (also brought by the Spirit, 16:12–13). Disciples thus know 'God's heart.' When they therefore pray, their desires and God's will harmonize, making them participants in God's efforts in the world (15:16; cf. 15:7)."[5] It is those who share and remain in Jesus' interests, aims, and outlook who are granted the privilege of asking whatever they wish in prayer. And those who remain in this friendship will be granted the very things they wish for (15:7). Thus, they do not pray as mere servants (15:15) but as friends who are granted access to relational space with Jesus. They do not pray as uninterested observers but as committed followers who desire to honor their friendship with Jesus.

The Evangelist indicates that by virtue of their friendship with Jesus, the disciples are granted the privilege of speaking plainly and boldly to God. As noted, in the Fourth Gospel the concept of παρρησία is not explicitly used in connection with prayer between believers and Jesus, but the phrases "whatever you ask" and "whatever you wish" both imply boldness in approaching God and offering petitions to him in prayer. In this model the disciples may boldly petition God knowing that no request is too great if it is consonant with Jesus' name and if it is issued out of loyalty to his cause (14:12–14). Perhaps, then, it is within the paradigm of boldness of speech that the Johannine concept of greater works can be more fully understood. It has been suggested that the so-called greater works are greater in the sense that they will be more frequent in their occurrence and more widespread in their distribution. If this is the case, I would like to suggest that such works must be prayed for in order to manifest through the disciples. On one hand, praying for such works may be too ambitious or perhaps unrealistic. Yet given the finalization of Jesus' hour of glorification (17:1), the completion of his work (19:30), the nature of the disciples' intimate friendship with him (15:13–15), and his promise to do whatever one asks for, it is not difficult to see why a disciple would boldly offer such great requests that would result in such works.

Further, Jesus' prayer of thanksgiving (John 6:11; 11:41) demonstrates that no request is too great if it is offered in the context of a relationship

---

5. Burge, *John*, 387.

with God that aims at the elucidation of his glory and the increase of his honor among men. As such, the concept of *mimesis* becomes relevant to the discussion. The disciples were called into a relationship of imitation, that is, they were commanded to mimic Jesus and follow his example in word and deed. As Jesus offered bold prayers to the Father, so the disciples were to offer bold prayers through the Son to the Father. In fact, one may approach God boldly to make petitions according to Jesus' indwelling word because, in effect, if Jesus sanctioned it then Jesus will do it. In this model, the pressure is placed on God to do whatever he promised to do. With this in mind, prayer offered in Jesus' name and informed by Jesus' words may be congruent with what God has already willed to do through the Spirit-Paraclete. The promise of 14:13–14; 15:7, 16; 16:23 is that the one who makes requests in Jesus' name and in alignment with his will may have his prayers answered.

The Specific Results of Prayer

The assumption of Johannine prayer is that it can be heard, it will be responded to, and it will yield specific "results." But what are those results, and how are they obtained? By simply stating that Jesus will answer prayer offered in his name, the Evangelist removes uncertainty and ambiguity from the discussion. His desire centers on adopting a mode of prayer that yields goods/results that are consonant with the will of the Father as revealed through Jesus, the Son. Hence, the Evangelist is not concerned with answered prayer, generally, but with answered prayer that glorifies the Father, particularly. The paragraphs that follow will further discuss how the desired result (of God's glory) is achieved through the praying disciples.

Honor for God by Trusting/Depending on God

The prayers of Jesus are descriptive, that is, in some measure they elucidate the nature of the Father-Son relationship. Further, they also provide an example of the nature of the Father-Son-disciple relationship, that is, how believers are to relate to God on the basis of their union with Jesus. In particular, they provide a model of the posture, perspective, and attitude that one might imitate as prayer is offered to the Father according to the dictates of 14:13–14; 15:7, 16; 16:23–24. Thus, Jesus' prayers are indicative, descriptive, and didactic. As Jesus gave thanks to the Father (6:11), so the disciples should thank him and express their gratitude for his goodness and generosity. Because the Father always hears the Son and responds to him (11:41–42), so he will also hear and respond to those who pray in Jesus' name. As Jesus looked up to heaven as he prayed (17:1), so the disciples may assume the same posture in prayer and by doing so demonstrate their dependency on God. As Jesus prayed for God's name to be glorified (12:28), so the disciples should pray in a manner that aims at the elucidation of the glory of God in their lives.

Yet this laconic answer provokes further discussion concerning the relationship between faith, prayer, and the Father's glory. In light of the analysis performed in previous chapters, I suggest that God is glorified both in the disciples' offering of prayer and in God's answer to prayer. Such glory is wrought in the relational context where faith, trust, and dependence are expressed. Although the Evangelist never states that Jesus exercised faith in God, the nature of his relationship with the Father is elucidated by elements that are virtually (but not exclusively) synonymous with faith, namely, trust and confidence. Such elements are seen in John chapters 6, 11, 12, and 17 wherein Jesus offers prayers of thanksgiving and/or petition to the Father. As seen throughout the Fourth Gospel, Jesus knew that God always heard him, and he therefore trusted the Father to respond to him, the nature of his requests notwithstanding. Since Jesus' will was in conformity with the Father's, there was no vacillation in his asking or the Father's granting. Further, since Jesus' desire centered on honoring his Father, the Father's desire, in turn, centered on glorifying himself through his Son. Yet by praying to the Father, Jesus demonstrated his dependence on the Father, and by depending on the Father, Jesus the Son brought honor to the Father. In one sense then, God's reputation was esteemed and enhanced in the prayers of Jesus even before the answer was visible. In sum, whether one observes the case of the feeding of the five thousand or the raising of Lazarus, the Father was honored as Jesus offered prayers that were indicative of his complete trust in the Father.

As seen throughout the Fourth Gospel, the disciples' relationship with God was forged on the basis of their faith/trust in him. Such faith involves not only believing in him but also trusting him. As indicated by the Evangelist, faith is not static but is rather a dynamic existential disposition of the heart that moves one to act and speak in a manner that honors God. True faith locates one in relational space with God where desires and requests are vocalized. In particular, faith in God provides the basis for offering bold, effectual prayer to God that places a demand on God's promise to answer. Yet how does such faith relate to God's glory and honor? In short, one glorifies God by trusting that God will do whatever he has promised. The very act of offering requests that are forged on the basis of Jesus' words not only presupposes faith in God but also demonstrates trust in God's character and trustworthiness.

Moreover, since the aim was to increase God's honor among men, such prayer would be offered in some form before men (as in the case of Jesus' prayer at Lazarus's tomb). In this understanding, the content of one's prayer could include words of thanksgiving but is most likely centered on requests and petitions. However, the Evangelist does not insist that one's prayers must be offered audibly and publicly. One may express his trust/faith in God by assuming a certain posture in prayer. As Jesus looked to heaven (John 17:1), so the disciples may look to heaven as an expression of their dependence on God. The same may be said of prayer that is offered with arms/hands extended toward heaven. On the other hand, one may kneel or bow in the space of prayer in order to offer his requests either audibly or silently. Yet as noted above, the Evangelist's main concern is for prayer to be offered on the basis of Jesus' person and name, not in a particular posture or place.

As far as the Fourth Gospel is concerned, the glory of God is most clearly revealed as God answers prayer. This is most notably seen in Jesus' prayer at Lazarus's tomb but is also the corollary of prayer that is offered in Jesus' name. In the context of 14:12–14, God's glory is linked not just to prayer in general but to prayer that results in the performance of greater works in particular. The same is true of answered prayed in 15:7–8. As such, the occupation of God's house with new converts/disciples inevitably brings greater honor to the Father, who sent the Son, hears the Son, and accepts prayers offered on the basis of his work and through the brokerage of his name. From this theological and existential basis, then, prayer that seeks the Father's honor is ultimate while personal honor is penultimate. For the Evangelist, true and effectual prayer is the sort that seeks after the spiritual well-being of the world instead of personal gain. It is never individualized but is rather contextualized to the interests and growth of God's family. In the final analysis, prayer is the means by which God-honoring requests are verbalized and actualized. It is the means by which one makes requests that aim at increasing God's honor and elucidating his glory before men.

The Maintenance of Relationship and God's Mission

Among the monotheistic religious traditions analyzed in the present work, relationship is essential. Part and parcel of the maintenance of one's relationship with God involves the confession of sin against God and the offering of praise, thanksgiving, and petition to God. The former genre of prayer involves the verbal concession that one has offended God and is therefore in need of pardon from God so that his relationship with him may be restored. Prayers of thanksgiving and praise acknowledge and esteem God for his benevolent nature and/or his deeds performed on the worshipper's behalf. Petitionary prayer centers on asking God to do what he has already promised to do. It may be argued that each sort of prayer aims at the maintenance of one's relationship with God. As such, both the OT and NT are replete with examples of each genre of prayer. Yet it is noteworthy to mention that prayer as confession of sin is absent from the Fourth Gospel. Instead of prescribing prayers that center on being restored to a relationship with God, the Evangelist highlights the necessity of remaining in a relationship with Jesus by faith (John 14:1, 12; 15:1–7; 16:1). As believers remain in union with God, they become recipients of the nourishment provided by Jesus, the vine, and receive the tender care of the Father-gardener. In this model, relational intimacy and permanency are guaranteed as one remains in Jesus by faith in his person and his words. Conversely, the one who fails to remain is like a branch that withers, is cast away, and is burned (15:6). One should not expect that his prayers to God will be heard or answered.

Accordingly, if faith in God grants one access to relational space with God, then prayer is the means by which one maintains communication with God within that space. While faith unites one to God, prayer serves as the existential medium through which one maintains relational intimacy with God and bears much fruit (15:8). Prayer, then, is not at odds with faith in God but is rather the corollary of it. Through prayer a channel of vertical communication between the disciples and God is opened through which one's desires and requests are verbalized. Though one cannot see God, he may speak freely to God as he remains in union with him by faith. Therefore, the Farewell Discourse precludes the possibility of a static, distant relationship with God, Jesus' departure notwithstanding. Moreover, since relationship with God is ultimate, not only would one's prayer center on the advancement of God's mission through the production of more disciples but it would also center on the protection of God's mission through the preservation (or maintenance) of established disciples. In this understanding, one may pray for a greater quantity of branches on the vine, but one may also pray for the preservation and health of the branches attached to the vine. That Jesus desired the preservation of his disciples is seen in his prayer to the Father before the hour of his suffering and departure. He states in John 17:11–12:

> 11 καὶ οὐκέτι εἰμὶ ἐν τῷ κόσμῳ, καὶ αὐτοὶ ἐν τῷ κόσμῳ εἰσίν, κἀγὼ πρὸς σὲ ἔρχομαι. Πάτερ ἅγιε, τήρησον αὐτοὺς ἐν τῷ ὀνόματί σου ᾧ δέδωκάς μοι, ἵνα ὦσιν ἓν καθὼς ἡμεῖς. 12 ὅτε ἤμην μετ' αὐτῶν ἐγὼ ἐτήρουν αὐτοὺς ἐν τῷ ὀνόματί σου ᾧ δέδωκάς μοι, καὶ

ἐφύλαξα, καὶ οὐδεὶς ἐξ αὐτῶν ἀπώλετο εἰ μὴ ὁ υἱὸς τῆς ἀπωλείας, ἵνα ἡ γραφὴ πληρωθῇ.

Jesus says further concerning those who would come to believe in 17:20–23:

> 20 Οὐ περὶ τούτων δὲ ἐρωτῶ μόνον, ἀλλὰ καὶ περὶ τῶν πιστευόντων διὰ τοῦ λόγου αὐτῶν εἰς ἐμέ, 21 ἵνα πάντες ἓν ὦσιν, καθὼς σύ, πάτερ, ἐν ἐμοὶ κἀγὼ ἐν σοί, ἵνα καὶ αὐτοὶ ἐν ἡμῖν ὦσιν, ἵνα ὁ κόσμος πιστεύῃ ὅτι σύ με ἀπέστειλας. 22 κἀγὼ τὴν δόξαν ἣν δέδωκάς μοι δέδωκα αὐτοῖς, ἵνα ὦσιν ἓν καθὼς ἡμεῖς ἕν· 23 ἐγὼ ἐν αὐτοῖς καὶ σὺ ἐν ἐμοί, ἵνα ὦσιν τετελειωμένοι εἰς ἕν, ἵνα γινώσκῃ ὁ κόσμος ὅτι σύ με ἀπέστειλας καὶ ἠγάπησας αὐτοὺς καθὼς ἐμὲ ἠγάπησας.

With this in mind, the Johannine model of mission involves not merely the multiplication of disciples but also the oneness within the Father-Son-disciple relational sphere. As relationships are maintained, prayers will be offered, fruit will be produced, and the Father-gardener will receive honor. In this model, prayer may be viewed as causal link between production of more disciples, the preservation of existing disciples, and their promotion of the glory of God in the world. Of course, the preservation of the disciples' relationship with God had little to do with their earthly comfort or the longevity of their earthly life. Instead, preservation must be understood in the context of remaining faithful to God and to his mission. While on the cross Jesus uttered the short prayer, "I thirst" (19:28), which I have shown is a statement that indicates Jesus' desire to complete the will of God in the midst of his suffering. In short, Jesus offered a prayer for strength to complete the mission assigned to him by the Father and to bring glory to his name (12:28). In his final prayer from the cross, Jesus prayed, "It is finished" (19:30). As shown, this prayer is a statement of finality: Jesus' mission is complete, the sacrifice has been offered, the Spirit will be sent, and the Father is glorified through the Son's obedience.

But just as Jesus faced his hour of suffering at the hands of the Romans, so the disciples would face hardship at the hands of the world and certain antagonistic Jews (15:18–26; 16:2). Yet as Jesus endured his hour of suffering by prayer to the Father, so too the disciples could remain faithful to Jesus and endure their hour of suffering by praying to God in Jesus' name. Through prayer the Father would enable the disciples to complete their mission as they encountered hostile circumstances. By representing the absent Jesus through their words and works, the disciples would bring glory to God (12:28; 14:12–14; 15:7–8) and increase the honor of the Father in the world. It is within this context that the disciples were promised peace and the fullness of joy (14:27; 15:11; 16:24).

Moreover, the topic of faithfulness to God became especially relevant as the disciples faced the "little while" of not seeing but then seeing Jesus again (16:16). Accordingly, the disciples' faith/trust would also become relevant in light of the temporal duration that existed between asking and receiving in prayer. As such, the emphasis of 16:21a centers on the sorrow that the mother feels as labor pains ensue. A corollary of this sorrow likely involves anxiety about the future occasion of the delivery of her baby in the form of minutes and hours. The emotional state of the mother, then, found a place of relevance and similitude in the disciples as they experienced sorrow over Jesus' disappearance and death, but such travail may have also been experienced as they awaited an answer to prayer. Yet their travail would be temporary, and even in the midst of it, the disciples could find a sense of comfort knowing that joy awaits them. Jesus would reappear, and the reward of his appearance would center on the privilege of approaching the Father directly in Jesus' name and experiencing a fullness of joy that no one could take from them (16:22, 24). On one hand, one may assert that the disciples' joy is based on their ability to pray and receive, generally. However, as noted, Johannine prayer must be viewed within the larger context of Jesus' mission and the Father's family. Thus, the collective evidence of chapters 14–16 indicates that by maintaining their relationship with Jesus (that is, by remaining in Jesus by faith and by offering prayer in his name) the disciples become vessels through which God's family expands and God's name is glorified.

Personal Reflections

I would like to conclude by reflecting on how the topic of prayer is relevant in a world 1,900 years removed from the Johannine community. As such, the following paragraphs are more personal and reflective than academic. Several decades ago, singer-songwriter Joan Osborne popularized a song whose refrain proclaims God's greatness and goodness along with the following lyrics,

> What if God was one of us?
> Just a slob like one of us
> Just a stranger on the bus
> Tryin' to make his way home?[6]

6. Osborne, "One of Us."

In response, one might point to the Evangelist's prologue where he notes that God has indeed become one of us (John 1:1, 14). The eternal Word became flesh and rode the proverbial bus. On his way home, this divine stranger was subjected to rejection, evil, and suffering. Paradoxically, Jesus was affected by sin, but he was never infected with sin. It is indeed a breathtaking proposition that the transcendent creator-God entered into the brokenness of this world to become one of us. Yet, this is the reality portrayed by the Fourth Evangelist. With this in mind, our prayers are not issued in the name of a cold, distant God. Rather, they are offered in the name of the one who gave his life for us. As noted by an unknown author, you can trust someone who is willing to bleed for you. Therefore, I concur that God is great and that God is good.

But the Fourth Gospel does not merely present Jesus as the one who can identify with our problems; it presents him as the only one who can truly rectify our problems. At various points throughout my time of study and research, I was reminded of the sin that people commit and the hopelessness that many people experience in this fallen world. Nevertheless, the Evangelist reminds us that Jesus came as light in the midst of darkness (1:4–5) and to bring living water in the midst of spiritual famine (4:13–14; 7:37). He came to reveal, not conceal (1:18). He came to save, not condemn (3:17). And Jesus left us with his name, a name that encapsulates the nature of his person and work. He is in fact savior, redeemer, and Lord. Therefore, the Fourth Evangelist posits prayers in his name as the means by which the world is changed and lives are transformed. Through prayer the invisible God invades our visible world. In prayer we exchange our pain and brokenness for healing and wholeness. In prayer we are granted the privilege of not only petitioning God for our own needs, but also for the needs and welfare of others. Therefore, in light of the promises of the Fourth Gospel, one should view prayer as the first option instead of the last resort in times of need. In fact, the ubiquity of pain and suffering demands perdurability in our praying.

Moreover, after a careful reading of the Johannine text, I am convinced that no prayer request is too great if it is congruent with God's will and is offered for the purpose of bringing God glory. As I drew close to the text of the Fourth Gospel I became more aware of the generous nature of God, who is often more willing to give than we are to ask. If this is the case, then we should offer prayer requests that might sound ridiculous in hopes that God may in fact perform the miraculous. But what about prayers that go unanswered? What about prayers that seem to fall on deaf ears? While the Scriptures sufficiently elucidate the nature of the invisible God, they do not exhaustively communicate the will of God. Thus, faith not only involves believing that God exists, but it also involves believing that God is good and that he will answer at the proper time and in the appropriate fashion. Our eschatological hopes may be deferred, but they will not be denied. Notwithstanding, it is important to remember that prayer is not merely the means by which one obtains results from God; it is the medium through which one experiences intimacy and fellowship with God. The Fourth Evangelist labors to demonstrate that such fellowship is possible exclusively through God's Son, Jesus, the Christ.

As noted in the introduction to this book, I have taken Einstein's challenge to "find out about prayer." And based on the testimony of the Fourth Evangelist, I have concluded that the God who created the universe that Einstein observed is but a prayer away for those who draw near to him on the basis of their relationship with Jesus, his Son. It is my hope that this book will make a small contribution to the field of Johannine research and will serve to enlighten, encourage, and equip those who seek to draw close to God through prayer.

Bibliography

Akala, Adesola Joan. *The Son-Father Relationship and Christological Symbolism in the Gospel of John*. Paperback ed. Library of New Testament Studies. International Studies in Christian Origins 505. London: Bloomsbury T & T Clark, 2015.

Aland, Barbara, et al., eds. *The Greek New Testament* (UBS⁴). 4th rev. ed. New York: United Bible Societies, 1993.

Alderlink, Larry J., and Luther H. Martin. "Prayer in Greco-Roman Religions." In *Prayer from Alexander to Constantine: A Critical Anthology*, edited by Mark Kiley, 123–27. London: Routledge, 1997.

Alexander, Philip. "'The Parting of the Ways' from the Perspective of Rabbinic AD 70 to 135. Wissenschaftliche Untersuchungen zum Neuen Testament 66. Tübingen: Mohr Siebeck, 1992.

Aloisi, John. "The Paraclete's Ministry of Conviction: Another Look at John 16:8–11." *Journal of the Evangelical Theological Society* 47.1 (2004) 55–69.

Ashton, John. *Understanding the Fourth Gospel*. Oxford: Clarendon, 1991.

Aune, David E. "Prayer in the Greco-Roman World." In *Into God's Presence: Prayer in the New Testament*, edited by Richard N. Longenecker, 23–42. Grand Rapids: Eerdmans, 2001.

Balentine, Samuel E. *Prayer in the Hebrew Bible: The Drama of Divine-Human Dialogue*. Minneapolis: Fortress, 1993.

Barrett, C. K. *The Gospel According to St. John: An Introduction with Commentary and Notes on the Greek Text*. 2nd ed. Philadelphia: Westminster, 1978.

Beasley-Murray, George R. *John*. Word Biblical Commentary 36. Grand Rapids: Zondervan, 1999.

Becker, Jürgen. *Das Evangelium nach Johannes: Kapitel 11–21*. 3rd rev. ed. Ökumenischer Taschenbuchkommentar zum Neuen Testament 4.2. Würzburg: Echter, 1991.

Bennema, Cornelius. *Excavating John's Gospel: A Commentary for Today*. Eugene, OR: Wipf & Stock, 2005.

———. *The Power of Saving Wisdom: An Investigation of Spirit and Wisdom in Relation to the Soteriology of the Fourth Gospel*. Wissenschaftliche Untersuchungen zum Neuen Testament 2.148. Eugene, OR: Wipf & Stock, 2007.

Berkovits, Eliezer. "From Temple to Synagogue and Back." In *Understanding Jewish Prayer*, edited by Jacob Josef Petuchowski, 138–51. New York: Ktav, 1972.

Beutler, Johannes. *Das Johannesevangelium: Kommentar*. Freiburg im Breisgau: Herder, 2013. eBook.

———. *Do Not Be Afraid: The First Farewell Discourse in John's Gospel (John 14)*. New Testament Studies in Contextual Exegesis 6. Frankfurt: Peter Lang, 2011.
Biblia Hebraica Stuttgartensia: With Westminster Hebrew Morphology. (BHS/WHM 4.2). Electronic ed. Stuttgart; Glenside, PA: German Bible Society; Westminster Seminary, 1996. Logos Bible Software 8.
Bietenhard, H. "*ónoma.*" *TDNT* 694–700.
Bock, Darrell L. *A Theology of Luke and Acts: Biblical Theology of the New Testament.* Grand Rapids: Zondervan, 2012.
Bradshaw, Paul F. *Daily Prayer in the Early Church: A Study of the Origin and Early Development of the Divine Office.* Eugene, OR: Wipf & Stock, 1981.
Brodie, Thomas L. *The Gospel According to John: A Literary and Theological Commentary.* New York: Oxford University Press, 1993.
Brown, Raymond E. *The Death of the Messiah: From Gethsemane to the Grave; A Commentary on the Passion Narratives in the Four Gospels.* 2 vols. Anchor Bible Reference Library. New York: Doubleday, 1994.
———. *The Gospel According to John (I–XII): Introduction, Translation, and Notes.* Vol. 1. Anchor Bible Commentary 29. New Haven: Yale University Press, 2006.
———. *The Gospel According to John (XIII–XXI): Introduction, Translation, and Notes.* Vol 2. London: Chapman, 1970.
Brown, Tricia Gates. *Spirit in the Writings of John: Johannine Pneumatology in Social-Scientific Perspective.* Library of New Testament Studies. Journal for the Study of the New Testament Supplement Series 253. London: T & T Clark International, 2003.
Bruce, F. F. *The Book of the Acts.* Rev. ed. New International Commentary on the New Testament. Grand Rapids: Eerdmans, 1988.
———. *The Gospel and Epistles of John.* Grand Rapids: Eerdmans, 1983.
Brueggemann, Walter. *Great Prayers of the Old Testament.* Louisville: Westminster John Knox, 2008.
———. *The Psalms and the Life of Faith.* Edited by Patrick D. Miller. Minneapolis: Fortress, 1995.
Bryant, Michael L. "An Examination of Prayer in the Johannine Literature." PhD diss., Southeastern Baptist Theological Seminary, 2008.
Bultmann, Rudolf. "*alḗtheia, alēthḗs, alēthinós, alētheúō.*" *TDNT* 1:37–40.
———. *Das Evangelium des Johannes.* Göttingen: Vandenhoeck & Ruprecht, 1964.
———. *The Gospel of John: A Commentary.* Translated by G. R. Beasley-Murray. Edited by R. W. N. Hoare and J. K. Riches. Philadelphia: Westminster, 1976.
Burge, Gary M. *Interpreting the Gospel of John: Guides to New Testament Exegesis.* Grand Rapids: Baker, 1992.
———. *John.* NIV Application Commentary 4. Grand Rapids: Zondervan, 2009. Kindle ed.
Burkert, Walter. *Greek Religion.* Cambridge: Harvard University Press, 1985.
Camp, Phillip G. "Prayer in the Pentateuch." In *Praying with Ancient Israel: Exploring the Theology of Prayer in the Old Testament*, edited by Phillip G. Camp and Tremper Longman III, 21–36. Abilene, TX: Abilene Christian University Press, 2015.
Camp, Phillip G., and Tremper Longman III, eds. *Praying with Ancient Israel: Exploring the Theology of Prayer in the Old Testament.* Abilene, TX: Abilene Christian University Press, 2015.

Carson, D. A. *The Farewell Discourse and Final Prayer of Jesus: An Exposition of John 14–17*. Grand Rapids: Baker, 1980.

———. "The Function of the Paraclete in John 16:7–11." *Journal of Biblical Literature* 98.4 (1979) 547–66.

———. *The Gospel According to John*. Pillar New Testament Commentary. Leicester: InterVarsity; Grand Rapids: Eerdmans, 1991.

———, ed. *Teach Us to Pray: Prayer in the Bible and the World*. 1990. Reprint, Eugene, OR: Wipf & Stock.

Charlesworth, James H. "The Dead Sea Scrolls and the Gospel According to John." In *Exploring the Gospel of John: In Honor of D. Moody Smith*, edited by Alan R. Culpepper and C. Clifton Black, 65–97. Louisville: Westminster John Knox, 1996.

Charlesworth, James H., et al., eds. *The Lord's Prayer and Other Prayer Texts from the Greco-Roman Era*. Valley Forge, PA: Trinity, 1994.

Chazon, Esther. "Hymns and Prayers in the Dead Sea Scrolls." In vol. 1. of *The Dead Sea Scrolls After Fifty Years: A Comprehensive Assessment*, edited by Peter W. Flint and James C. VanderKam, 244–70. Studies on the Texts of the Desert of Judah 30. Leiden: Brill, 1998.

Chazon, Esther, and Moshe J. Bernstein. "An Introduction to Prayer at Qumran." In *Prayer from Alexander to Constantine: A Critical Anthology*, edited by Mark Christopher Kiley, 9–13. London: Routledge, 1997.

Coloe, Mary L. *God Dwells with Us: Temple Symbolism in the Fourth Gospel*. Collegeville, MN: Liturgical, 2001.

———. "The Nazarene King: Pilate's Title as the Key to John's Crucifixion." In *The Death of Jesus in the Fourth Gospel*, edited by G. Van Belle, 839–48. Bibliotheca Ephemeridum Theologicarum Lovaniensium 200. Leuven: Leuven University Press, 2007.

———. "Temple Imagery in John." *Interpretation* 63.4 (2009) 368–81.

Coloe, Mary L., and Tom Thatcher, eds. *John, Qumran, and the Dead Sea Scrolls: Sixty Years of Discovery and Debate*. Early Judaism and Its Literature 32. Atlanta: Society of Biblical Literature, 2011.

Countryman, L. William. "Jesus' 'High Priestly Prayer': John 17." In *Prayer from Alexander to Constantine: A Critical Anthology*, edited by Mark Christopher Kiley, 222–29. London: Routledge, 1997.

Crump, David. *Knocking on Heaven's Door: A New Testament Theology of Petitionary Prayer*. Grand Rapids: Baker Academic, 2006.

Cullmann, Oscar. *Das Gebet im Neuen Testament: Zugleich Versuch einer vom Neuen Testament aus zu erteilenden Antwort auf heutige Fragen*. 2nd ed. Tübingen: Mohr Siebeck, 1997.

Culpepper, R. Alan. *Anatomy of the Fourth Gospel: A Study in Literary Design*. Philadelphia: Fortress, 1983.

———. *The Gospel and Letters of John*. Nashville: Abingdon, 1998.

Danker, Frederick W., et al. *A Greek-English Lexicon of the New Testament and Other Early Christian Literature*. 3rd ed. Chicago: University of Chicago Press, 2000.

De Vries, Simon J. *1 Kings*. Word Biblical Commentary 12. Nashville: Thomas Nelson, 2003.

Derickson, Gary W. "Viticulture and John 15:1–6." *Bibliotheca Sacra* 153.609 (1996) 34–52. Online. https://www.dts.edu/download/publications/bibliotheca/BibSac-Derickson-ViticultureAndJohn15,1-6.pdf.

Diehl, Judith A. "The Puzzle of the Prayer: A Study of John 17." PhD diss., University of Edinburgh, 2007.

DiSante, Carmine. *Jewish Prayer: The Origin of Christian Liturgy*. Translated by Matthew J. O'Connell. Mahwah, NJ: Paulist, 1985.

Dodd, C. H. *The Interpretation of the Fourth Gospel*. Cambridge: Cambridge University Press, 1953.

Doohan, Helen, and Leonard Doohan. *Prayer in the New Testament: Make Your Requests Known to God*. Collegeville, MN: Liturgical, 1992.

Dunn, James D. G. *Baptism in the Holy Spirit: A Re-examination of the New Testament Teaching on the Gift of the Spirit in Relation to Pentecostalism Today*. Philadelphia: Westminster, 1970.

Elbogen, Ismar. *Jewish Liturgy: A Comprehensive History*. Philadelphia: JPS, 1993.

Etienne, Sister Anne. "Birth [Biblical Images, esp. John 16:16–22]." *Ecumenical Review* 34.3 (1982) 228–37.

Ferguson, Everett. *Background of Early Christianity*. 3rd ed. Grand Rapids: Eerdmans, 2003.

Finkel, Asher. "Prayer in the Jewish Life of the First Century as Background to Early Christianity." In *Into God's Presence: Prayer in the New Testament*, edited by Richard N. Longenecker, 43–65. Grand Rapids: Eerdmans, 2001.

Fitzmyer, Joseph A. "Abba and Jesus' Relationship to God." In *À cause de l'Évangile: Études sur les Synoptiques et les Actes offertes au P. Jacques Dupont, OSB., à l'occasion de son 70e anniversaire*, edited by Robert Gantoy, 15–38. Lectio Divina 123. Paris: Cerf, 1985.

Fowler, W. Warde. *The Religious Experience of the Roman People from the Earliest Times to the Age of Augustus*. Gifford Lectures for 1909–1910. London: Macmillan, 1911. eBook.

France, R. T. *Matthew: An Introduction and Commentary*. Tyndale New Testament Commentaries 1. Downers Grove, IL: InterVarsity, 1985.

Fretheim, Terence E. *The Suffering of God*. Philadelphia: Fortress Press, 1984.

Garcia Sison, Victor. *The Verb "Menéin" in the Theological Context of the Fourth Gospel*. Rome: Pontificia Studiorum Universitas a S. Thoma Aq. in Urbe, 1994.

Genette, Gérard. *Narrative Discourse: An Essay in Method*. Translated by Jane E. Lewin. Ithaca, NY: Cornell University Press, 1980.

Green, Joel B. "Persevering Together in Prayer: The Significance of Prayer in the Acts of the Apostles." In *Into God's Presence: Prayer in the New Testament*, edited by Richard N. Longenecker, 183–202. Grand Rapids: Eerdmans, 2001.

Haenchen, Ernst. *A Commentary on the Gospel of John 1–6*. Translated by Robert W. Funk. Edited by Robert W. Funk with Ulrich Busse. Hermeneia: A Critical and Historical Commentary on the Bible. Philadelphia: Fortress, 1984.

———. *A Commentary on the Gospel of John 7–21*. Translated by Robert W. Funk. Edited by Robert W. Funk with Ulrich Busse. Hermeneia: A Critical and Historical Commentary on the Bible. Philadelphia: Fortress, 1984.

Hammer, Reuven. *Entering Jewish Prayer: A Guide to Personal Devotion and the Worship Service*. New York: Schocken, 1994.

———. "A Legend Concerning the Origins of the Shema." *Judaism* 32.1 (1983) 51–55.

Hammerling, Roy. *A History of Prayer: The First to the Fifteenth Century*. Leiden: Brill, 2008.

Heiler, Friedrich. *Prayer: A Study in the History and Psychology of Religion*. Translated by Samuel McComb. Edited by Samuel McComb and John Edgar Park. London: Oxford University Press, 1932.
Hendriksen, William. *Exposition of the Gospel According to John: Two Volumes Complete in One*. New Testament Commentary. Grand Rapids: Baker, 1953.
Herrmann, Johannes, and Heinrich Greeven. "*eúchomai, euchḗ, proseúchomai, proseuchḗ*." *TDNT* 279–85.
———. "εὔχομαι, εὐχή, προσεύχομαι, προσευχή." *TDNT* 2:775–808.
Hoffman, Lawrence A., ed. *My People's Prayer Book: Traditional Prayers, Modern Commentaries*. Vol. 2. Woodstock, VT: Jewish Lights, 1998.
Horst, Pieter W. van der, and Judith H. Newman. *Early Jewish Prayers in Greek*. Edited by Loren T. Stuckenbruck. Commentaries on Early Jewish Literature. Berlin: de Gruyter, 2008.
Horton, Stanley M. *Acts: A Logion Press Commentary*. Springfield, MO: Logion, 2001.
Hunter, W. Bingham. "The Prayers of Jesus in the Gospel of John." PhD diss., University of Aberdeen, 1979.
Hurtado, Larry W. "The Place of Jesus in Earliest Christian Prayer and Its Import for Early Christian Identity." In *Early Christian Prayer and Identity Formation*, edited by Reidar Hvalvik and Karl Olav Sandnes, 35–56. Wissenschaftliche Untersuchungen zum Neuen Testament 336. Tübingen: Mohr Siebeck, 2014.
Hvalvik, Reidar. "Praying with Outstretched Hands: Nonverbal Aspects of Early Christian Prayer and the Question of Identity." In *Early Christian Prayer and Identity Formation*, edited by Reidar Hvalvik and Karl Olav Sandnes, 57–90. Wissenschaftliche Untersuchungen zum Neuen Testament 336. Tübingen: Mohr Siebeck, 2014.
Hvalvik, Reidar, and Karl Olav Sandnes, eds. *Early Christian Prayer and Identity Formation*. Wissenschaftliche Untersuchungen zum Neuen Testament 336. Tübingen: Mohr Siebeck, 2014.
Hwang, Won-Ha. "The Presence of the Risen Jesus In and Among His Followers with Special Reference to the First Farewell Discourse in John 13:31–14:31." PhD diss., University of Pretoria, 2007.
Jacobs, Louis. *Jewish Prayer*. 1955. Reprint, Eugene, OR: Wipf & Stock, 2008.
Janowitz, Naomi. *Magic in the Roman World: Pagans, Jews, and Christians*. London: Routledge, 2001.
Jeffers, James S. *The Greco-Roman World of the New Testament Era: Exploring the Background of Early Christianity*. Downers Grove, IL: InterVarsity, 1999.
Jeremias, Joachim. *Jerusalem in the Time of Jesus: An Investigation into Economic and Social Conditions During the New Testament Period*. Philadelphia: Fortress, 1969.
———. *The Prayers of Jesus*. London: SCM, 1967.
Johnson, Luke Timothy. *Among the Gentiles: Greco-Roman Religion and Christianity*. New Haven. Yale University Press, 2009.
———. *The Gospel of Luke*. Sacra Pagina Series 3. Collegeville, MN: Liturgical, 1991.
Johnson, Paul. *History of the American People*. New York: Harper Perennial, 1999.
Karris, Robert J. *Prayer and the New Testament: Jesus and His Communities at Worship*. New York: Crossroad, 2000.
Käsemann, Ernst. *The Testament of Jesus: A Study of the Gospel of John in Light of Chapter 17*. Philadelphia: Fortress, 1968.

Kebler, Werner H. *The Passion in Mark: Studies on Mark 14–16*. Edited by Werner H. Kebler. Philadelphia, Fortress, 1976.

Keener, Craig S. *The Gospel of John*. 2 vols. Peabody, MA: Hendrickson, 2003.

———. *Matthew*. IVP New Testament Commentary Series 1. Downers Grove, IL: InterVarsity, 1997.

Kerr, A. R. *The Temple of Jesus' Body: The Temple Theme in the Gospel of John*. Sheffield: Sheffield Academic, 2002.

Kiley, Mark Christopher, ed. *Prayer from Alexander to Constantine: A Critical Anthology*. London: Routledge, 1997.

Kittel, Gerhard, and Gerhard Friedrich, eds. *Theological Dictionary of the New Testament*. Translated by Geoffrey W. Bromiley. 10 vols. Grand Rapids: Eerdmans, 1964–1976.

———. *Theological Dictionary of the New Testament*. Translated by Geoffrey W. Bromiley. Abridged into 1 vol. by Geoffrey W. Bromiley. Grand Rapids: Eerdmans, 1985.

———. *Theological Dictionary of the New Testament*. Translated by Geoffrey W. Bromiley. 10 vols. Electronic ed. Bellingham, WA: Logos Bible Software, 2000.

Koenig, John. *Rediscovering New Testament Prayer: Boldness and Blessing in the Name of Jesus*. San Francisco: HarperSanFrancisco, 1992.

Kok, Jacobus (Kobus). *New Perspectives on Healing, Restoration, and Reconciliation in John's Gospel*. Biblical Interpretation Series 149. Leiden: Brill, 2017.

Köstenberger, Andreas J. *Encountering John: The Gospel in Historical, Literary, and Theological Perspective*. Paperback ed. Encountering Biblical Studies. Grand Rapids: Baker Academic, 2002.

———. "The 'Greater Works' of the Believer According to John 14:12." *Didaskalia* 6.2 (1995) 36–45.

———. *John*. Baker Exegetical Commentary on the New Testament. Grand Rapids: Baker Academic, 2004.

Kysar, Robert. *John*. Augsburg Commentary on the New Testament. Minneapolis: Augsburg, 1986.

Laney, J. Carl. "Abiding Is Believing: The Analogy of the Vine in John 15:1–6." *Bibliotheca Sacra* 146.581 (1989) 55–66.

Lincoln, Andrew T. "God's Name, Jesus' Name, and Prayer in the Fourth Gospel." In *Into God's Presence: Prayer in the New Testament*, edited by Richard N. Longenecker, 155–82. Grand Rapids: Eerdmans, 2001.

Lindars, Barnabas. *The Gospel of John*. London: Marshall, Morgan & Scott, 1972.

Lochman, Jan Milič. *The Lord's Prayer*. Translated by Geoffrey W. Bromiley. Grand Rapids: Eerdmans, 1990.

Lohse, Eduard. *Vater Unser: Das Gebet der Christen*. Darmstadt: Wissenschaftliche Buchgesellschaft, 2009.

Longenecker, Richard N. *Into God's Presence: Prayer in the New Testament*. Grand Rapids: Eerdmans, 2001.

Longman, Tremper, III. "Prayer in the Psalms." In *Praying with Ancient Israel: Exploring the Theology of Prayer in the Old Testament*, edited by Phillip G. Camp and Tremper Longman III, 87–100. Abilene, TX: Abilene Christian University Press, 2015.

Louw, Johannes P., and Eugene A. Nida. *Greek-English Lexicon of the New Testament: Based on Semantic Domains*. 2nd ed. 2 vols. New York: United Bible Societies, 1996.

Malherbe, Abraham J. *Social Aspects of Early Christianity.* 2nd ed. Eugene, OR: Wipf & Stock, 2003.
Malina, Bruce J. *The New Testament World: Insights from Cultural Anthropology.* 3rd ed. Louisville: Westminster John Knox, 2001.
Malina, Bruce J., and Richard Rohrbaugh. *Social-Science Commentary on the Gospel of John.* Social-Science Commentary. Minneapolis: Augsburg Fortress, 1998.
Marshall, I. Howard. *Acts: An Introduction and Commentary.* Tyndale New Testament Commentaries 5. Downers Grove, IL: InterVarsity, 1980.
———. "Jesus—Example and Teacher of Prayer in the Synoptic Gospels." In *Into God's Presence: Prayer in the New Testament*, edited by Richard N. Longenecker, 113–31. Grand Rapids: Eerdmans, 2001.
Martin, Bernard. *Prayer in Judaism.* New York: Basic, 1968.
Martin, Ralph P. *Worship in the Early Church.* Rev. ed. Grand Rapids: Eerdmans, 1974.
Martyn, J. L. *History and Theology in the Fourth Gospel.* 3rd ed. New Testament Library. Louisville: Westminster John Knox, 2003.
Matlock, Michael D. *Discovering the Traditions of Prose Prayers in Early Jewish Literature.* Library of Second Temple Studies 81. New York. T & T Clark International, 2012.
Meeks, Wayne A. *The First Urban Christians: The Social World of the Apostle Paul.* New Haven: Yale University Press, 1983.
Michaels, J. Ramsey. *The Gospel of John.* New International Commentary on the New Testament. Grand Rapids: Eerdmans, 2010.
Migliore, Daniel L., ed. *The Lord's Prayer: The 1991 Frederick Neumann Symposium on the Theological Interpretation of Scripture.* Princeton Seminary Bulletin, Supplementary Issue 2. Princeton, NJ: Princeton Theological Seminary, 1992.
Mihoc, Vasile. "Prayer to Jesus in the New Testament." In *Das Gebet im Neuen Testament: Vierte europäische orthodox-westliche Exegetenkonferenz in Sâmbăta de Sus, 4.–8. August 2007*, edited by Hans Klein et al., 165–83. Wissenschaftliche Untersuchungen zum Neuen Testament 249. Tübingen: Mohr Siebeck, 2009.
Millar, Gary J. *Calling on the Name of the Lord: A Biblical Theology of Prayer.* New Studies in Biblical Theology 38. Downers Grove, IL: InterVarsity, 2016.
Miller, Patrick D. *They Cried to the Lord: The Form and Theology of Biblical Prayer.* Minneapolis: Fortress, 1994.
Moloney, Francis J. *Glory Not Dishonor: Reading John 13–21.* Minneapolis: Fortress, 1998.
Morris, Leon. *The Gospel According to John: The English Text with Introduction, Exposition and Notes.* New International Commentary on the New Testament. Grand Rapids: Eerdmans, 1971.
———. *The Gospel According to Matthew.* Pillar New Testament Commentary. Grand Rapids: Eerdmans, 1992.
Moule, H. C. G. *The High Priestly Prayer: A Devotional Commentary on the Seventeenth Chapter of St. John.* 1907. Reprint, Grand Rapids: Baker, 1978.
Nestle, Eberhard, et al., eds. *Novum Testamentum Graece.* 27th ed. Stuttgart: Deutsche Bibelgesellschaft, 1993.
Newman, Barclay M., and Eugene A. Nida. *A Handbook on the Gospel of John.* New York: United Bible Societies, 1980.
Neyrey, Jerome H. *Give God the Glory: Ancient Prayer and Worship in Cultural Perspective.* Grand Rapids: Eerdmans, 2007.

———. *The Gospel of John*. New Cambridge Bible Commentary. New York: Cambridge University Press, 2007.

Neyrey, Jerome. H., and Eric C. Stewart, eds. *The Social World of the New Testament: Insights and Models*. Peabody, MA: Hendrickson, 2008.

Nilsson, Martin P. *A History of Greek Religion*. Translated by F. J. Fielden. Oxford: Clarendon, 1925.

O'Day, Gail R. "'I Have Overcome the World' (John 16:33): Narrative Time in John 13–17." *Semeia* 53 (1991) 153–66.

Osborne, Joan. "One of Us." Written by Eric Bazilian. Track 6 on *Relish*, CD, Blue Gorilla Records/Mercury, 1995.

Ostmeyer, Karl-Heinrich. *Kommunikation mit Gott und Christus: Sprache und Theologie des Gebetes im Neuen Testament*. Edited by Jörg Frey. Wissenschaftliche Untersuchungen zum Neuen Testament 197. Tübingen: Mohr Siebeck, 2006.

———. "Prayer as Demarcation: The Function of Prayer in the Gospel of John." In *Das Gebet im Neuen Testament: Vierte europäische orthodox-westliche Exegetenkonferenz in Sâmbăta de Sus, 4.-8. August 2007*, edited by Hans Klein et al., 233–47. Wissenschaftliche Untersuchungen zum Neuen Testament 249. Tübingen: Mohr Siebeck, 2009.

Penner, Jeremy. *Patterns of Daily Prayer in Second Temple Period Judaism*. Edited by Florentino García Martínez. Studies on the Texts of the Desert of Judah 104. Leiden: Brill, 2012.

Peterson, David G. *The Acts of the Apostles*. Pillar New Testament Commentary. Grand Rapids: Eerdmans, 2009.

Petuchowski, Jakob J., ed. *Understanding Jewish Prayer*. New York: Ktav, 1972.

Polhill, John B. *Acts: An Exegetical and Theological Exposition of Holy Scripture*. New American Commentary 26. Nashville: Broadman & Holman, 1992.

Pulleyn, Simon. *Prayer in Greek Religion*. Oxford Classical Monographs. Oxford: Clarendon, 1997.

Reif, Stephan C. *Judaism and Hebrew Prayer: New Perspective on Jewish Liturgical History*. Cambridge: Cambridge University Press, 1993.

Rosenblatt, Marie-Eloise. "The Voice of the One Who Prays in John 17." In *Scripture and Prayer: A Celebration for Carroll Stuhlmueller*, edited by Carolyn Osiek and Donald Senior, 131–44. Wilmington, DE: Glazier, 1998.

Sadananda, Daniel Rathnakara. *The Johannine Exegesis of God: An Exploration into the Johannine Understanding of God*. Beihefte zur Zeitschrift für die neutestamentliche Wissenschaft und die Kunde der älteren Kirche 121. Berlin: de Gruyter, 2004.

Sanders, E. P. "Defending the Indefensible." *Journal of Biblical Literature* 110.3 (1991) 463–77.

Sandnes, Karl Olav. *Early Christian Discourses on Jesus' Prayer at Gethsemane: Courageous, Committed, Cowardly?* Supplements to Novum Testamentum 166. Leiden: Brill, 2016.

Sarason, Richard S. "The 'Intersections' of Qumran and Rabbinic Judaism: The Case of Prayer Texts and Liturgies." *Dead Sea Discoveries* 8.2 (2001) 169–81.

Schenke, Ludger. *Johannes Commentar*. Kommentare zu den Evangelien. Düsseldorf: Patmos, 1998.

Schlier, H. "ἀμήν." *TDNT* 1:335–38.

———. "amén." *TDNT* 53–54.

Schnackenburg, Rudolf. *The Gospel According to St. John: Commentary on Chapters 13–21*. Translated by David Smith and G. A. Kon. New York: Crossroad, 1982.

Schnelle, Udo. *Das Evangelium nach Johannes 4*. Theologischer Handkommentar zum Neuen Testament. Leipzig: Evanelische Verlagsanstalt, 2016.

Schuller, Eileen M. "Prayer, Hymnic, and Liturgical Texts from Qumran." In *The Community of the Renewed Covenant: The Notre Dame Symposium on the Dead Sea Scrolls*, edited by Eugene Ulrich and James VanderKam, 153–74. Christianity and Judaism in Antiquity 10. Notre Dame: University of Notre Dame Press, 1994.

———. "Prayer in the Dead Sea Scrolls." In *Into God's Presence: Prayer in the New Testament*, edited by Richard N. Longenecker, 66–90. Grand Rapids: Eerdmans, 2001.

Smith, Dennis E. *From Symposium to Eucharist: The Banquet in the Early Christian World*. Minneapolis: Fortress, 2003.

Staudt, E. "Prayer and the People in the Deuteronomist." PhD diss., Vanderbilt University, 1980.

Steinsaltz, Adin. *A Guide to Jewish Prayer*. New York: Schocken, 2000.

Steudel, Annette. "The Houses of Prostration 'CD' XI, 21–XII, 1—Duplicates of the Temple." *Revue de Qumrân* 16.1 (1993) 49–68. Online. http://www.jstor.org/stable/24609082.

Streett, Andrew. *The Vine and the Son of Man: Eschatological Interpretation of Psalm 80 in Early Judaism*. Emerging Scholars. Minneapolis: Fortress, 2014.

Thompson, Marianne Meye. *John: A Commentary*. New Testament Library. Louisville: Westminster John Knox, 2015.

Thompson, Michael E. W. *I Have Heard Your Prayer: The Old Testament and Prayer*. Peterborough: Epworth, 1996.

Thüsing, Wilhelm. *Herrlichkeit und Einheit. Eine Auslegung des Hohepriesterlichen Gebetes Jesu (Johannes 17)*. Welt der Bibel 14. Düsseldorf: Patmos, 1962.

Thyen, Hartwig. *Das Johannesevangelium*. Edited by Andreas Lindemann. 2nd ed. Handbuch zum Neuen Testament 6. Tübingen: Mohr Siebeck, 2015.

Turner, M. M. B. "Prayer in the Gospels and Acts." In *Teach Us to Pray: Prayer in the Bible and the World*, edited by D. A. Carson, 58–83. 1990. Reprint, Eugene, OR: Wipf & Stock, 2002.

Twelftree, Graham H. *People of the Spirit: Exploring Luke's View of the Church*. Grand Rapids: Baker Academic, 2009.

Van Belle, G., ed. *The Death of Jesus in the Fourth Gospel*. Bibliotheca Ephemeridum Theologicarum Lovaniensium 200. Leuven: Leuven University Press, 2007.

Van der Watt, Jan G. "The Ethos of Being Like Jesus: Imitation in 1 John." In *Ethos und Theologie im Neuen Testament: Festschrift für Michael Wolter*, edited by Jochen Flebbe and Matthias Konradt, 415–40. Göttingen: Vandenhoeck & Ruprecht, 2016.

———. *Family of the King: Dynamics of Metaphor in the Gospel According to John*. Biblical Interpretation Series 47. Leiden: Brill, 2000. eBook.

———. *An Introduction to the Johannine Gospels and Letters*. T & T Clark Approaches to Biblical Studies. London: T & T Clark, 2007.

———. "Mimesis or Imitation in Ethical Dynamics." Lecture notes, Radboud University, Nijmegen, Netherlands, December 2014.

———. "Narrative and Ethics." Lecture, Radboud University, Nijmegen, Netherlands, June 2015.

———. "Salvation in the Gospel According to John." In *Salvation in the New Testament: Perspectives on Soteriology*, edited by Jan G. van der Watt, 101–131. Supplements to Novum Testamentum 121. Leiden: Brill, 2005.

———. "Some Reflections on the Historicity of the Words 'Laying Down Your Life for Your Friends' in John 15:13." In *Glimpses of Jesus through the Johannine Lens*, edited by Paul N. Anderson et al., 481–92. Vol. 3 of *John, Jesus, and History*. Early Christianity and Its Literature 18. Atlanta: SBL, 2016.

Wengst, Klaus. *Das Johannesevangelium: Kapitel 11–21*. Theologischer Kommentar Zum Neuen Testament 4.2. Stuttgart: Kohlhammer, 2001. Kindle ed.

Werline, Rodney Alan. *Penitential Prayer in Second Temple Judaism: The Development of a Religious Institution*. Early Judaism and Its Literature 13. Atlanta: Scholars, 1998.

Westcott, Brooke Foss. *The Gospel According to St. John: The Greek Text with Introduction and Notes*. 1908. Reprint, Grand Rapids: Eerdmans, 1954.

Wilckens, Ulrich. *Das Evangelium nach Johannes*. NTD 4. Göttingen: Vandenhoeck & Ruprecht, 2000.

Witherington, Ben, III. *John's Wisdom: A Commentary on the Fourth Gospel*. Louisville: Westminster John Knox, 1995.

Wright, N. T. "The Lord's Prayer as a Paradigm of Christian Prayer." In *Into God's Presence: Prayer in the New Testament*, edited by Richard N. Longenecker, 132–54. Grand Rapids: Eerdmans, 2001.

Wylen, Stephen M. *The Jews in the Time of Jesus: An Introduction*. New York: Paulist, 1996.

Yancey, Philip. *Prayer: Does It Make Any Difference?* London: Hodder & Stoughton, 2006.

Zaleski, Philip, and Carol Zaleski. *Prayer: A History*. Boston: Houghton Mifflin, 2005.

Zumstein, Jean. *Kreative Erinnerung: Relecture und Auslegung im Johannesevangelium*. Translated by Esther Straub. Zurich: Pano, 1999.

www.ingramcontent.com/pod-product-compliance
Lightning Source LLC
Chambersburg PA
CBHW051638230426
43669CB00013B/2357